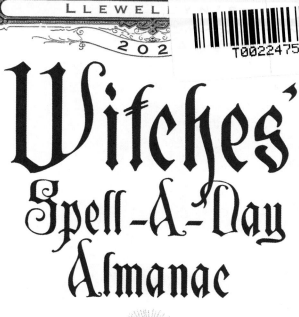

LLEWELL

202

Witches'
Spell-A-Day
Almanac

Holidays & Lore
Spells, Rituals & Meditations

© 2023 Llewellyn Worldwide Ltd.
Cover design by the Llewellyn Art Department
Interior art © 2018 Laura Tempest Zakroff: pages 9, 29,
49, 71, 91, 111, 129, 149, 169, 191, 215, 237
Spell icons throughout © 2011 Sherrie Thai
You can order Llewellyn books and annuals from *New Worlds*,

Llewellyn's catalog. To request a free copy of the catalog, call toll-free
1-877-NEW WRLD or visit our website at www.llewellyn.com.
ISBN: 978-0-7387-6905-9
Llewellyn is a registered trademark of Llewellyn Worldwide Ltd.
2143 Wooddale Drive
Woodbury, MN 55125

Printed in China

Contents

A Note on Magic and Spells

The spells in the *Witches' Spell-A-Day Almanac* evoke everyday magic designed to improve our lives and homes. You needn't be an expert on magic to follow these simple rites and spells; as you will see if you use these spells throughout the year, magic, once mastered, is easy to perform. The only advanced technique required of you is the art of visualization.

Visualization is an act of controlled imagination. If you can call up in your mind a picture of your best friend's face or a flag flapping in the breeze, you can visualize. In magic, visualizations are used to direct and control magical energies. Basically the spellcaster creates a visual image of the spell's desired goal, whether it be perfect health, a safe house, or a protected pet.

Visualization is the basis of all good spells, and as such it is a tool that should be properly used. Visualization must be real in the mind of the spellcaster so it allows him or her to raise, concentrate, and send forth energy to accomplish the spell.

Perhaps when visualizing you'll find that you're doing everything right, but you don't feel anything. This is common, for we haven't been trained to acknowledge—let alone utilize—our magical abilities. Keep practicing, however, for your spells can "take" even if you're not the most experienced natural magician.

You will notice also that many spells in this collection have a somewhat light tone. They are seemingly fun and frivolous, filled with rhyme and colloquial speech. This is not to diminish the seriousness of the purpose, but rather to create a relaxed atmosphere for the practitioner. Lightness of spirit helps focus energy; rhyme and common language help the spellcaster remember the words and train the mind where it is needed. The intent of this magic is indeed very serious at times, and magic is never to be trifled with.

Even when your spells are effective, magic won't usually sparkle before your very eyes. The test of magic's success is time, not immediate eye-popping results. But you can feel magic's energy for yourself by rubbing your palms together briskly for ten seconds, then holding them a few inches apart. Sense the energy passing through them, the warm tingle in your palms. This is the power raised and used in magic. It comes from within and is perfectly natural.

Among the features of the *Witches' Spell-A-Day Almanac* are an easy-to-use "book of days" format; new spells specifically tailored for each day

of the year (and its particular magical, astrological, and historical energies); and additional tips and lore for various days throughout the year—
including color correspondences based on planetary influences, obscure
and forgotten holidays and festivals, and an incense of the day to help
you waft magical energies from the ether into your space. Moon signs,
phases, and voids are also included to help you find the perfect time for
your rituals and spells. (All times in this book are Eastern Standard Time
or Eastern Daylight Time.)

Enjoy your days and have a magical year!

Spell-A-Day Icons

New Moon

Full Moon

Abundance

Altar

Balance

Clearing, Cleaning

Garden

Grab Bag

Health, Healing

Home

Heart, Love

Meditation, Divination

Money, Prosperity

Protection

Relationship

Success

Travel, Communication

Air Element

Earth Element

Fire Element

Spirit Element

Water Element

2024 Spells at a Glance by Date and Category*

	Health, Healing	Protection	Success	Heart, Love	Clearing, Cleaning	Balance	Meditation, Divination
Jan.	21, 26	16	1, 10, 15, 28	17	3, 4, 8	2, 27, 30, 31	6, 12, 13
Feb.	6, 15	21, 23, 28	5, 16, 29	14	3, 25	18	12
March	4	9, 30	23, 24, 31	8	3, 5, 6, 12, 20	13, 18, 19, 21	11
April	5	10, 25	18, 28	6, 12, 17	27	4, 7, 14, 20, 21	1, 2, 24
May		16, 26	11	9, 14	18, 28	4, 10, 29	3, 13, 19, 20, 22
June	3, 22	11, 15, 23	13, 30	16, 26	5, 7, 24	12, 28, 29	4, 8
July	19	6, 8, 17, 24, 26, 30, 31	14, 16	20	28	18, 29	15
Aug.	17, 29	3, 31	12, 25, 26	9	10, 28, 30	16	6, 14
Sept.	4	7, 18	8, 12		6, 26	22, 23	15, 19
Oct.	24			28	8, 18, 19		6, 13, 31
Nov.	7	23, 27, 29	30	2, 14, 25	3, 22	6, 17	5, 9, 12, 16, 26
Dec.	2, 10, 28	13	20	25, 27		6, 9, 14, 17	5, 11

*List is not comprehensive.

2024

Year of Spells

January

Happy New Year! The calendar year has begun and even though we may be in the depths of winter (in the Northern Hemisphere) or the height of summer (in the Southern Hemisphere), we stand at the threshold of fifty-two weeks filled with promise. Legend has it that this month is named to honor the Roman god Janus, a god of new beginnings and doorways, but it is also associated with Juno, the primary goddess of the Roman pantheon. Juno was said to be the protectress of the Roman Empire, and Janus (whose twin faces look to both the past and the future simultaneously) encourages new endeavors, transitions, and change in all forms. Since this month marks the beginning of the whole year, we can plant the seeds for long-term goals at this time, carefully plotting the course of our future success.

In the United States, there are three important holidays occurring in January: New Year's Day, Martin Luther King Jr. Day, and Inauguration Day. Each of these days exemplifies powerful change and transition. The dawn of a new year heralds a fresh start, and whether snow-covered or bathed in summer heat, January offers renewed possibilities for all.

Michael Furie

January 1
Monday

3rd ♍

Color of the day: Silver
Incense of the day: Narcissus

New Year's Day – Kwanzaa ends

Ring in the New Year Spell

Cast this spell on New Year's Day to manifest good luck throughout the year ahead. You'll need a calendar, a blue ink pen, and a bell.

Place the calendar before you, then close your eyes and take some deep breaths to help you relax before you begin. When you're ready, pick up the pen. Turn to each month of the calendar and think about what you want that month to bring. Choose a keyword or symbol to represent your wish for each month, and inscribe it on the calendar page beside or above the name of the month or on the picture portion. Envision yourself experiencing the month of your dreams as you slowly form the word or symbol on the calendar page. Ring the bell and state in simple terms what you welcome each month to bring.

As you turn the calendar page at the beginning of each new month, ring the bell again as you focus on your wish for the days ahead.

Melanie Marquis

January 2
Tuesday

3rd ♍
☽ v/c 6:36 pm
☽ → ♎ 7:47 pm

Color of the day: Gray
Incense of the day: Cedar

Replenishing Breath Exercise

Today is World Introvert Day. Most of us are actually a mix of both introverted and extroverted, depending on the situation and our personal comfort levels. Even if you feel you're definitely an extrovert, exploring the introvert perspective can help you practice better boundary setting and self-care.

This is easier to do when you're more aware of the energy you're taking in from the world and how you're distributing it. Focused breathing is an easy way to do this.

To recharge yourself, take a deep breath in, feeling the external air fill your core. Exhale softly, imagining that your breath is adding a layer to the outside of your body instead of being dispersed into the world. Inversely, if you're feeling overstimulated, take a gentler breath in, and exhale in a strong, short burst, visualizing excess/unwanted energy leaving your body and releasing tension. You can repeat either option up to three times if you need to.

Laura Tempest Zakroff

January 3
Wednesday

3rd ♎

4th Quarter 10:30 pm

Color of the day: White
Incense of the day: Lavender

Unblocking Ritual

Today, perform this simple unblocking ritual to proactively reestablish a swift and harmonious life momentum after the recent Mercury retrograde period. (Mercury went retrograde on December 13, 2023, and resumed direct motion on January 1.)

First, open all the doors inside your home. If anything is obstructing a door's full range of motion, such as furniture, remove it so the door can open all the way. Safely light any scent of incense you have on hand. Carry the incense, with a dish or sufficiently large incense holder beneath it, to the threshold of one open door, and cleanse the entire inside of the door with the smoke. As you do this, feel that you are getting stuck energy moving and opening doorways of opportunity and blessings in your life. Repeat with each additional door on the inside. Finally, open your front door all the way and repeat the process with the threshold of your front door. Close your door and extinguish the incense. Smile and feel grateful for your newly activated life flow.

Tess Whitehurst

January 4
Thursday

4th ♎

Color of the day: Turquoise
Incense of the day: Apricot

Yuletide Undecorating

Decorating often feels magical, undecorating not so much. But it doesn't have to be that way. Putting away the Yuletide decorations can be a magical experience, too!

As you box up your lights, stockings, and other holiday decorations, take a moment to connect with your most treasured items before packing them away. Hold them close to your heart and reflect on the energies and history those items contain. If that energy makes you feel loved and wanted, open yourself up to it, absorbing it into yourself. As you pack away each item, give thanks to it for being a part of your holiday.

Once everything has been packed up, draw a pentacle on the outside of every storage box while visualizing you and your loved ones celebrating Yuletide with those items again next year and saying:

We celebrated Yuletide with good cheer
And shall do so again come next year!
Our memories have been packed away,
But in our hearts they'll always stay.
Blessed be!

Amanda Lynn & Jason Mankey

January 5
Friday

4th ♎︎

☽ v/c 6:41 am

☽ → ♏︎ 7:39 am

Color of the day: Purple
Incense of the day: Yarrow

A Purification Spell

During the winter our homes are closed up and may trap dark energies. This spell will help cleanse your living space.

You'll need one bayberry-scented candle. Safely light the candle. Gaze into the flame. Visualize a white light coming out of the flame growing until it surrounds your home. See the white light absorbing any negative energy until it is all harmlessly gone. Relax and breathe deeply. When you've returned to a calm daily state of mind, safely extinguish the flame. Your home is now free of unwanted energies. Put the candle away and use it for other positive magic.

James Kambos

January 6
Saturday

4th ♏︎

Color of the day: Blue
Incense of the day: Sandalwood

Divination Tea Spell

The beginning of the year is an excellent time to perform divination for information on how the rest of the year will go. This tea will help you open your third eye and open up to the messages that you most need to hear. To prepare the tea, you will need the following:

- 1 part mugwort
- 2 parts hibiscus
- 1 part nettle

Boil water, and as the water heats up, mix the herbs together in a bowl, holding the intention of seeing clearly. Put the tea mixture into a strainer, place this in a teapot, and pour the hot water over the herbs.

As the tea steeps, set up your space for divination. Set out candles if you so desire, and get ready to step into divinatory space.

Carefully and intentionally pour yourself a cup of tea from the pot. Sit down in front of your divination method of choice and see what unfolds. Make sure you take notes!

Phoenix LeFae & Gwion Raven

January 7
Sunday

4th ♏

☽ v/c 3:22 pm

☽ → ♐ 4:08 pm

Color of the day: Yellow
Incense of the day: Frankincense

Winter Wind Cleansing

The nature of winter is cold and clean. The dry air is clear so that everything is easy to see. By day, the sun sparkles on the snow. By night, the stars twinkle sharp in the sky. Winter brings clarity of thought and vision.

For this spell you need only yourself and an open space outdoors where the wind blows free. It doesn't have to be a fierce wind; even a breeze will do. Dress appropriately for the weather. Just make sure you can still feel the air on some part of your body.

Stand outside and turn your face into the wind. Feel it flowing over and around you. Then say:

Winter wind, wild wind,

Blow so clean and clear;

Sweep my body and mind

Free of doubt and fear.

Visualize wind blowing through you and clearing away anything that doesn't belong, such as negative thoughts, stray bits of foreign energy, unhelpful ideas, and so on.

When you feel refreshed and clean, go back indoors and warm up.

Elizabeth Barrette

NOTES:

January 8
Monday

4th ♐

Color of the day: White
Incense of the day: Clary sage

I'm Done with These

It has been a week since New Year's Day, time enough to settle into 2024 and January. Maybe you made some New Year's resolutions to start some new routines. But with the waning moon, now is the time to do a quick tidying up, psychically, of yourself, your habits, your space, and your intentions, letting go of what you no longer need and banishing it.

Write a list of anything that needs to stop or be let go of. Fold the list in half, with the words folded in and no longer visible. Say:

I am done with these.

Burn the paper (over the toilet or sink, for safety), saying:

I now release.

Flush the toilet or rinse the sink, saying:

You are banished now.
And I am free. So mote it be.

Dallas Jennifer Cobb

January 9
Tuesday

4th ♐

☽ v/c 1:24 pm
☽ → ♑ 8:33 pm

Color of the day: Red
Incense of the day: Cinnamon

Banish Blockages

The new year is over a week behind us now. Have you stuck to your resolutions? It's okay if you haven't, but don't completely abandon them. This simple charm will help you to get back on track, and it uses everyday items that you probably already possess or can acquire easily:

- 1 egg
- 1 black felt tip pen
- A sheet of newspaper from this year
- A rolling pin or hammer

Crack the egg. You can eat the contents, since you'll be working with the shell and not the actual egg. Take the pen and write on the shell what knocked you off track. Place the eggshell in a sheet of newspaper and wrap it up, then smash it with the rolling pin or hammer. Envision everything blocking your progress being broken down into manageable pieces, so you can get where you want to be. Finally, dispose of the shell (still wrapped in newspaper) somewhere off your

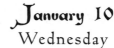

property, so you've got that restrictive energy well and truly out of your way!

Charlie Rainbow Wolf

NOTES:

January 10
Wednesday

4th ♑

Color of the day: Topaz
Incense of the day: Lilac

Annual Grimoire Blessing

One of my professors in graduate school always said, "If you have no plan, you plan to fail." There are many annual guidebooks, and they can really set you on the right track. Alongside your chosen annual, keep a grimoire. A grimoire is a magickal book of your own design and making, where you record your workings, notes, results, and ideas. This year, challenge yourself not only to purchase, design, and obtain a grimoire, but also to keeping it going the entire year. Your grimoire is an extension of you and your practice, so it should look and feel like you and your intent.

If you've never had a grimoire, a great way to start is to look for a blank lined book that calls out to you. Purchase it, bring it home, and bless it with a magick wand. Recite:

You are mine and I am yours.
Together we will hold, create,
and keep my magick alive as
I embark on the new year.

Stephanie Rose Bird

January 11
Thursday

4th ♑

New Moon 6:57 am

☽ v/c 9:33 pm

☽ → ♒ 10:01 pm

Color of the day: Green
Incense of the day: Balsam

Loving Attention

The new moon is a powerful time for setting intentions, but this month let's engage this practice with a twist. Often when we set intentions, we're focusing on something we want to change, fix, or accomplish—there's an emphasis on *doing*. From now until the next full moon (on the 26th), choose instead something that you'll give your attention to, shifting the emphasis to simply *being present* with it.

For instance, perhaps you choose to focus on your relationship with money or a particular family dynamic. Select objects to represent this focus, and place them on your altar or somewhere you'll regularly see. Spend time daily, even just a minute or two, paying attention to your area of focus, perhaps looking at the items and noticing, without judgment, any thoughts or feelings that arise. Or you might light a candle on a heat-proof surface and say, "I acknowledge you, (describe the focus area)." Don't leave the candle unattended.

Acceptance is the prerequisite to change, and spending a moon phase simply being present can pave the way for profound shifts.

Melissa Tipton

NOTES:

January 12
Friday

1st ≈

Color of the day: Pink
Incense of the day: Mint

Spreading Joy and Beauty Around

Here we are, a couple weeks into a new year. How much beauty and joy are you seeing these days? Many people are, alas, being negative and political, speaking hurtful thoughts and performing hurtful acts. Let's spread some joy around!

Visualize yourself wearing Joseph's technicolor coat. It's covered with stripes and patches and spangles of every color, shining, gleaming, glittering, nearly singing. Write messages of joy on every patch and spangle. This beautiful coat does not inspire jealousy, as it did among Joseph's brothers, but rather joy, beauty, and glory in everyone who sees it. Visualize yourself wearing this coat every time you go out. Fluff and wave it as you walk so that patches and spangles fly off. Some land on the ground and plant seeds from which flowers immediately sprout. Others fly toward the people you pass, touching their hearts with joy and beauty. Greet these people. Let your dream coat spread the joy and beauty we so much need today.

Barbara Ardinger

January 13
Saturday

1st ≈

☽ v/c 4:59 am
☽ → ♓ 10:29 pm

Color of the day: Brown
Incense of the day: Patchouli

Powerful Number 13

Today is the first number 13 day of the year! Superstitions abound regarding this number. There's no 13th floor in buildings, and we're told to look out for bad tidings when this day appears on the calendar. Yet the number 13 is also the number of a baker's dozen (you get an extra baked good for free), it's the number of full moons in a year, and the dollar bill is loaded with number 13 symbolism!

For this spell you will need thirteen small stones, a small clear quartz crystal, a white candle, and a fireproof candleholder. Arrange the stones in a circle. Place the white candle in the holder, then set it in the center of the circle, along with the crystal. Light the candle. Say:

Candle flame burning bright,

On this thirteenth day I do delight

In the joyous expression
of divine mysteries

That surround, enfold, and bless me.

Extinguish the candle when done.

Najah Lightfoot

January 14
Sunday

1st ♓

Color of the day: Gold
Incense of the day: Almond

Renewing Your Spiritual Path

The dark of winter can often bring with it unease and apathy. It's not unusual for us to feel stagnant in our spiritual practices. You can tap into the power of the day, Sunday, to access your spiritual goals and manifest them into reality.

Create a sachet with a small piece of cloth, a string, and a few herbs you have in your cabinet. You can use rosemary, oregano, and sage. Feel free to include other herbs you have if they call to you to do so. Once you have the herbs, place them in the center of the cloth. Know that you are ready to move forward out of this place of stagnation, and as you tie the string to secure the edges of the cloth, say:

I am ready to move past this place of stagnation and into one of growth.

Keep the sachet where you can see it daily to remind you of your commitment.

Charlynn Walls

January 15
Monday

1st ♓

☽ v/c 11:33 pm
☽ → ♈ 11:49 pm

Color of the day: Gray
Incense of the day: Hyssop

Martin Luther King Jr. Day

Erasing Racism "Peace by Piece"

Today is Martin Luther King Jr. Day. On this day of remembrance for both the revolutionary person and the freedom he helped inspire, it's good to examine our own internal racism, no matter our ethnic or cultural origins.

Today, take time to reflect on your own viewpoints concerning racism. Contemplate how deeply embedded racist ideas truly are worldwide. We are not free from these, as racist ideas of all varieties are so insidious that we often don't even recognize our own!

To add a small light of hope to the progression of erasing racism around the world, sit silently in front of a small black, tan, or brown candle safely burning. Silently ask the universe to help you better understand racism. Dedicate yourself to more deeply researching these issues.

When ready, ignite and deeply focus on a pink candle. (The black, tan, or brown candle represents people of color, while the pink candle symbolizes peace and equanimity.)

Declare eight times:

Racism buried deep in our minds, I hereby realize and banish all kinds. The world must unite through power and might; judgments so wrong must transform into right.

Allow the supervised candles to safely burn out on their own.

Raven Digitalis

NOTES:

January 16
Tuesday

1st ♈

Color of the day: Black
Incense of the day: Basil

Exfoliation Spell

Sometimes extra cleansing is needed and our regular routine just won't cut it. For this spell you will need a quarter cup of salt (sea salt is ideal, but any salt will do) and a tablespoon of olive oil.

Mix the ingredients in a small bowl. Take three deep breaths and then use the first two fingers of your dominant hand to draw a pentacle in the mixture. Focus on clearing out stuck energy and cleansing power. Repeat this process three times.

Take the mixture into the shower, keeping it out of the spray of water. Wash your body as you normally do. When complete, use the salt and oil to exfoliate your skin. Make sure you get behind your knees, the bottoms of your feet, the bottom of your spine, and the back of your neck.

Rinse off with water as hot as you can handle and then turn the water all the way to cold once you are fully rinsed off.

Phoenix LeFae & Gwion Raven

January 17
Wednesday

1st ♈

2nd Quarter 10:53 pm

Color of the day: Yellow
Incense of the day: Bay laurel

Love Finder Charm

Use this charm to attract new opportunities for love and romance. Take a piece of rose quartz and hold it close to your heart as you imagine yourself brimming with love and adoration. Pour these feelings into the crystal. Anoint the crystal with a few drops of jasmine oil as you imagine yourself being loved, admired, and appreciated. Place a pink candle in a secure holder on a fireproof surface. Light the candle and carefully hold the crystal over the flame briefly as you envision scenes of love and romance. Place the crystal directly next to the candle as you continue to visualize the romance you wish to experience.

Snuff out the candle when you're finished visualizing, or stay with the candle until it burns out on its own. Carry the rose quartz with you until your wishes are fulfilled, then return the crystal to nature.

Melanie Marquis

January 18
Thursday

2nd ♈

☽ v/c 3:03 am

☽ → ♉ 3:12 am

Color of the day: White
Incense of the day: Mulberry

Magical Money Planning

Instead of dreading or avoiding the topic of money, thinking of earning money as a boring but necessary chore, or just blindly hoping for the best, today you're going to get excited about money. Remember, you can choose to relate to money as an energetic currency and play around with the process of using your magic to magnetize it. With lighthearted and joyful expectation, clarify your financial intentions and goals.

Light a green candle and light or diffuse some wealth-drawing incense or oil, such as cinnamon, patchouli, vetiver, or clove. Call on a deity related to wealth, or just call on the Goddess or God. Then answer the following in a journal or notebook. Be sure to phrase all your answers in the present tense, as if already true:

How much money are you choosing to make this year? How are you choosing to make it? What would you like to spend it on or how would you like to invest it? How will you feel when you do this?

Tess Whitehurst

January 19
Friday

2nd ♉

Color of the day: Rose
Incense of the day: Rose

To Stir a Magical Daily Brew

Believe it or not, today is National Brew a Potion Day! While the word *potion* tends to conjure up ideas of a bubbling cauldron full of mysterious and magical ingredients, much of what we craft to eat and drink, as well as the medications we take, are also technically products of potions. You can also add a bit of magic to something you already brew daily, such as your morning coffee or tea, just by how you stir it!

Had a bad dream or need to clear your head? Stir your cup (with a spoon or stirring wand) counterclockwise three to nine times, dispersing the unwanted thoughts. Need to muster up some confidence for the day? Stir clockwise six times. Feel like you need a little extra protection or focus? Stir a pentagram into your cup. You could also stir in a sigil for whatever goal you may be working on. Then drink and enjoy your brew as usual!

Laura Tempest Zakroff

January 20
Saturday

2nd ♉

☽ v/c 8:57 am

☽ → ♊ 8:58 am

☉ → ♒ 9:07 am

Color of the day: Indigo
Incense of the day: Magnolia

Inauguration Day

Spirit of Coexistence

Each culture views the Divine in their own way. Some revere one deity, while others revere many. Some religions are small and personal, while others are large and communal. It is important that people respect each other's beliefs and work on getting along.

Take some time today to manifest the spirit of coexistence. On your altar, place a symbol of your religion in one quarter. Choose three other religions and place symbols of them in the other three quarters. Study a little about them, if you wish, so you can understand them better. Think about how the quarters of a circle exist in balance with one another. They are all equal, not trying to push each other away. Visualize a world in which everyone respects each other and lives in peace. What would that look like? What would be your place in such a world? Then think of one small thing you can do to move in that direction, and do it.

Elizabeth Barrette

January 21
Sunday

2nd ♊

Color of the day: Orange
Incense of the day: Heliotrope

Winter, Be Gone!

There are some people who love winter, and others who are more than ready for it to be done by the end of January. There's no way to speed up the change of the seasons, but you can connect to more tropical energies when the winter blues have got you down.

For this exercise you'll need a candle, a playlist of summer songs, and a drink that reminds you of warmer weather. Start by safely lighting the candle and saying:

Today I chase the winter blues away!

Start your playlist and take a big sip of your drink. Let the music and your drink seep into you, and think about the memories they conjure up.

Stare into your candle for a bit and let the flame remind you of warmer days ahead. Imagine the candle flame as the sun in the sky, warming your skin. Drink, listen to music, and look at the flame until your winter blues have gone away. Blow out the candle when you are done. Repeat as necessary during the cold time of year.

Amanda Lynn & Jason Mankey

January 22
Monday

2nd ♊
☽ v/c 3:40 pm
☽ → ♋ 4:51 pm

Color of the day: Silver
Incense of the day: Lily

Mirror, Mirror Spell

This spell combines scrying and protection. It is a tool to see what is coming up behind you that you're unaware of. Sometimes this spell gives you information about situations of your own making. Other times you receive clues about baneful work others may be casting in your direction. It's a powerful spell that will give you clear insight.

Here's what you'll need:

- A black four-inch candle and candleholder
- Matches
- A 2-by-2-inch mirror

Gather your materials and head to the bathroom. Set the candle in the holder on the bathroom counter and light it. Hold the mirror in your left hand. Turn off the lights. Hold the mirror a few inches behind the candle and angle it so you can see over your left shoulder. Stare into the mirror. Whisper, "What do I need to know that is hidden from me?" or "Who do I need to look out for?"

Peer into the mirror until you feel complete. Remember any images, thoughts, sounds, or other sensory clues that come to you. Turn on the lights, then douse the candle with water and dispose of it.

Phoenix LeFae & Gwion Raven

NOTES:

 January 23
Tuesday

2nd ♋

Color of the day: Maroon
Incense of the day: Bayberry

Sacred Self-Care Spell

The waxing moon moves into Cancer. The moon rules Cancer, providing a double dose of maternal, nurturing, and emotionally watery energy. But Cancerian energy is not just about caring for others. Use it to care for yourself.

Whether you shower or bathe, use the opportunity to purify, neutralize, and anoint. Gather some salt and some oil. (Table salt is fine, but use sea or Epsom salt if you have it. Olive oil can be used, but a few drops of essential oil in a carrier will feel luxurious.) Remove your clothing and step into the tub. Rub salt over your body, especially your elbows, knees, and feet. Say:

Salt, purify me.

Run some water and rinse off the salt, saying:

I release what is rough and tough.

Shower or bathe as usual, and after rinsing off and before getting out of the tub, gently anoint your body with oil. Say:

I anoint myself everywhere, invoking sacred self-care. Blessed be.

Dallas Jennifer Cobb

 January 24
Wednesday

2nd ♋

☽ v/c 5:58 pm

Color of the day: White
Incense of the day: Marjoram

Magnifying What Works

One powerful way to increase good fortune is to take time each day to focus on what is working well in your life. It's easy to fixate on what we don't like or are trying to change, but sometimes this can lead to getting mired in a "not-working" mindset where we're more in tune with what we don't want and less aware of what we do.

For one week, spend time in the morning or evening writing down three things that are working in your life, and be specific. These can be big or small, such as your car or the public transportation that gets you to work each day or the way you feel when your pet looks at you with their adorable face.

Challenge yourself to do this with something you don't like. Can you break the situation down and find one to three aspects that are working? This shift in perspective ignites creative problem-solving abilities as we train our focus on pathways, however small, of ease and efficacy rather than on obstructions.

Melissa Tipton

January 25
Thursday

2nd ♋

☽ → ♌ 2:37 am

Full Moon 12:54 pm

Color of the day: Crimson
Incense of the day: Jasmine

Full Moon Magick

It's a cold, winter moon if you live in the Northern Hemisphere of planet Earth. It's a bright, warm moon if you live in the Southern Hemisphere. But no matter where you live, whether north or south, it's the full moon and magick is afoot!

The full moon creeps up on us, pulling back the veil of our psyche and dreams and infiltrating our subconscious. I always seem to have some sort of crying jag or emotional fit before or during a full moon, no matter how hard I try to control the energies around me. And perhaps that is the issue.

For this spell, all you need to do is give yourself permission—permission to be you. You can dance, scream, cry, laugh, watch a funny or scary movie, light a bunch of a candles, or do nothing at all. Allow yourself the blessing of knowing you are enough under the light of this full moon.

Najah Lightfoot

January 26
Friday

3rd ♌
☽ v/c 4:19 pm
Color of the day: Coral
Incense of the day: Thyme

Break a habit Spell

If you have a bad habit that you can't seem to get rid of, this spell may help. You'll need:

- A sheet of white paper
- A blue ink pen or blue colored pencil
- A tray or sink
- An ice cube, crushed ice, or snow

First write the habit on the paper. Include any details. Next place the paper in a tray or in the sink. Now rub the ice or snow all over the text you just wrote on the paper. Rub it until the writing begins to fade. Wrap the paper into a wad, and if possible include any fragments of unmelted ice or snow along with the paper. Throw the paper and any ice or snow into the trash. Even better, if you can, throw the paper in a trash can located away from your home.

James Kambos

January 27
Saturday

3rd ♌
☽ → ♍ 2:11 pm
Color of the day: Gray
Incense of the day: Ivy

howling at the Moon

New Year's Eve and New Year's Day start this month off with a bang—one of the biggest and showiest bursts of energy of the entire year. Here we are today almost at the end of January. You may be wondering what there's left to do in your spiritual practice. Well, there's plenty!

We are at the gibbous moon phase of Wolf Moon (the first full moon in January). What an excellent time for replenishing the soul. This is the day for building on the new energies around you and purging what you don't need. Try this:

Go outside tonight and turn your eyes up toward the darkened sky.

Howl three times, each time thinking of what you wish to give up. Imagine yourself surrendering the useless aspects of your life to the universe as you howl.

Focus on Wolf Moon and howl for each of the three things you are releasing back into the universe.

Stephanie Rose Bird

 January 28
Sunday

3rd ♍

Color of the day: Amber
Incense of the day: Marigold

The Magic Parking Space Word

No matter where we live, if we drive a car, we need to park it somewhere. Whether we're at work or at the mall or at home in an urban neighborhood that has more multi-family dwellings than there are parking spaces, we need to park our car.

Speak the Parking Space Word:

ZZZZZAAAAAZZZZZ.

Speak it loud and with great energy. It seems to work best if you plan ahead and say where you want to park. Speak the Word, therefore, when you turn a corner or enter the parking lot:

ZZZZZAAAAAZZZZZ.
Parking space at _____.

Be aware that the Word doesn't always work immediately. Sometimes you have to drive around the block or around the lot. Repeat the Word every time you turn a corner. It will work.

Barbara Ardinger

January 29
Monday

3rd ♍

☽ v/c 6:20 pm

Color of the day: Lavender
Incense of the day: Rosemary

Raven Magic

Today in 1845, Edgar Allan Poe published his poem "The Raven." Ravens are considered to be very powerful magic. Some cultures see them as positive, while others view them as harbingers of doom. When I lived in England, it was said that a raven landing on your house was good luck. This spell invites good raven magic into your home. You'll need a feather duster (preferably black, like the raven) and some fresh basil—the supermarket should have both.

Tear the basil leaves into pieces, and as you do, recite:

I have no doubt, I will not be without.

Still chanting, drop the basil leaves onto the floor by your doors, then use the feather duster to sweep them over the threshold. Leave them where they lie, and let the wind take them away. If you live in an apartment complex, sweep them over the threshold of your unit, then take them outside and leave them inconspicuously outside the main entrance.

Charlie Rainbow Wolf

 January 30
Tuesday

3rd ♏

☽ → ♎ 3:04 am

Color of the day: Scarlet
Incense of the day: Ylang-ylang

Knocking Down the Walls

When we are hurt, we often put up walls to protect ourselves from pain and heartache. Sometimes we do not even realize that we have built up these walls as a coping mechanism. It can be difficult to remove them once they are up. This spell will help you do just that so you can be open to your full potential.

You will want to create a visual model of the wall you want to remove. You can get creative here and use Legos or kinetic sand, or you can simply draw a picture of a wall on a piece of paper. As you remove the pieces of your wall, say:

Brick by brick, stone by stone,
I remove this wall to open myself up
to the possibilities that await me.

(If I were drawing a picture, it would look like a pile of bricks next to the wall, with a hand out to remove the next one.)

Charlynn Walls

January 31
Wednesday

3rd ♎

Color of the day: Brown
Incense of the day: Honeysuckle

Dance to Release Stagnation

For many readers, namely those in the Northern Hemisphere who don't live in a tropical environment, this midwinter time of year can feel depressing or stagnant. It's time to dance!

First, determine your intention. What do you wish to draw within yourself for the spring and beyond? Then decide on a selection of upbeat music you enjoy. It should have a running time of at least ten minutes. Next, find a time when you will be alone and able to let loose.

Finally, like the Lady Gaga song, just dance. No eyes, no judgment. Create your own small chant to repeat out loud and in your mind while dancing; repeat this to seal your spell.

Raven Digitalis

February

The word *February* is based on the Latin *februa* and refers to the Roman festival of purification of the same name. This festival later became integrated with February's infamous Lupercalia. Since ancient times, February has been observed as a month of cleansing, cleaning, purification, and preparation for the warm months ahead. We see the Celtic Imbolg (Candlemas) celebrated in February to perpetuate the summoning of solar light. In many parts of the world at this time, the promise of sunlight seems bleak, even imaginary. The world around us is slowly awakening from its wintery slumber, and some semblance of excitement begins to grow in the hearts of those attuned to the seasonal tides.

Daylight hours are short in February, so this time of year can sometimes feel depressive. We must actively cultivate our inner light through regular exercise, solid sleep, meditation, yoga, ritual, studying, artwork, and planning ahead for the year. When performing magickal work this month, remember that your energy levels may be lower than usual and you must summon your own inner light to strengthen and illuminate your efforts. Do whatever it takes to stay on top of your game, keep energized, cultivate happiness, and embrace February's cleansing rebirth!

Raven Digitalis

February 1
Thursday

3rd ♎

☽ v/c 4:03 am

☽ → ♏ 3:37 pm

Color of the day: Purple
Incense of the day: Myrrh

Imbolc Sundown Candle Spell

Imbolc traditionally begins at sundown on February 1. With many parts of the world still coated in rain or snow, we honor this changing of the seasons with the glowing of a candle flame. For this spell you will need a tealight candle, some sprigs of greenery if you have any available (to help with atmosphere), and a clean space on your windowsill. On the windowsill place the tealight and greenery. Safely light your candle and say:

*Around the world, winter is
taking its last breaths,*

*And stirrings of spring rise
from the darkness.*

*I light this candle to honor
the wisdom and inspiration
that comes from new life.*

*As the wheel of the Earth
moves, I move with it.*

Close your eyes and think about what new things you are preparing for in your life. Place your hands close to the flame, letting the heat remind you of passion and motivation for the coming season. Sit and meditate for as long as you feel is necessary, then blow out your candle if it is still burning.

Amanda Lynn & Jason Mankey

NOTES:

February 2
Friday

3rd ♏

4th Quarter 6:18 pm

Color of the day: White
Incense of the day: Violet

Imbolc – Groundhog Day

Invoking Springtime

Instead of seeing today as midwinter, let's see Imbolc as the first day of spring. No matter where you live, look out the window. If it's snowing, look under the snow and see the sprouting green leaves. Imagine your yard in its springtime splendor.

Gather your coven (or work alone) to invoke springtime. Place two candles on your altar, one dark and one light (white or yellow). Light the dark candle and go around the circle, giving thanks for winter's rest. Use the dark candle to ignite the light candle, then safely extinguish the dark candle and remove it from the altar. As the light candle burns, read this excerpt from John Keats:

Open afresh your round of starry folds,

Ye ardent marigolds!

*Dry up the moisture from
your golden lids,*

For great Apollo bids

*That in these days your
praises should be sung*

*On many harps, which
he has lately strung.*

Talk about the signs of spring and the music of Apollo's harps. Let the candle burn safely down, then open the circle.

Barbara Ardinger

NOTES:

February 3
Saturday

4th ♏

☽ v/c 10:24 pm

Color of the day: Black
Incense of the day: Rue

Improve Your Luck

Today is Setsubun, a Shinto observance of spring. For luck in this belief system, like in many, beans play an important role. Today's magickal work involves numerology, beans, and a chant.

First, lightly roast two cups of beans in a cast-iron pot over a fire outdoors or on a cookie sheet in the oven set at 350 degrees F. The type of beans is of your choosing but should align with your ancestry, preferred recipes, or options available in the pantry. For example, as an African American, I might select black-eyed peas. Then let your beans cool to room temperature.

Fill your hands with the beans and spread them in and around your sacred space. (An altar or favorite personal space works well.) As you sprinkle them, chant:

Devils out, happiness in!

(In Japanese this is *Oni wa soto, fuku wa uchi!*) Afterward, cook the number of beans that corresponds with your age until tender, and eat them. This should improve your luck.

Stephanie Rose Bird

February 4
Sunday

4th ♏

☽ → ♐ 1:28 am

Color of the day: Gold
Incense of the day: Eucalyptus

Magical Purpose

An altar can be as simple as a collection of beautiful objects, but there's also power in creating a space that's designed to support magical work. You can build a "working" altar by starting with a blank slate and adding only the items that have a specific magical function. For instance, you might include a ritual blade to banish or "cut away" unwanted energies, or a cup or bowl to contain energy. The space can be set up however you choose; the key is to have a clear reason for including each item.

Then consecrate each object for its chosen purpose. Begin by focusing on your breath, coming to a centered, focused state of mind, then visualize the object carrying out its intended function—for example, seeing the blade cutting through unwanted energy and dispelling it. Maintain the image as the energy of this function builds within you, then hold the object in both hands, sending the energy into the object as you say:

I call upon this (item) to (state the purpose). So mote it be.

Melissa Tipton

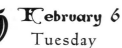

 February 5
Monday

4th ♐

Color of the day: Ivory
Incense of the day: Neroli

Achieve Your Goals Spell

As we move toward spring, it's a good time to "plant" your goals to achieve success. For this spell you'll need a plain sheet of paper and a small handful of garden or potting soil. Begin by writing a few of your goals on the paper. Stick to a small number, maybe three or four. Read them over. Are they what you really want? Are they realistic?

Next, sprinkle the soil over the paper, covering the goals you just wrote. Set the paper aside for a few days. Then, when you feel the time is right, shake the soil off into a small dish. Lay the paper aside. Keep the soil in the dish on your altar. For about a week, occasionally feel the soil with your fingers as you meditate on your goals. After a week, discard the soil, outside if possible. Keep your list of goals. After you realize them, you may discard the paper too.

James Kambos

February 6
Tuesday

4th ♐

☽ v/c 12:06 am
☽ → ♑ 7:08 am

Color of the day: White
Incense of the day: Geranium

Draw It Out Healing Spell

Use this spell to help cleanse your body of baneful energies and spark healing. Take a washcloth dampened with cool water and rub it slowly over your skin, beginning at your face and then going down your neck, across your chest and down each arm, down your torso, and down each leg. Then boil this washcloth in a pot of heavily salted water. As the washcloth boils, drink a glass of cold, filtered spring water, envisioning the refreshing liquid cleansing your body with each drink. Let the washcloth boil for a few minutes, then turn off the heat and pour out the water. Allow the washcloth to cool, then wring it out and tie it into a hard knot. Place this near your bed until the illness has passed, then either dispose of it or run the washcloth through the laundry and donate it.

Melanie Marquis

February 7
Wednesday

4th ♑

Color of the day: Yellow
Incense of the day: Lilac

Altar Blessing

An altar provides a focus for mystical practice. It can provide a place for worship, spellcasting, or whatever else you need. In the process, however, it tends to pick up stray bits of energy. Over time, these can build up enough to become distracting, rather like bug spots on a windshield. So an altar needs to be cleaned and blessed periodically.

Begin by removing all the things on the altar—candlesticks, statuettes, bowls, and so on. Take off the altar cloth. If it's washable, wash it. If not, just shake it out, and consider whether it's shabby enough to need replacing. Wipe off the altar with a suitable cleaner. Then say:

Altar shining clean and bright,

Blessed be by sacred light.

Hold the holy items high,

Here between the earth and sky.

Magic flowing fair and free,

As I will, so mote it be.

Finish by putting a clean cloth over the altar. Then set your items back in their customary places.

Elizabeth Barrette

February 8
Thursday

4th ♑

☽ v/c 2:52 am

☽ → ♒ 8:59 am

Color of the day: Green
Incense of the day: Clove

Dark Moon Problem-Solver

Try this with any problem for which no obvious solution seems to be in sight. Light a candle and call on the Goddess (or call on the Divine in another way). On a scrap of paper, write:

Thank you for solving the issue with _____ in an even better way than I ever could have envisioned. I am so grateful that I never have to worry about it again.

Fold or roll up the paper and place it in your cauldron or in a small box with a lid. As you literally close the lid on the problem, feel that you are releasing all energy related to the issue and entrusting the problem to the Goddess (or the Divine). Extinguish the candle.

Leave the box or cauldron closed at least until the next dark moon. During that time, do your best to release all worry to the Divine while taking action (or taking no action) as you feel guided. Once the problem is solved, recycle the paper.

Tess Whitehurst

February 9
Friday

4th ♒

☽ v/c 5:59 pm

New Moon 5:59 pm

Color of the day: Rose
Incense of the day: Vanilla

Dark Moon Chocolate

Today is both a new moon and Chocolate Day (as part of the celebratory week leading up to Valentine's Day)—which is a pretty tasty combination! The new moon is an excellent time to shift our focus inward, which can be great for healing but may cause anxiety as well, especially if we can only seem to focus on what we've done wrong. A little dark chocolate can help bring some sweetness and grounding to the energy.

There's a wide variety of dark chocolate bars and morsels available, so find one you like, preferably something with easy bite sizes that stores well so you can have the chocolate handy. When you need it, pull out a piece and say:

In the darkness, I taste the sweet.

Whole and magic, I am complete.

Clear your mind and focus only on the flavor, fully enjoying the sensation of the chocolate in your mouth. Then take a cleansing breath and know good things will come.

Laura Tempest Zakroff

February 10
Saturday

1st ♒

☽ → ♓ 8:42 am

Color of the day: Gray
Incense of the day: Pine

Lunar New Year (Dragon)

Lunar New Year Luck Spell

Today is the start of Lunar New Year. The year runs until January 28, 2025, and is the year of the Wood Dragon. Symbolized by gold and silver and associated with the direction east, the Wood Dragon welcomes abundance and new beginnings. In China, the dragon symbolizes nobility, power, and the emperor, and promises a lucky, abundant, and powerful year.

Today, invoke lucky Wood Dragon energy to bless the year, and your life, with abundance, wealth, power, and noble energy. Traditionally a red envelope containing money is gifted to children or elders, wishing them prosperity and luck. Find some red paper (maybe you have leftover Yule or Christmas wrap) and use it to fold money into. Make a gift to a child or elder. As you give wealth and prosperity, you bless and magnetize yourself simultaneously. As the Wiccan Rede decrees, what you send out returns to you threefold.

Dallas Jennifer Cobb

February 11
Sunday

1st ♓

Color of the day: Yellow
Incense of the day: Hyacinth

holy Smoke! An Incense Blessing

I have been obsessed with super-fine, high-quality incense—both stick and resin—since the age of fifteen. I attribute this to a past life, but whatever the case, there is something special about genuine, non-synthetic smoke sanctifying a room, home, or outside space.

Simply collect all the incense you have. Feel free to be a connoisseur like me by tossing out the "fake" stuff.

Face the east. Holding your hands over all your incense, take deep breaths and, when centered, declare the following six times:

Creatures of air, power of the east, the incense before me is enchanted with life and all that I intend. And so it is!

Raven Digitalis

February 12
Monday

1st ♓

☽ v/c 7:32 am

☽ → ♈ 8:26 am

Color of the day: Silver
Incense of the day: Clary sage

You Are What You Eat

This spell is easily incorporated into daily or regular food magic practices. You are connecting yourself to the food you eat and all the unseen forces that brought you here, right now. When you eat, say:

As I eat this _____ (name whatever food you are about to eat), I acknowledge that all food is energy and potential as I am energy and potential.

All food nourishes my spirit.

All food comes from interconnected and unseen processes, human-made, earth-made, and universe-made.

I am the result of an unbroken chain of circumstances stretching back through infinite time and stretching forward to this moment.

I am the mystery of the universe made flesh.

As I eat this food, I invoke myself as the spirit and potential of all things.

Then eat and remember that you and the universe are inseparable.

Phoenix LeFae & Gwion Raven

February 13
Tuesday

1st ♈

Color of the day: Black
Incense of the day: Ginger

Mardi Gras (Fat Tuesday)

A Kitchen Blessing Spell

In England, this day is known as Shrove Tuesday or Pancake Tuesday. It's the time of feasting before the Lenten sacrifices. Flat, crepe-like pancakes with fresh lemon juice and sprinkled sugar are eaten. This spell blesses the place where food is prepared and where people often gather together.

You'll need a new broom (I like an old-fashioned corn broom for this, but any broom will do), lavender oil, and salt. In the morning, rub lavender oil where the whisks of the broom join the handle, and say:

*I anoint thee with oil that
thy work may be blessed.*

After the evening meal, sprinkle salt on the kitchen floor. Use the new broom to sweep it up. (If you have a carpet, put down a mat and sprinkle salt onto that.) As you sweep, say:

To purify and provide, so mote it be.

Gather the salt that has been swept and place it outside the main entrance. The kitchen has been blessed.

Charlie Rainbow Wolf

February 14
Wednesday

1st ♈

☽ v/c 5:21 am
☽ → ♉ 10:02 am

Color of the day: Topaz
Incense of the day: Marjoram

Valentine's Day – Ash Wednesday

The Language of Love

Today is Valentine's Day, a day geared toward a show of love for others. However, we need to make sure we take care of ourselves first so we can attract the love we truly need and deserve into our lives.

On this day, before you share it with another, take a ritual bath or shower. Use a bath bomb or shower melt with a scent that you associate with love and that relaxes you. As you immerse yourself in the water, repeat to yourself three times:

I am love. I am loved.

Let the water drain away along with any of your doubts that you are unworthy. Go about your evening and know you are attracting the right energy to you.

Charlynn Walls

February 15
Thursday

1st ♉

Color of the day: White
Incense of the day: Nutmeg

hammer Time!

It's hammer time! MC Hammer brought the groove and those fabulous pants to life when he recorded his world-famous song "U Can't Touch This" in 1989. On this Thursday (Thor's Day), let us release the icy cold grip that winter has on us by putting on our favorite music and dancing around a little. Dance as best as you can, in whatever way is appropriate for you. And if you've got a pair of those fabulous pants, all the better!

We all need a bit of inspiration sometimes to move our bodies. For some of us, especially us older folks or those for whom movement may be difficult, just moving a little to our favorite song can do wonders. So bring some good juju magic to this day by playing your favorite song and getting your groove on!

Najah Lightfoot

February 16
Friday

1st ♉

☽ v/c 10:01 am

2nd Quarter 10:01 am

☽ → ♊ 2:39 pm

Color of the day: Purple
Incense of the day: Cypress

What Do We Believe In?

In the play *Peter Pan*, when Tinker Bell drinks the poison intended for Peter and her light begins to fade, the audience saves her life by applauding. I even clap for her when I'm watching the DVD.

We may not be able to literally save lives with applause, but we can cheer and encourage people and save their energetic lives by applauding. When you hear a speech, even an informal one, on a topic you support—applaud. When you hear music sung or played beautifully—applaud. When you see an action or even a gesture that will help people—applaud. When you witness an event, even a minor one, that's uplifting and bright—applaud.

What do we believe in? Maybe the fairies live in all of us. Can you feel yours? We need their light, their energy, their beauty, their magic. When we glimpse a fairy acting in someone's body, speaking in their voice—applaud.

Barbara Ardinger

February 17
Saturday

2nd ♊

Color of the day: Indigo
Incense of the day: Sage

honoring Wood Dragon

The energy of Wood Dragon is upon us in 2024. This is a complex dragon that embodies honor and nobility and symbolizes success and power. Wood Dragon is green and is symbolic of spring.

Today, if you have a censer, place a piece of sandalwood incense inside of it on white-hot charcoal. Swing this counterclockwise in your living room. As an alternative, wave a few lit sticks of sandalwood incense in the room in the same manner, using a safe incense holder to avoid fire.

As you move counterclockwise, chant:

*Wood Dragon, I use my powers
to invoke your spirit.*

*Let me ride your rising energy
and draw from your intuition.*

Help me conjure luck.

*With every step, let your
power and energy flow.*

Repeat the chant thrice. Extinguish the incense.

Stephanie Rose Bird

NOTES:

February 18
Sunday

2nd ♊

☽ v/c 10:21 pm

☽ → ♋ 10:25 pm

☉ → ♓ 11:13 pm

Color of the day: Orange
Incense of the day: Juniper

Absolute Potential

At the top of the Qabalistic Tree of Life is Kether, a plane of absolute potential. Here, energy exists before form, with the ability to become anything, and it can dissolve stuck or rigid elements in our lives, returning them to a state of greater fluidity and potential.

This is especially helpful when something seems unbalanced. Perhaps you've been pouring time and effort into a relationship or project, but you don't feel like you're getting much in return. Surrendering this energy to the potentiality of Kether loosens the imbalanced configuration, allowing the energy to re-form in new, more beneficial ways.

On a piece of paper, write a description of the situation. Tap into how you feel when you're embroiled in this dynamic, and feel the paper soaking up that energy like a sponge. Light a white candle, then touch the paper to its flame, letting it burn to ash on a heatproof surface. Feel the energy releasing, free to organize in new, more functional ways. Snuff out the candle and dispose of the ash once it's fully cooled.

Melissa Tipton

NOTES:

February 19
Monday

2nd ♋

Color of the day: Gray
Incense of the day: Lily

Presidents' Day

happy home Spell

Cast this spell to encourage a happy home. Obtain a selection of crystals. You might choose clear quartz, rose quartz, smoky quartz, citrine, or amethyst. Have each person in your household select one crystal to place in each common room in your house, so that everyone has a representative crystal in every room that the family shares. Have each household member hold their crystals while thinking of something that makes them feel happy. Then have everyone place their crystals in a single dish in each room as happy wishes for the family are made and shared. Let each person also choose a crystal to place alone within their own personal, private living space. Encourage your household members to make a happy wish for themselves as they place their personal crystal in their own private living area.

Should conflicts arise, sprinkle rosemary, salt, lavender, or water on the communal dishes of crystals to help stabilize and calm things down. If a general gloom or dreariness falls over the house, anoint the stones with lemon juice or place them on a bed of basil. The crystals should help everyone feel positive and wanted within the home.

Melanie Marquis

NOTES:

February 20
Tuesday

2nd ♋

Color of the day: Maroon
Incense of the day: Cedar

Universal Understanding Spell

One of the greatest peace songs of all time is "Universal Soldier." The writer of this song is Buffy Sainte-Marie, and today is her birthday. Let's honor her and this song by getting to understand one another better. Sit at your altar and safely light a blue candle. Ground and center, then say:

Peace and understanding
begin with me.

Now I will spread
understanding universally.

Peace and understanding are the key.

Safely extinguish the candle. Begin to act on the words you just said. Here are some ideas. Go to an international cultural fair, and talk to people from different backgrounds and eat different foods. Buy books by authors of ethnicities other than your own. Take time to learn another language. Many colleges offer international coffee hours where you can meet students from other lands, so try attending. Together we can bring about universal understanding.

James Kambos

February 21
Wednesday

2nd ♋

☽ v/c 1:38 am

☽ → ♌ 8:40 am

Color of the day: White
Incense of the day: Lavender

Invoking Daily Solar Protection

To begin your day in a balanced mental, emotional, and spiritual vibe, simply go outside to a location where you won't be bothered for a few minutes. Bring an offering of your favorite dried herb or flower. This exercise is a morning procedure for solar energetic shielding.

Six is the number of the Sun as a planet in esoteric Qabalah. Standing to face the eastern Sun, take six deep breaths in through the nose and out through the mouth. Gently focus on the Sun. Say the following six times:

Conquering Sun, O holy one, ignite
my day no matter what comes!

Finish by crossing your arms across your chest, with your right hand on your heart. Take six more deep breaths while seeing sunlight surrounding you. Bow and give thanks to conclude.

Raven Digitalis

February 22
Thursday

2nd ♌

☽ v/c 11:18 pm

Color of the day: Crimson
Incense of the day: Carnation

National Margarita Day

Jimmy Buffet may have you believing that a margarita's magic is related mainly to attempting to heal a broken heart and failing. Well, maybe there's some truth to that. But for this spell, you're going to work with the magical properties of agave and lime to strengthen and bless one or more of your friendships. Agave brings sweetness and a sense of shared adventure. Lime is used for blessing and empowering, as it's aligned with the strength and beauty of the sun. Invite one or more friends over and make everyone a margarita with any recipe you prefer. (You don't have to use agave nectar unless you want to, because tequila is made from agave.) As you blend or shake, send energy into the cocktail and whisper or think these words:

Bless this friendship (or these friendships). May it (they) be sweet, bright, and filled with laughter and love. Thank you.

Serve, toast your friend(s), and then enjoy (responsibly). Repeat as desired.

Tess Whitehurst

February 23
Friday

2nd ♌

☽ → ♍ 8:38 pm

Color of the day: Coral
Incense of the day: Alder

Put It on Ice

February is in the dead of winter, a time of hibernation and withdrawal. It only makes sense to utilize the power of the season to help us with a protection spell. When we are threatened, it can be prudent to take active steps to ensure we are safe and secure. This spell is for when you know who is making an active attack either online or in real life. You can use a picture of the person in question or their name written on a piece of paper.

Place the picture or written name in an ice tray or a ziplock bag. Fill the container with water so it covers the picture or name. Place in the freezer and forget about it. This will help the person cool off and hopefully forget their vendetta. If necessary, follow up with the proper law enforcement/judicial procedures in addition to the spell for good magical hygiene.

Charlynn Walls

☾ February 24
Saturday

2nd ♍

Full Moon 7:30 am

Color of the day: Blue
Incense of the day: Sandalwood

Moon Wisdom

Today is the full moon of February. This phase brings things to fruition. It correlates with wealth and prosperity. The full moon is round like a silver coin. It is the peak of all that has come before.

This is a good time to meditate on your accomplishments and how you achieved them. Take a silver coin, such as a nickel, dime, or quarter. Hold it in your hand to use as a focus. Sit in a chair or on a floor cushion.

Think back over the past two to four weeks. Consider the financial decisions you have made. How much money have you earned? How much have you saved? What temptations have you avoided? What have you invested in? How have these choices contributed to your prosperity?

Turn over the coin in your hand, round and silver as the moon. What mistakes have you made? How can you avoid repeating them? Carry the coin into the next month as you continue working on your prosperity.

Elizabeth Barrette

February 25
Sunday

3rd ♍

Color of the day: Yellow
Incense of the day: Almond

What No Longer Serves Me

After yesterday's full moon, it's time to observe your internal energy. The shift from a robust culmination energy to a waning vibe can be a harsh one. You may feel depressed or empty, sad or lost. But this is a powerful force to consciously harness.

Take time today to sit in silence and reflect on anything you need to reduce, let go of, release, or be done with. Are you relying too much on caffeine? Time to reduce reliance. Do you flop on the couch in front of the TV all evening? Rethink that. Do you hang out with less than uplifting people? Release them.

Cultivate awareness. Make a list. Know what no longer serves you.

And for the next fourteen days, until the next new moon on March 10, use the waning energy of the moon to help you release, reduce, let go of, or be done with what no longer is needed.

Dallas Jennifer Cobb

▽ February 26
Monday

3rd ♍

☽ v/c 2:35 am

☽ → ♎ 9:29 am

Color of the day: White
Incense of the day: Rosemary

Wash Those Cares Away

The waning moon is a good time for some self-care. I often feel as if the full moon drains my energy a bit. I've gotten used to this rhythm and use it to turn inward. For this spell you'll need a bath or shower, plus a bath bomb, a shower steamer, or a drop of essential oil (to add to the bathwater or shower basin). Jasmine, sandalwood, and myrrh are the best fragrances, but any lunar herb will suffice.

The spell is simple. Enjoy the shower or bath. Let the water soothe away cares and frustrations. If you are showering, envision the negative emotions and stresses of the day washing down the drain as the water engulfs you. If you are in a bathtub, feel the water drawing the tension and drama away from you, then pull the plug while you are still in the bath so you can feel those energies disappearing down the plughole.

Charlie Rainbow Wolf

NOTES:

February 27
Tuesday

3rd ♎︎

☽ v/c 1:22 pm

Color of the day: Scarlet
Incense of the day: Basil

Remember Your Dreams Spell

Dreams can reveal a lot of information. Through dreams, our subconscious speaks to us and the language of magick comes through. However, it's not always easy to remember dreams. The first step is to keep a journal next to your bed. Any time you wake up, write down what you remember, even if this is just colors, concepts, or feelings.

You can seed your dreams before going to bed in order to ask for specific help. Early in the day, get a small bowl. Put the following items in the bowl:

- 1 pinch of dried mugwort
- 1 pinch of dried lavender
- 1 pinch of dried rose

Then fill the bowl with water.

Using the first two fingers of your dominant hand, draw an invoking pentacle over the water. Lean close to the bowl and whisper the question or advice that you seek during sleep. Place the bowl of water in the freezer.

Before going to sleep that night, take out the bowl of frozen water and put it under your bed. When you wake up, immediately write down anything on your mind. Take a bath, adding in the water from the bowl, and allow yourself to meditate on the dreams you had.

Phoenix LeFae & Gwion Raven

NOTES:

Ḟebruary 28
Wednesday

3rd ♎

☽ → ♏ 10:09 **pm**

Color of the day: Brown
Incense of the day: Honeysuckle

Bully, Be Gone!

National Pink Day (or Pink Shirt Day) started with a show of solidarity by two Canadian boys wearing pink shirts to support another student who was being bullied. It is a day dedicated to breaking the bullying cycle that is found not only in school but outside the classroom as well.

Unfortunately, bullies can even be found in the magical practitioner community, especially among those who are power-hungry or insecure in their own practice, so they seek to dominate and abuse others.

Taking some inspiration from National Pink Day, here's an anti-bullying charm. On a small pink candle (a tealight votive or smaller), inscribe the name of the bully. Light the candle and repeat this chant three times, then let the candle burn out safely:

Hurtful words and vicious deeds,

Bruised egos make angry seeds.

Cool your rage or find the door.

Be gone! A bully no more!

Laura Tempest Zakroff

Ḟebruary 29
Thursday

3rd ♏

Color of the day: Purple
Incense of the day: Balsam

Leap Day

Embracing Leap Day Magic

Leap Day is one of the more mysterious days in our calendar. What makes it most interesting is that it is the rarest day, only existing every four years. We believe that this day is most auspicious for manifesting some longer-term spells.

One simple spell is to write a letter to your future self describing all the things you want to manifest in your life over the next four years. Take a pen and a piece of paper and jot down where you see yourself in the coming years, being as vague or specific as you wish. Your goals can be magical or mundane, whichever you like, but definitely keep them to a realistic standard. Put the paper in an envelope and seal it with a pentacle by drawing one on the envelope closure. Store the letter in a place you will remember and look forward to the sense of accomplishment you will feel when you open it in four years!

Amanda Lynn & Jason Mankey

March

M arch is upon us! March is a month of unpredictable weather. Will the weather spirits decide to bring us a last hurrah of winter in the form of a blustery snowstorm or instead bring us signs of spring's beginning in the form of budding trees and perhaps rain showers sprinkled with mild, sunny days? There really is no telling! However, for those of us who follow the Wheel of the Year, the spring equinox is a time of new beginnings, regardless of the weather.

Rituals of spring and new beginnings will take place around the globe this month. Druids still gather at Stonehenge to welcome the rising sun on the morning of the equinox. March also is the time to celebrate the festival of Holi, popular in India and Nepal. People engage in paint fights, covering each other in festive splatters of vibrant color, welcoming the arrival of spring and all its vibrancy.

In March, however you choose to celebrate, work the magick of new beginnings!

Blake Octavian Blair

March 1
Friday

3rd ♏

Color of the day: White
Incense of the day: Orchid

User-Friendlier Technology

If, like me, you're older than twelve, you may find technology bewildering when you get a new device or an upgrade. To make this new technology more understandable and easier to work with, fill it with magic.

Lay the new device on your altar. Center yourself and then surround the device with a circle of indigo (third-eye chakra) energy. Strengthen the circle, then expand so it's a big indigo bubble with your device in the center. Speak the following invocation:

O, (name of device),
New Technology—

O, Smart Technology—

Be friendly.

Be accessible!

Take my hand

And lead me through your mysteries,

Through your vocabulary,

Through your apps and upgrades.

O, Helpful Technology—

Be kind to me.

Be user-friendly.

Make me your partner.

So mote it be!

Sit with the indigo bubble with the device in the center and visualize yourself using the device comfortably and with confidence. When you feel ready to proceed, open the bubble and the circle and pick up the device. Do something!

Barbara Ardinger

NOTES:

March 2
Saturday

3rd ♏

☽ v/c 2:47 am

☽ → ♐ 8:56 am

Color of the day: Black
Incense of the day: Ivy

Wind and Knot Spell

This spell is similar to the ones that sailors used to cast to capture the power of the wind in ancient times. When they needed more wind for their sails, they'd untie a knot that they had tied in their sails.

Use this spell when you need to give your spells a boost of energy. You'll need one square handkerchief or piece of fabric. Go outside on a windy day with your handkerchief or fabric. Hold it up to the sky and say:

Wind that blows across the land,
wind that blows across the sea,

With your mighty power, favor me.

Now quickly tie the handkerchief or fabric into a knot. If you want more knots, repeat the charm. When you cast a spell that needs more power, untie one of your knots as you reach the spell's climax.

James Kambos

March 3
Sunday

3rd ♐

4th Quarter 10:23 am

Color of the day: Gold
Incense of the day: Marigold

Spring Fresh Floor Wash

Spring is the cleaning season. It's time to wash away the old energy of winter and bring in a breath of fresh air. You can do this is by creating a magical floor wash. Despite the name, it will clean many different surfaces, including wood, linoleum, and glass. This works with a wet mop, a sponge, or a dish rag.

In a bucket, combine 1 gallon hot water, ½ cup white vinegar, 2 tablespoons lemon juice, and 5 drops essential oil. Lemon, peppermint, and tea tree oils all have cleansing, uplifting qualities. Stir counterclockwise to combine, which helps dispel any negative energies.

Clean from the back of the room or house toward the door. Mop floors and wipe down tables, countertops, and cabinets. Clean bathroom fixtures too. Mop right over the threshold on the way out, to remove dirt and unwanted energies. When you're done cleaning, if you have a yard you can throw the remaining floor wash into the grass. Otherwise, pour it down the toilet.

Elizabeth Barrette

March 4
Monday

4th ♐

☽ v/c 10:41 am

☽ → ♑ 4:15 pm

Color of the day: Ivory
Incense of the day: Narcissus

A Prayer for the Living

In March of 1918, the first case of the Spanish flu was documented. We've just come through another similar pandemic. These are good reminders not to take health—on either a personal or a global level—for granted.

For this healing spell you will need:

• A white taper or pillar candle

• A knife or athame

• A box of matches

• A heatproof plate or dish

Using the knife, first carve a heart into the candle, followed by an equal-armed cross and then a circle. (The arrangement doesn't matter as long as the three emblems are on the candle.) Light the candle and let some of the wax drip onto the heatproof dish, then secure the candle onto the plate using the melted wax.

Stare into the flame and project good energy toward yourself, toward your loved ones, toward those you know, toward your country, toward the world. There's a lot of toxic posi-tivity (and negativity) out there, but this spell will help to restore balance. When the meditation is finished, pinch the flame out with your fingers or use a candle snuffer.

Charlie Rainbow Wolf

NOTES:

March 5
Tuesday

4th ♑

Color of the day: Red
Incense of the day: Ylang-ylang

Five in Motion Spell

Regardless of whether March marks for you the shift from winter into spring or summer into fall, it's a good time to clear yourself energetically. We'll use the Tarot and the body to achieve this cleanse. The fives in the Minor Arcana point to the need to break a cycle. These cards are a call to shift how you think, feel, perceive, or act in order to move forward.

I recommend doing this clearing in the morning or evening, but it can work any time you need to realign. You can stand, sit, or lie down. Take three slow breaths while considering the five external points of your body: feet, hands, and head—all connecting back to the heart. Focus on each part of the body in turn as you say:

One foot forward to be confident.

One foot following in harmony.

One hand giving to create change.

One hand receiving to accept aid.

One mind open to new directions.

All in union with my heart to guide.

Take one more cleansing breath to finish and you're done!

Laura Tempest Zakroff

March 6
Wednesday

4th ♑

☽ v/c 2:35 pm

☽ → ♒ 7:38 pm

Color of the day: White
Incense of the day: Marjoram

Magickal Springtime Floor Wash

Although it may not officially be spring yet, many of us in the Northern Hemisphere can certainly feel spring springing, day by day, hour by hour. Let's start utilizing that energy for spring cleaning!

Simply boil water, then add a wee bit of sea salt and vinegar, concluding with one cup of makeshift tea designed with your intentions at hand. Add this to your mopping water. This tea is not meant for drinking, as you will add it to your mopping bucket. Do not allow the tea to steep for more than a few minutes, as it may stain the flooring. The tea should be made using one or more herbs that correspond to your cleansing intentions, such as lavender for peace, mint for purification, and/or hot pepper for chasing out bad vibes.

Sing a favorite song over the brew, loudly declare your intentions, and visualize the concoction glowing with light. Blissfully mop your floors and throw the rest of the brew outside on your front porch or point of entry.

Raven Digitalis

March 7
Thursday

4th ♒

Color of the day: Turquoise
Incense of the day: Jasmine

Pisces Power!

Let's celebrate the people of Pisces, the sign of the two fishes. Pisces is the sign of ethereal, mysterious, old souls with kind, deep, sensitive hearts. It relates to ancient wisdom and the energy of Neptune and the deep sea. However, not all fish swim in the sea. Some swim in rivers or high mountain lakes. Pisces people know how to swim away and disappear in plain sight. Have you ever tried to catch a fish with your bare hands? It ain't gonna happen.

Today, during Pisces season, give thanks for these watery human creatures who are so deeply enchanting. Vibe with the element of water, be it snow, rain, or water from your tap, for all water flows from nature.

Najah Lightfoot

March 8
Friday

4th ♒
☽ v/c 1:56 pm
☽ → ♓ 8:03 pm

Color of the day: Pink
Incense of the day: Mint

Automatic Writing for Self-Love

Today is Friday, the day of the week that is associated with Venus and corresponds with love of all kinds. Let's take a journey down the road of self-love and appreciation and do some automatic writing with that in mind.

Put on some good music (maybe the Cure's "Friday I'm in Love"), dress up in something that makes you feel good, and perhaps even light some scented candles to set the mood. When you feel comfortable and relaxed, connect with the meaning of self-love and get inspired to let go of any inhibitions. Pull out your journal or a piece of paper and just let the divine inspiration flow. Don't worry too much about being coherent. The point of this exercise is just to write down whatever comes to you.

And remember this is about *you*. You are writing down what you love and appreciate about yourself. When you're finished, read the entry and allow yourself to shine in how you are seen through the eyes of the divine.

Amanda Lynn & Jason Mankey

March 9
Saturday

4th ♓

Color of the day: Gray
Incense of the day: Sage

Binding Spell for Defense

Use this spell to stop threatening or harmful adversarial actions against you. You'll need a rusty nail and a black piece of string. Hold the string between your fingertips and focus on the adversary you wish to stop. Think of the string as actually encapsulating the very essence of this foe. Tie nine knots along the length of the string as you say:

This is my enemy tied up in knots.

Then tie the string just beneath the nailhead, and wrap it around the length of the nail as you say:

This is my enemy losing direction.

Tie off the end of the string with a quadruple knot as you say:

This is my enemy stopped for good.

Drive the nail all the way down into firm dirt, somewhere away from your property where you won't go again. Stomp on the spot as you say:

This is my enemy bound forever,
unable to harm me, unable to hurt.

Cover the nailhead completely with dirt so that it's no longer visible.

Melanie Marquis

 March 10
Sunday

4th ♓

New Moon 5:00 am
☽ v/c 3:45 pm
☽ → ♈ 8:19 pm

Color of the day: Amber
Incense of the day: Hyacinth

Daylight Saving Time
begins at 2:00 a.m. –
Ramadan begins at sundown

Mindful Consumption

With the Muslim holy month of Ramadan beginning at sundown, this is a great time to contemplate the value of fasting. During the entire month of Ramadan, Muslims refrain from eating from dawn until dusk to remember the less fortunate and reinforce gratitude.

Intermittent fasting has become quite popular for weight loss and cleansing. Can you dedicate part of the day to consciously fast from something? It doesn't have to be food. It could be fasting from social media, television, shopping, or news media. By consciously abstaining from these things, you will cultivate an awareness of those less fortunate, intense gratitude for what you have access to, and an understanding of what you consume daily (and sometimes mindlessly).

Dallas Jennifer Cobb

March 11
Monday

1st ♈

Color of the day: Lavender
Incense of the day: Hyssop

Astral Travel

Since today is a Monday, we can tap into the energies of the Moon. This is an excellent time to work a spell that will help us travel in the astral plane. This meditation will help us connect with our spiritual guides/teachers. Keep a pad of paper and pen next to you so you can record what happens. Minimize distractions. Put on soft music or enjoy silence if you prefer. You will want to be in a relaxed state in a place where you are comfortable, as you may be sitting for a while. State your intention aloud:

I am traveling to meet my spiritual teachers who will guide me to achieve my highest good.

Close your eyes and listen to the soft rhythm of the music in the background as you feel yourself rise out of your body. Reach out and connect with your spiritual teacher. Listen and absorb what they share with you. When you are ready, think about your physical body and your physical environment, and return there. Record what you have learned to reflect on later.

Charlynn Walls

March 12
Tuesday

1st ♈

☽ v/c 7:08 am
☽ → ♉ 8:28 pm

Color of the day: Gray
Incense of the day: Ginger

Energetic Unplugging

When our choices feel bound up in what other people think or expect of us, it's helpful to use energetic techniques to support real-world action as we disentangle our power from external influences.

Cast a magic circle: Stand facing north, and sense energy welling up from the earth into your body. Then let energy cascade down from the sky, entering your crown and filling your body. Allow these energies to combine, flowing into your dominant hand. With arm outstretched and index finger pointed, visualize drawing a line of energy in the air as you turn clockwise, and repeat for a total of three revolutions. Your circle is now cast.

Now envision a challenging situation, like you're painting a picture with thought and emotion. When this feels complete, see an electrical outlet with a cord plugged into this mental picture. This is a cord to your energy field, and with intention, unplug it, detaching your power from the situation.

Release the circle: As if you're opening a curtain, "grab" the energy and move counterclockwise. Be open to intuitive messages prompting real-world actions that will support this energetic unplugging.

Melissa Tipton

NOTES:

March 13
Wednesday

1st ♉

Color of the day: Yellow
Incense of the day: Bay laurel

Make a Balance Ladder

Witch's ladders have been employed by magick workers since at least the seventeenth century. They are made with rope, often three feet long. Tied into the rope every few inches are knots, feathers, sticks, hair, fur, and all manner of charms, stones, and baubles. Witch's ladders are used for protection, summoning, sending messages to spirits, and warding off onlookers.

This take on a Witch's ladder helps create balance. First get thirty-six inches of rope or twine. Collect items representing balance for your life. These can be anything: a coin for continued wealth, acorns for timely growth, a feather for spontaneous flights of fancy, a red clown nose for laughter, herbs from your window box for abundance, a train ticket for travel, or a key symbolizing a safe home. Tie the items to the rope from bottom to top. If everyone in the household is participating in the magick, create this together. Hang the ladder in a conspicuous place. If the ladder is for personal use, hang it in a secret place where only you can see it.

Phoenix LeFae & Gwion Raven

March 14
Thursday

1st ♉

☽ v/c 6:29 pm

☽ → ♊ 11:16 pm

Color of the day: White
Incense of the day: Clove

The Summer Day

Today is Dita e Veres ("The Summer Day"), one of the most celebrated pagan days in Albania. This marks the end of winter and honors nature's ability to regenerate. Zana Malit, Muse of the Mountain and the goddess of hunting, forests, and nature, only comes out of her temple today. Let's invoke Zana Malit's spirit.

Put a large bowl of spring water in the middle of the floor. Collect four 3-to-4-inch pillar candles in the colors orange, yellow, blue, and green. Orange and yellow represent the rising and setting sun and summer energy, blue is for the sky and mountains and the spirit of peace, and green is for the verdancy and growth of summer.

Put the candles in fireproof holders. Whisper "Zana Malit, bless this space" as you place the blue candle to the north of the bowl, the orange candle to the east, the green candle to the south, and the yellow candle to the west.

Light each candle as you think of what they represent, and chant "Zana Malit" as you focus your eyes on the water.

Put your hands in prayer position at your heart center and reflect. Open your arms out to your sides, palms up, and say "Welcome, Zana Malit, growth and warmth," as you face the north, west, south, and east of the bowl of water. Dip into the bowl with your fingers. Snuff out the candles.

Stephanie Rose Bird

NOTES:

 March 15
Friday

1st ♊

Color of the day: Purple
Incense of the day: Thyme

Your Grimmerie

In the musical *Wicked*, the Grimmerie is the book that only Elphaba can read. In one scene, she picks it up, moves downstage away from unsympathetic characters, opens it at random, and recites a string of nonsense syllables that put wings on the monkeys. Traditional witches call this book a Book of Shadows.

We all need a Grimmerie in which we record the magical work we do, plus our thoughts and ideas about magic. Whether you use a journal with pages of real paper or put it on your phone, your Grimmerie must be confidential and protected. (Do *not* post it on social media.)

To charge your Grimmerie, hold it between your hands and visualize a stream of energy from your root chakra moving into the Grimmerie and enlivening it with basic, practical magic. Move up through your chakras, bringing the qualities of each one to your book. Finally, release the chakra energy and begin to write the first of the splendid ideas, spells, and other acts of magic you will record in your Grimmerie.

Barbara Ardinger

March 16
Saturday

1st ♊

Color of the day: Blue
Incense of the day: Magnolia

Daffodil Mood Boost

Daffodil magic is strong. These cheerful flowers are aligned with the goddess Persephone, who—like daffodils—gets to burst forth from the underworld at the earliest dawn of spring. Today, boost your mood and clear away gloominess left over from the winter months by bringing a pot of daffodils into your home. (These are often easily obtainable in markets around this time of year.) Stand in front of a sunny window while holding the pot. Inhale the daffodils' scent and drink in their beauty. Relax and allow your personal energy to be transformed by this simple act. Feel, imagine, or sense the vibrational medicine of the living blossoms permeate and bless your aura. Say:

> *Persephone, goddess of spring, please shine the radiant light of your spirit into my heart and home through these floral allies and emissaries. Thank you.*

Close your eyes and envision golden sunlight filling your consciousness and home. Place your daffodils in bright, indirect light (or plant them outside) and care for them lovingly.

Tess Whitehurst

▽ March 17
Sunday

1st ♊

2nd Quarter 12:11 am

☽ v/c 12:43 am

☽ → ♋ 5:40 am

Color of the day: Yellow
Incense of the day: Frankincense

St. Patrick's Day

Touch the Earth Spell

To charge your spirit to prepare yourself for magic, there are times when you just really need to get in touch with the Earth. This ritual is for those moments. When you won't be disturbed, go outside. It could be your backyard, a park, or a forested area. Breathe deeply as you ground and center. Then say:

Trees and land, rocks and sand,

Empower me with this command.

Now drop to your knees and place your hands upon the Earth. Smell its rich scent and feel its power entering you. Smell and feel the Earth until you're almost dizzy. Now you are ready for magic!

James Kambos

☉ March 18
Monday

2nd ♋

Color of the day: Silver
Incense of the day: Clary sage

Monday Magick

Monday, Monday. This day begins during the period of the waxing moon. Traditionally, Monday was the start of the workweek, but now the world clock runs 24/7. People work remotely thanks to technology, and a person's workday can end or begin at any time of the day or night. This spell will help boost your Monday energy.

You will need:

- A white candle
- Florida Water (to cleanse your candle)
- A fireproof candleholder
- A clock (This can be a digital image, a printed image, or a watch.)
- A lighter or matches
- A place where you will not be disturbed

Upon arising, wipe the candle upward and then downward with Florida Water. Allow it to dry and place it in the holder.

Light the candle and hold your clock image or watch in your hand. Say:

> On this Monday, I charge my time to be sacred and all mine.
>
> I move through the hours of time and space with love and patience and a little grace!

Extinguish the candle when done.

Najah Lightfoot

NOTES:

March 19
Tuesday

2nd ♋

☽ v/c 2:52 pm

☽ → ♌ 3:33 pm

☉ → ♈ 11:06 pm

Color of the day: Scarlet
Incense of the day: Cinnamon

Spring Equinox – Ostara

Sense of Balance

This is Ostara, the Spring Equinox. Day and night stand equal, with day growing as we approach the warm season. Balance is something we all need in life. Take some time today to practice with it.

For this exercise, you need about a dozen small to medium rocks. It helps if they are flat enough to have a top and a bottom. Lay the largest rock on a flat piece of ground. Move it around until it's as stable as you can make it. Set the next-smaller rock on top. Feel for its balance point with your hands and your subtle senses. Shift as needed until it stays put. Continue placing smaller rocks in the same way. How high can you go before they fall over?

This is the same sense of balance you need in your life to make sure you don't have too many or too few things. Feel for the position that creates security. Practice on the equinoxes, when it's easier to sense.

Elizabeth Barrette

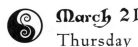

 March 20
Wednesday

2nd ♌

Color of the day: Brown
Incense of the day: Lilac

Bursting the Ties That Bind

When a relationship ends, emotional cords often still bind the exes together. Many people don't even realize this is happening, which is one reason they get stuck in their grief or anger. Attachment is real. This spell will help to dissolve any residual energy between the two of you.

You will need a red or black balloon. Put the opening of the balloon over your faucet and fill it with water.

Stand naked in your (empty) bath or shower. Slowly turn counterclockwise in a spiral motion, holding the balloon above your head to start and gradually moving it down toward your feet. As you spin, chant the words "I erase the ties that bind." Don't let the balloon pop!

When you reach your feet, stomp on the balloon to burst it. If it's not full enough to pop, you may prick it with something. Let the water flow down the drain, taking the now-severed attachment with it. Dispose of the balloon's carcass as far away from your home as possible.

Charlie Rainbow Wolf

 March 21
Thursday

2nd ♌

Color of the day: Purple
Incense of the day: Carnation

Balancing Mind, Body & Spirit

Here we are in the midst of Vernal Equinox vibrations! Newness is growing all around us and, naturally, also within us. To both honor and take witchy advantage of the energies afoot, perform the following exercise alone or with a friend or group.

Take an unfertilized egg from a humanely raised and free-range chicken or other bird. Rub this all over your body (or assist others if appropriate), imagining your accrued astral "muck" entering the egg(s).

While rubbing with the egg(s), whisper the following as many times as you'd like:

*Muck and junk now must flee;
enter this egg, so mote it be.*

Holding the egg in your right hand, see it surrounded by toxic-looking energy. Visualize additional astral detritus entering and surrounding it.

Finish by forcefully throwing the egg(s) at a tree, shouting, "Be gone!" Then walk away without looking back.

Raven Digitalis

March 22
Friday

2nd ♌

☽ v/c 2:34 am

☽ → ♍ 3:42 am

Color of the day: Coral
Incense of the day: Vanilla

Mending Fences

As we go through life, we inevitably have people come in and out of our lives. Some of the individuals were acquaintances and others were dear friends, but for one reason or another, we drifted apart. Other times we may have had a more explosive falling-out.

Since today is Friday, we will tap into the energies of Venus (the planet associated with this day of the week) to try and repair a relationship we valued. If you have an item that reminds you of this friend, you will want to use it as a focal point for the spell. Hold the chosen item to your heart and say:

Reaching out through time and
space, I call you. You are my friend
and I hold you in my heart.

Repeat until you feel you have reached out to the person. Follow up with a phone call, email, message, or letter to see if they are ready to hear what you have to say.

Charlynn Walls

March 23
Saturday

2nd ♍

Color of the day: Indigo
Incense of the day: Pine

Purim begins at sundown

Spirit of Esther Incense

Tonight is the beginning of Purim, a holiday in the Jewish faith honoring Esther, who was a young Hebrew woman living in Persia. She became queen yet still risked her life in order to thwart a planned genocide of her people. You can read the whole story in the Book of Esther, which has inspired many modern retellings. It was one of my favorite stories growing up and a good reminder to be true to ourselves and our community despite whatever dangers we may face.

Make an incense blend inspired by Esther to help you be brave, fight for what's right, and be true to your heart. You will need:

- 1 portion myrrh resin

- 1 portion frankincense resin

- 1 portion dried rose petals or rose hips

- 1 portion coriander seeds

- 1 portion dried pomegranate seeds (or a little juice)

Mix everything together in a mortar and pestle. Burn on a charcoal tablet in a proper holder. (Allow to dry first if you use juice.) You can also take these ingredients and infuse them in olive oil for an anointing oil.

Laura Tempest Zakroff

NOTES:

March 24
Sunday

2nd ♍

☽ v/c 11:49 am

☽ → ♎ 4:37 pm

Color of the day: Gold
Incense of the day: Heliotrope

Palm Sunday

Victory

As the beginning of Holy Week in the Christian tradition, Palm Sunday commemorates Christ's entrance into Jerusalem. Palm branches, seen as symbols of victory and triumph, were laid before him.

We all have complicated lives. We work, play, socialize, create, and enjoy recreation. But how often do we stop and take stock of our victories?

Today, take time to reflect: What have you overcome? Where is your victory? How do you triumph?

It may be something small and seemingly simple, like finally winning in Scrabble against your Great-Aunt Minnie, or something life-changing, like overcoming your fear of walking alone at night. Often, our greatest victories are over things that others don't know about and can't see— things that we hold internally, like old wounds, trauma, and fears.

Today, name some of your victories, great or small. Know that Palm Sunday commemorates triumph and victory, and claim your holy celebration.

Dallas Jennifer Cobb

NOTES:

☾ March 25
Monday

2nd ♎

Full Moon 3:00 am

Color of the day: Gray
Incense of the day: Neroli

Lunar Eclipse

Self-Reflection Lunar Eclipse Spell

Traditional astrologers feel that doing magick during an eclipse is inauspicious. In magickal workings, eclipse energy can come across as confusing. It can be harder to navigate the waters of an eclipse over those of other full moons. The belief is that the eclipse energy is inconsistent and magick worked during these moments is unreliable.

However, self-reflection is a good thing during a lunar eclipse. By using the energy of the darkness to go within and take stock, you can connect with pieces of your life that you might have been ignoring, avoiding, or putting off. It's not necessarily a good time to take action on these things, but it is a good time to take stock.

During the eclipse, take out your journal and write this:

So far, this year has been _____.

Write until you feel complete. Then write this:

Lately, I have been feeling _____.

Write until you feel complete.

When you are finished, set your journal aside. The next day, take out your journal and read over what you wrote. Notice anything interesting or important that you feel you need to pay attention to.

Phoenix LeFae & Gwion Raven

NOTES:

March 26
Tuesday

3rd ♎

☽ v/c 7:09 pm

Color of the day: Black
Incense of the day: Bayberry

Pathmaking Spell

Use this spell to create a physical path when weeds or grass need to be removed, as well as a metaphorical path when current obstacles are blocking your progress.

Cut out enough pieces of cardboard to cover the areas you want to convert into a path. If you don't have a yard or garden where you need to create a path, you can adapt the spell by using small flat stones instead of cardboard, arranging them on top of the soil surrounding an indoor potted plant.

Using a washable marker or pencil, draw a symbol or write a word on each stone or piece of cardboard to represent a blockage or obstacle you wish to remove. Place the cardboard or stones with the blank side facing upward and the symbols or words facedown. Think about the words or symbols that represent your obstacles being enveloped in darkness, facing the ground and blocked from any light. If you're using cardboard, weigh it down so it won't blow away, and leave it in place until the vegetation beneath dies away, making it easy to prepare the ground for your new pathway. Dispose of the cardboard or add it to the compost as you say:

The weeds are gone! The path is made!

If you're using the stones and potted plant substitution, wait until you've fully cleared the obstacles, then remove the stones, wash off any remaining markings, and return them to the earth away from your property.

Melanie Marquis

NOTES:

March 27
Wednesday

3rd ♎

☽ → ♏ 5:03 am

Color of the day: White
Incense of the day: Lavender

Money Magnet

For this spell you'll need a magnet of any kind. Holding the magnet in both hands, close your eyes and visualize a door. This door opens to the flow of money, mediated by the highest good. In your mind's eye, open the door and feel the multi-directional flow of money moving through and around you. Soak in this energy and move it down and out through your hands, charging the magnet. Continue until the magnet feels fully saturated.

Place the magnet somewhere visible, and every time it catches your eye, tap into that feeling of the flow of money. As this magnet draws the energy of money to you, allow yourself to be inspired to take tangible actions. For instance, perhaps your intuition urges you to apply for a new job or start listing your artwork online. Be on the lookout for little (and big!) nudges that help you welcome more money into your life.

Melissa Tipton

March 28
Thursday

3rd ♏

Color of the day: Green
Incense of the day: Mulberry

Call Forth and Manifest

The season of spring has arrived! In my state of Colorado, March is one of the snowiest months, so we get excited thinking about the planting of gardens and flowers. You may live in a climate where you can already sow seeds in the ground. If so, lucky you! Either way, you can use this spell to bless your seeds as the physical manifestation of things you'd like to see blossom into reality.

For this spell you will need a packet of seeds. Hold some seeds in your hand and say:

Little seeds you may be.

You hold the essence of life to be.

May you blossom by the sun.

May you thrive in the moonlight,

Little seeds grow into big things, by day and by night!

Now follow the directions for planting the seeds. Some seeds need to be soaked overnight, and some can be planted directly in the ground after the last frost.

Najah Lightfoot

March 29
Friday

3rd ♏

☽ v/c 11:40 am

☽ → ♐ 3:52 pm

Color of the day: Rose
Incense of the day: Alder

Good Friday

Sacrifice for Thanks

The holidays of Good Friday and Passover are about sacrifice. Christians believe that Jesus sacrificed his life for the good of others, and they commemorate that on Good Friday. Passover is a commemoration of the time when the Jewish people marked their doorposts with the blood of a sacrificial lamb, sparing them from the Angel of Death.

Most magical traditions today don't demand sacrifice, but making a small sacrifice can be powerful magic. For this spell you will need a small bit of food or drink that you truly enjoy. (The leftovers you weren't going to eat don't count!) Once you've picked out your food or drink, take it outside to a secluded spot where you can leave it on the ground undisturbed. (Bushes work great for this!)

Before sharing your sacrifice, thank any higher powers (deities, ancestors, spirits, fey, the Earth/natural world) you work with for the blessings in your life. Ask for nothing in return. Simply leave

your offering as a sign of thanks. Reciprocity is real, and the powers you serve will give blessings to you in return.

        Amanda Lynn & Jason Mankey

NOTES:

March 30
Saturday

3rd ♐

Color of the day: Brown
Incense of the day: Patchouli

Cascarilla Protection Magick

People are decorating eggs around this time. In Hoodoo and Santeria, two paths with West African roots, ground eggshells called cascarilla ("cas-ka-Ree-yah") are used for different purposes, including banishing spirits, clearing, and protection.

To create cascarilla, set your oven to 225 degrees F. Grind a dozen clean, dry eggshells, preferably from a black hen. Place on a cookie sheet. Bake until brittle and crumbly. Remove from the oven, let cool, then grind with a mortar and pestle to pulverize.

Place the cascarilla powder in a bowl. Add a little spring water (just enough to make a paste). Use this paste to draw a tiny *x* on each of your windows and make a thin line on each of your thresholds. This will keep harmful spirits away from your home.

Stephanie Rose Bird

March 31
Sunday

3rd ♐

☽ v/c 8:16 pm

Color of the day: Orange
Incense of the day: Eucalyptus

Easter

Easter Lily Clearing Ritual

Clear away blocks to your most divinely designed success with this space clearing ritual. All you need is an Easter lily in a vase. (Lilies are extremely poisonous to cats and dogs, so if you have a pet, don't risk it. Use a white rose instead.)

If it's sunny out, first go outside and hold the flower in sunlight for a minute or two. Sense or imagine it drinking in the cleansing, empowering light of the sun. Whether it's sunny or not, ask the Goddess and God to bless the flower and to help you employ it to clear the space in your home and remove all blocks to success. Open your front door all the way. With the flower still in the vase, wave the flower around the threshold. Move inside, close the door, and walk around each area of your home in a roughly counterclockwise direction, sweeping the area with the bloom. Finally, place the flower on your altar or in a central location in your home.

Tess Whitehurst

April

This month we move from dark to light, from cold to warm, from brown to green. April is a magical month that starts with April Fools' Day and ends on the eve of May Day, begins with a joke and ends with an outdoor sleep-out. Here in Ontario, Canada, the average temperature at the beginning of April is close to freezing. It's common to have snow on the ground. Throughout April a magical transformation occurs: the temperature climbs as high as 66 degrees Fahrenheit (19 degrees Celsius) and flowers bloom.

Post-equinox, the days grow longer. Between April 1 and 30, the daylight increases from 12 hours and 46 minutes to 14 hours and 8 minutes. As the sun travels northward, it climbs in the sky. Not only do days lengthen, but shadows shorten as well. It is inviting to get outdoors. Like the plants that need sunlight to conduct photosynthesis, we humans need sunlight to help manufacture vitamin D.

This month, make time to enjoy the outdoors. Get out in the daylight, take evening walks in the twilight after dinner, contemplate your garden, and turn your face toward the sun at every chance. With winter coming to an end, now is your time to transform.

Dallas Jennifer Cobb

April 1
Monday

3rd ♐

☽ → ♑ 12:05 am

4th Quarter 11:15 pm

Color of the day: White
Incense of the day: Narcissus

April Fools' Day – All Fools' Day

honoring the Fool Within

All Fools' Day (or April Fools' Day) has a reputation for being a day of pranks and practical jokes—which means you should probably double-check the publication date of that too-good article you just saw on the internet. But what if on this day we embraced the energy of the Fool from the Major Arcana instead—while also viewing this card in a new light? Rather than seeing the Fool as a figure about to step off a cliff, consider that they're stepping down from the heavens to the top of a mountain, beginning their exciting journey down into the world. This shift can help us change our own perspective when facing both difficulties and opportunities.

Pull the Fool card out from your Tarot deck and place it upon your altar for meditation. To represent the tools of the Minor Arcana, collect:

• A stick of incense (for wands)

• A candle (for swords)

• A glass of water (for cups)

• A salt or a spice (for pentacles)

Now recognize each with these words:

I breathe the aroma of life.
(Light the incense.)

I am guided by the light within me.
(Light the candle.)

May I always be refreshed.
(Drink the water.)

May my life be rich and flavorful.
(Taste the salt or spice.)

Laura Tempest Zakroff

NOTES:

April 2
Tuesday

NOTES:

4th ♑

Color of the day: Gray
Incense of the day: Geranium

Elemental Meditation

U se this meditation to strengthen your magickal connection to the Earth.

Go outside with a candle in a holder, a cone of incense on a fireproof dish, a small dish of salt, and a glass of water. Sit or stand with your feet touching the earth. Light the candle and watch the flame as you think of all the light in the world in its many forms. Meditate for a while on the nature of this light. Next, drink the glass of water as you meditate on all the forms of water in the world. Next, touch the ground and touch the salt. Feel the energies resonating and think of all the matter that makes up the planet. Finally, light the incense as you meditate on the air that envelops our planet, and the motion and growth it facilitates. Meditate on how these aspects of nature are all present and active in your own body.

When you're finished, put out the candle and the incense and pour any remaining water on the earth. Add the salt to a bath or use it to season food.

Melanie Marquis

April 3
Wednesday

4th ♑

☽ v/c 1:40 am

☽ → ♒ 5:08 am

Color of the day: Topaz
Incense of the day: Marjoram

Fae Altar Spell

The spring is an excellent time to start communicating with the Fae. All it takes is a little awareness and consistency on your part. This spell is best done outdoors, but if that isn't possible, place this working near a window. Once you create the altar, the work has just begun.

When the altar is in place, you will need to maintain that spot, spend time there, and make sure to give offerings. This is the real work of having a relationship with the Fae: paying attention to them.

Spend the day collecting items that feel connected to the Fae realms. Ideally these will be items that are natural, such as charms, trinkets, acorns, seeds, plants, or anything else that makes you think of the Fae. Try to avoid anything plastic. Make sure you have something that can be used as a receptacle for offerings.

Go to the area where you will be creating your Fae altar. Clear and/ or clean the space with the intention that this will be where you commune with the Fae. Speak out loud your desires. Speak from your heart, telling the Fae that you want to be in relationship with them.

Begin to place the items in a way that is pleasing to you. For the last step of this spell, place an offering or libation out for the Fae. Say out loud that this offering is for them and you will be giving them offerings regularly.

Allow yourself some time to simply sit in this area. Notice anything interesting or odd that may happen while you are there. Notice any feelings that arise. When you feel complete, go about your day.

Phoenix LeFae & Gwion Raven

April 4
Thursday

4℞ ≈

Color of the day: Crimson
Incense of the day: Myrrh

Embody the Goddess/God

Somatics is the practice of tuning in to the body, developing a mind-body connection, in order to recognize clues to the internal (emotional or psychological) state coming from an external alignment, posture, or practice. Many psychotherapeutic practitioners use somatics to work with people experiencing extreme trauma. Somatics can also be used proactively. Instead of looking for signs in the body that speak about internal states, we can use the body to create an internal state.

Today, embody your inner Goddess/God. Stand with your feet wider apart than your hips. Engage your butt muscles (gluteus maximus) so your pelvis pushes slightly forward. Place your hands on your hips. Roll your shoulders back and down, lifting your chest slightly. Turn your palms out and tip your chin up slightly. Look to the horizon. Consciously breath and feel the power of this stance, and notice how it uplifts your spirit.

Thou art Goddess.
Thou art God.

Dallas Jennifer Cobb

NOTES:

April 5
Friday

4th ≈

☽ v/c 1:40 am

☽ → ♓ 7:13 am

Color of the day: Purple
Incense of the day: Yarrow

Doorway to health

Choose a door that you walk through often, and charge it with the intent of healing by standing in front of the doorway and visualizing the opening filling with light in the color(s) of your choice, any that you associate with healing. As the doorway glows with brilliant light, say:

This doorway is a portal

To health and wellness true.

My body, mind, and spirit

In harmony they will be.

Perfect health on every level

Each time that I walk through.

Throughout the day, when you walk through the door, let this be an invitation for a reset, perhaps focusing on your breathing for a moment and bringing loving attention to your wellbeing. You might use an affirmation to reinforce this healing mindset, such as "I am in balance and harmony in body, mind, and soul."

Pay attention to any insights that arise regarding your health. For instance, perhaps you realize that a particular relationship is very draining and you need to set clear boundaries, or maybe you're inspired to try a new herbal supplement.

Melissa Tipton

NOTES:

April 6
Saturday

4♅ ♓

Color of the day: Indigo
Incense of the day: Sage

Pet Remembrance Jar

Few experiences are harder than losing a pet. Cats, dogs, and all the other animals we cohabitate with are most certainly family! This jar spell serves as a way to reconnect with a pet that has passed away.

For this spell you will need a clean wide-mouth jar (like a Mason or jelly jar), a picture of your pet, and things that remind you of your pet. Slip the photo into the jar so you can easily and clearly see the image of your pet. Behind the image place mementos of your pet. This might include their favorite dry treats or toys. You can also write down some cherished memories and add those to the jar. If you have some of your pet's hair in a brush or other item, add that as well.

Once your jar has been filled, screw on the lid and say your pet's name out loud and tell them you love them. Place the jar on an altar or other safe space and pick it up every time you miss your pet and need to feel their energy.

Amanda Lynn & Jason Mankey

 April 7
Sunday

4♅ ♓

☽ v/c 4:27 am
☽ → ♈ 7:25 am

Color of the day: Yellow
Incense of the day: Marigold

Witches' Day Off

Today's aspects seem to be guiding us to relax and enjoy some beer. First of all, it's National Beer Day. And, of course, it's Sunday. What's more, it's a dark moon, which has been called the Witches' day off. As if that weren't enough, Mercury is retrograde. While Mercury retrograde gets a bad rap, these periods actually help us to align with divine timing and to stop forcing things so we can take life in stride. With all this in mind, pour yourself a beer. (A nice chamomile tea blend would be a great substitute.) Hold it in both hands. Breathe, close your eyes, and channel bright golden light into the beverage. (You can imagine it coming down through the crown of your head, entering your heart, and moving down through your hands into the drink.) Open your eyes, raise your glass, and say:

> Goddess of moon, God of
> the sun, nourish my soul
> with relaxation and fun.

Then savor.

Tess Whitehurst

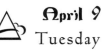

 April 8
Monday

4t♄ ♈
𝕹ew 𝕸oon 2:21 pm
☽ v/c 10:39 pm
Color of the day: Gray
Incense of the day: Rosemary

Solar Eclipse

Drawing Down the Sun

For this eclipse spell you'll need water and a clear bottle. I use filtered tap water and a lidded Mason jar. You'll also need a black pen and a sticky note or piece of masking tape.

The beauty of this spell is you don't have to be there for it to work. Write on the sticky note or masking tape what you want the water to absorb from the eclipse. Perhaps you want better career prospects, or a bit more financial stability, or just some of the sun's vitality. Stick your intent on the bottle full of water, then set it in a position where it will be in the sun during the eclipse.

Use this water as an elixir. Add a bit to your morning beverage to revitalize it, give a drop to plants to help them grow, or put some in a beloved pet's water as a pick-me-up. It's got compelling energy stored in it. It will give anything you do an extra boost of power.

Charlie Rainbow Wolf

April 9
Tuesday

1st ♈
☽ → ♉ 7:23 am
Color of the day: White
Incense of the day: Cinnamon

Ramadan ends

Daisy Air Magick Spell

Our flower of the month, the daisy, is a cheerful flower. It is a magickal flower. Take nine fresh daisies in your dominant hand. Think of your romantic desires. Do you seek a new partner? Do you want a relationship with loyalty, purity, and honor?

Focus on your intention for the relationship you have or want as you pull off the petals of the daisies one at a time. Go outside. Hold the petals in both hands and make your wish. On the ground, draw the word(s) that is most emblematic of the intent you've set. (You can trace them in sand or dirt.) After about five minutes have passed, get on your hands and knees and blow away the word(s). Let your intention manifest by the power of the air element. So mote it be!

Stephanie Rose Bird

April 10
Wednesday

1st ♉

Color of the day: Brown
Incense of the day: Lilac

Pin on Protection

Today is Safety Pin Day, celebrating an invention originally patented on April 10, 1849. Since then, it has provided a safer way of fastening things, but it also represents protection. Ukrainians put them on children's clothes to repel evil spirits. Some folks wear them for good luck. A more recent use in public spaces indicates that the wearer is a "safe person" who will help if asked.

Safety pins appear in many crafts, especially beadwork. This makes it fun and easy to wear them for magical, social, or decorative purposes. Get some coiless safety pins or ones with removable heads. Fill the back of the pin with small beads, then seal the wire with a crimp bead to prevent the others from moving. Black, white, and cobalt blue are colors of protection, especially when combined to make eye beads. Now you can pin your pretty protective charm to a hat or sweater. A similar approach works with the type of cloak pin that resembles a safety pin, but you need bigger beads.

Elizabeth Barrette

April 11
Thursday

1st ♉

☽ v/c 6:04 am
☽ → ♊ 8:59 am

Color of the day: Turquoise
Incense of the day: Nutmeg

Feeling Lucky

Luck is one of the energies we can tap into today, as it is a Thursday, the day of the week associated with Jupiter. We can all benefit from getting a little extra boost of luck. So whatever you need to accomplish today, this week, or this year, you can achieve that with this spell.

Find a small item that you can carry with you as a good luck charm. This could be any item of significance. You could use a ring, a pendant, or a stone. (Aventurine and holey stones work very well.) Take the item and hold it between both of your hands. As you concentrate on adding energy to the object, say:

I create my own luck. When it is needed, so it will be.

Charlynn Walls

April 12
Friday

1st ♊

Color of the day: Rose
Incense of the day: Rose

Love Wrap Charm

Use this simple charm to cast the most powerful magick of all: love. By surrounding people, your town, or even the world with love, you are raising vibrations that have the power to support, sustain, and uplift us.

Take a moment to clear your head, then think of someone or something you love dearly. Let this feeling of love fill your heart completely, then focus on the essence of this energy. Let this loving power expand. Imagine the loving feeling in your heart radiating out from your body to grow infinitely larger. Envision this love literally enveloping the specific people or places you want your charm to affect. If you're thinking of a certain person, imagine the loving energy wrapping around them like a gentle hug. If you're envisioning the whole world, imagine the loving energy completely surrounding the planet like a glowing sphere. When you've radiated as much love from your heart as you can muster, let the final traces of the loving feelings settle back in your own heart. Give yourself a hug or a pat on the back to seal the charm.

Melanie Marquis

April 13
Saturday

1st ♊

☽ v/c 10:46 am
☽ → ♋ 1:45 pm

Color of the day: Black
Incense of the day: Sandalwood

Childlike Wonder and Awe

Today is Saturday and it's the cycle of the waxing moon. Saturdays always seem to feel like a day to run around and do fun things. Along with the pep in your step that the spring brings, a Saturday during this season makes you want to cast all obligations aside and do something just for you. So that's what you should do today!

Proclaim that today is your day. If you can set aside the entire day, that's wonderful. If this is not possible, see if you can carve out an hour or even a half hour for yourself. There is only one you. Use this day to be kind to yourself and to do something that ignites your childlike wonder and awe.

Najah Lightfoot

April 14
Sunday

1st ♋

Color of the day: Amber
Incense of the day: Heliotrope

Who Are You?

For his 1965 musical *On a Clear Day You Can See Forever*, lyricist Alan Jay Lerner wrote that we can "rise up and see" who we are and have been. (The musical is partly about reincarnation.) We can, he wrote, see ourselves more clearly. Here in 2024, when everything seems to be murkier than ever, too many people seem to be clueless about who they are. Declare your intention to seek that forever vision. Look for clarity.

Find a peaceful spot, perhaps outdoors, and breathe deeply to center yourself. Rise above yourself and enter into a magical state of questioning and answering. Look around. What's the big picture where you are? Rise up and look closely through that forever lens at yourself, past and present, maybe future. What do you see? Use the clarity to see who you truly are. When you come back down to earth, look around again and speak aloud who you are. Now resolve to always act through that clarity.

Barbara Ardinger

April 15
Monday

1st ♋

2nd Quarter 3:13 pm
☽ v/c 7:22 pm
☽ → ♌ 10:24 pm

Color of the day: Lavender
Incense of the day: Lily

A Tool for Empaths

Those of us who identify as empaths have no choice but to absorb emotional energy around us at any given time. I should know, as I've written two books on the subject and also co-created the Empath's Oracle.

We highly empathic souls have an incredible stone at our disposal: black tourmaline. To ease social anxiety in public situations and protect your energy in public, simply wear or carry this stone. Be sure to cleanse it first with water and smoke, and tell it your intentions.

Repeat this working as often as you'd like (and indeed it is a spell!), but be sure *not* to wear or carry black tourmaline daily due to its potency. We must remain protected, not energetic hermits!

Raven Digitalis

April 16
Tuesday

2nd ♌

Color of the day: Maroon
Incense of the day: Cedar

Under the Rose

Roses are often associated with love and love spells, but they also figure prominently in spells for secrecy and silence. Roses have been closely linked to Harpocrates, the god of silence. When swearing a person to secrecy or engaging in actions you wish to keep secret, make an oath "under the rose."

Gather rose petals, stem roses, or cut rose flowers from bushes. Place them in a cloth bag, or gather the roses in a bundle and tie with black yarn or string. The fresher the roses, the more potent the spell.

As you gather with others to manifest your secret magick, place the bundle of roses above your heads. Hang the roses like you would mistletoe in a doorway or from the ceiling. Work the spell under the roses, and all present will be oathbound not to reveal what was done, discussed, or revealed.

Phoenix LeFae & Gwion Raven

April 17
Wednesday

2nd ♌

Color of the day: Yellow
Incense of the day: Honeysuckle

A Pansy Love Spell

Pansies are known for being a powerful love-attracting ingredient in love magic. For this spell you'll need a pack of seeds or a small bouquet of pink, burgundy, or red pansies. A mix is fine, too. You'll also need a sheet of paper. Place the seeds or cut pansies on your altar. Concentrate on the type of person you wish to attract, but don't think of a specific person. Then on the paper, write these words:

Pansies pink, pansies red,

Bring me the one who will turn my head.

Find me the one who will light a spark.

Find me the one who will warm my heart.

Keep the pansies for three days. If you have a pack of seeds, plant them in a garden or pot. If you have cut pansies, compost them or throw them out. Keep the written charm hidden, and read it now and then. When you find a partner, carefully burn the paper in the flame of a pink candle. When the ashes cool, throw them out. Keep the candle for future spellwork.

James Kambos

April 18
Thursday

2nd ♌

☽ v/c 8:02 am

☽ → ♍ 10:10 am

Color of the day: Purple
Incense of the day: Apricot

Bring It to Me Spell

Use this magick to attract what you desire. You will need:

* 1 handful basil
* 3 quartz crystal points
* A 6-inch circle of yellow, green, white, or red fabric
* A 6-inch piece of yellow, green, white, or red string

Place the basil and crystals in the center of the fabric circle. Hold your hands over the herbs and crystals as you think of what you want to attract. Envision having whatever it is, and feel the emotions this will bring. Send this energy through your hands and into the basil and quartz points. Gather the edges of the fabric and twist the top to form a bundle with the basil and crystals inside. Tie the bundle around the top with the string to secure. Carry this with you as a charm to attract to you what you want.

Melanie Marquis

 April 19
Friday

2nd ♍

☉ → ♉ 10:00 am

Color of the day: White
Incense of the day: Violet

Spirits of Place

Whether you live amid asphalt and skyscrapers or forests and fields, every place is inhabited by spirits of the land. Partnering with these spirits can benefit both you and them, creating more harmony and dissolving obstructions. In a meditative state, make your intention known:

Spirits of this land, I seek to partner with you in perfect love and perfect trust.

Allow time for a connection to be felt, perhaps repeating this intention over multiple days. Be patient, especially if this is your first time connecting with the spirits of this place.

When the connection is made, start a conversation like you would with a person; get to know each other. Over time, you can ask if there's something the spirits need to support their health and healing. Perhaps they want litter picked up or pollinator-friendly flowers planted. Maybe their request is more energetic in nature, such as regular offerings of love. In return, the spirits may offer healing, blessings, or insights.

Melissa Tipton

April 20
Saturday

2nd ♏

☽ v/c 8:20 pm

☽ → ♎ 11:08 pm

Color of the day: Gray
Incense of the day: Pine

Peace Garden Spell

With so much chaos going on around us, it can be hard to focus on the positive and peaceful aspects of life. For this spell all you need is yourself and a garden, either yours or a community garden you like to visit.

Find a cozy and quiet place in the garden and sit down to relax. Look at all the lush life growing abundantly around you in collective harmony. Witness and experience all the flora and fauna cohabitating, and allow that energy to fill you up as you remember the abundance and beauty that life has to offer. Feel your hands on the soft grass, smell the aroma of any scented flowers in bloom, and listen for any birds or bees flying around the garden. Close your eyes and take in all the serenity of this place and know that peace does exist and is readily available. When you are ready, take this energy with you and spread it to others throughout the day.

Amanda Lynn & Jason Mankey

April 21
Sunday

2nd ♎

Color of the day: Gold
Incense of the day: Almond

Creatively heal the World

World Creativity and Innovation Day promotes the importance of fresh, new, and out-of-the-box thinking with regard to sustainability and climate change. Today, take a moment to come up with some creative ways you can personally support our beloved planet Earth. If weather permits, take a notebook or journal outside and sit on the grass or under a tree. (Otherwise find a comfy spot where you can gaze out the window.)

Breathe and connect with the elements in your environment, one by one. First, *earth*: soil, rocks, plants, and trees. Then *air*: birds, insects, clouds, and the feeling of the air on your skin. Then *fire*: the sun and sunlight. Then *water*: any body of water or the awareness of moisture in the air, earth, and plants. Finally, *spirit*: the first four elements combined, as well as the conscious aliveness that interweaves all of it. Then contemplate how you can become an even better steward of the land and planet. List these ideas in your notebook. When this feels complete, thank each element in turn.

Tess Whitehurst

▽ April 22
Monday

2nd ♎

☽ v/c 7:24 pm

Color of the day: Silver
Incense of the day: Hyssop

Earth Day – Passover begins
at sundown

honor the Land Spirits

While today is Earth Day, which brings attention to environmental issues on a global scale for one day, as Witches, it is vital that we be stewards of the land on a daily basis. We are a part of Earth, not separate from it. We can all tend to the spirits of the land around us, regardless of whether we're in a city, in the suburbs, or out in the woods. While we can make offerings to the land, such as gifts of water and native seeds, one of the best things we can do as human beings is gather and remove trash. This gesture may not seem like an offering, but it is an act of service and an offering of our time.

One easy way to do this regularly is when you go on walks and hikes, always bring a compact reusable bag to collect items that can be recycled, as well as a disposable bag for trash that cannot. I guarantee the land spirits will appreciate your efforts, as will the plants, animals, and other visitors.

Laura Tempest Zakroff

☽ April 23
Tuesday

2nd ♎

☽ → ♏ 11:20 am

Full Moon 7:49 pm

Color of the day: Black
Incense of the day: Ginger

health Moon

The full moon marks its maximum swell of energy. That makes today a good time for spells that benefit from high power. One option focuses on health and healing. You can recharge your body's energy reserves with moonlight. While this is no substitute for good self-care, it can give you a quick boost. Take advantage of the warming spring to bare some skin. A T-shirt and/or shorts will help you absorb more energy. Go outside when the moon is in the sky and stand in a place where the it can shine on you. Face the moon and say:

Full moon, bright moon,

Let me be your cup.

Full moon, bright moon,

Fill my body up.

Feel the energy sinking into you. Turn your back to the moon and repeat the verse again. Visualize the moonlight boosting your health so your body can take good care of itself. Once you feel full, cover up and go back indoors.

Elizabeth Barrette

April 24
Wednesday

3rd ♏

Color of the day: White
Incense of the day: Lavender

Be the Magic

Magic is all around us, but we can't always see it. Today, look at the world through "magical" glasses. Look for signs, be aware of synchronicities, pay attention to symbols, and notice omens.

If you receive $7.77 in change at the grocery store, go look up the magical significance of these numbers. If a fox darts across the road in front of you, seek the meaning of this totem animal. If the license plate on the car ahead of you says *BELIEVE*, pause and do that. If you find a twenty-dollar bill in the pocket of your jacket, count your blessings.

When we open our eyes to see magic everywhere, the energy does not disappoint. The more we seek to see, the more we see. The more we seek to believe, the more we believe. And the more magic we practice, the more magic there is.

Be the magic.

Dallas Jennifer Cobb

April 25
Thursday

3rd ♏

☽ v/c 7:17 pm

☽ → ♐ 9:37 pm

Color of the day: Green
Incense of the day: Jasmine

A Protective Witch Bottle

The Sun is now in Taurus, an appropriate time for dealing with things that are material, grounded, and tangible. Use this spell to make a powerful protection amulet to place in your home. I have heard that traditionally Witch bottles were placed in chimneys, but not everyone has one of those these days. To make your Witch bottle, you will need:

- An empty, clear Christmas ornament (I prefer glass over plastic) or a small clear glass jar with a lid
- Some sea salt
- Some old rusty nails
- Some black peppercorns
- A pinch of dried parsley

One by one, add the ingredients to the container, saying:

This strengthens and protects me and all I hold dear.

Close the top. Place the container in the chimney, under the stairs, in the crawl space, or under the stoop, or bury it in the soil. Do not speak of it and do not revisit it. Should you move, make another Witch bottle rather than take this one with you.

Charlie Rainbow Wolf

NOTES:

 **April 26**
Friday

3rd ♐

Color of the day: Pink
Incense of the day: Cypress

Sweet Dreams

Dreams free of nightmares are highly sought after. There are ways you can employ herbs to make this wish come true. First, fill a nice-size bowl with a mixture of rose water and spring water and place it under your bed. Push it under the middle of the bed. This is an invitation to the gods, goddesses, and water spirits.

Next, make a sweet dreams sachet. Rub ⅓ cup chamomile flowers, lavender buds, and jasmine or hops gently between your hands into a bowl. (Do not use hops if you are in recovery from alcohol.) This releases the natural essential oils in the herbs. Breathe into the bowl the intention to have sweet and meaningful, intuitive dreams. Take handfuls of the herbal blend, and into each one, breathe gently all your hopes for the blend. Put the herbs back in the bowl. Place the herbal blend in a sachet or two and put beneath your pillow. Sweet dreams!

Stephanie Rose Bird

April 27
Saturday

3rd ♐

Color of the day: Brown
Incense of the day: Sage

Sweep It Away

Some people like to clean, while for others it's a chore they'd rather not do. Either way, having the right tools can make a big difference. And when it comes to cleaning, what magickal Witch doesn't know the power of a broom? Today we are going work some broom magick!

This day on the calendar occurs during the waning moon cycle, which is when the moon is moving from full to new—a good time for letting go. This is a good spell for cleansing your home or office space.

You will need:

• 3 tablespoons salt

• A refreshing essential oil of your choice

• 1 cup water

• A broom

Add the salt and three drops of the essential oil to the water, then pour the water over the broom bristles. Use the broom to sweep your floors or any place that needs cleansing.

Najah Lightfoot

 ## April 28
Sunday

3rd ♐

☽ v/c 3:31 am

☽ → ♑ 5:37 am

Color of the day: Amber
Incense of the day: Frankincense

Master Number, Big Plan

The good news is that today's date adds up to a master number: 4 (month) + 2 + 8 (day) + 2 + 0 + 2 + 4 (year) = 22. That's the Master Builder. Power on all planes. Practical idealism. Do you have an ambition? A big plan? A promotion? A new job? A proposal of marriage? An adventure? Today's the day to start creating your path to fulfillment of your big plan.

Grab a pen and some paper (or your new Grimmerie from March 15) and cast a working circle around yourself. Lay bay and oak leaves for power and success in the elemental corners. Add malachite and green tourmaline (ditto), and lay a silver dollar in the north. Declare your intention (plan) out loud. Now call ideas to come to you. Write them down. Make necessary revisions to your notes. When you have a satisfactory plan, face north, speak your intention again, then clap your hands once and push hard to send the energy into motion and manifestation.

Barbara Ardinger

April 29
Monday

3rd ♑

Color of the day: Gray
Incense of the day: Rosemary

Gossip Stoppit!

A short yet effective variation of an ancient anti-shit-talking spell is to take any dry leaf (or leaves) that you can write on with a permanent marker. The ideal is bay leaf. Then simply write the origin (or origins) of the gossip being stirred. If this is unknown, simply (or additionally) write words like "gossip," "lies," and "slander" on any of the leaves.

Then safely burn the leaf (or leaves), stating:

Accountable for my speech, I declare with honor. May others' false words be banished this hour!

To add a boost, sprinkle some slippery elm root on the leaves' ashes. Repeat the spell any time you see fit.

Raven Digitalis

▽ **April 30**
Tuesday

3rd ♑
☽ v/c 11:19 am
☽ → ♒ 11:20 am

Color of the day: Red
Incense of the day: Bayberry

Passover ends

A Fern Spell

If you have a secret to keep, a fern can help you. Ferns are ancient and have been on Earth since almost the beginning of time. They are laden with mystery, and for this reason they are ready to hear and keep our secrets.

For this spell you'll need a small potted fern and one small rock. When you won't be disturbed, hold the rock. Now tell the fern your secret. Add any details you can think of. As you do this, project the secret into the rock. When done, press the rock into the soil of the potted fern. You and the fern are now bonded. Tend the plant and nurture it. When the time comes that you no longer need to keep the secret, remove the rock from the soil. Return the rock to nature by gently placing it outside. Continue to tend the fern. You are now bonded with one of Earth's most ancient living entities.

James Kambos

May

Welcome to the famously merry month of May! Though it was originally named after the Greek fertility goddess Maia, the Catholic Church has since designated this month as sacred to the Virgin Mary, even referring to her as "the Queen of May" during this time. Day one of this flower-filled month is the beloved holiday of Beltane, during which the veil that usually conceals the world of the fairies fades, and our power to make contact with them reaches its yearly peak. Indeed, May's birth flower is a fairy favorite: the lily of the valley. As for our skies, this month they host the Eta Aquariids meteor shower, which reaches its peak around May 6 and is most visible before the sunrise.

May is also the month when the light half of the year begins to assert itself in earnest, and we sense the days lengthening, the sun growing warmer, and the leaves filling out the trees. This allows us to gaze bravely into our own brilliance and to courageously release anything that has been holding us back from being our most radiant, expansive, beautiful selves. Indeed, May's bright presence reminds us to claim the vital prosperity that is our birthright and our natural state.

Tess Whitehurst

May 1
Wednesday

3rd ♒
4th Quarter 7:27 am
Color of the day: Yellow
Incense of the day: Lilac

Beltane

A Garland of Marigolds

Making floral wreaths of spring flowers is as old as spring itself. The flowers you choose can influence the magick you are creating. Marigolds are associated with prophecy and psychic ability. Weaving and wearing a garland filled with marigolds will bring insight, through dreams, of what might blossom for you in the spring and early summer. Wear the garland all day, or as long as possible, and put it under your pillow overnight. You will need:

- Green floral wire

- Fresh marigolds (usually sold in packs of four or six, or picked from your garden)

- Some thin ribbon and a selection of lavender, roses, and green vines (optional)

Make a circle of the floral wire big enough for your head, and decorate it with the marigolds. You can also add ribbons, foliage, and anything else that strikes your fancy.

Phoenix LeFae & Gwion Raven

May 2
Thursday

4th ♒
☽ v/c 5:28 am
☽ → ♓ 2:52 pm
Color of the day: Purple
Incense of the day: Nutmeg

Connect with Your higher Power

Today is the National Day of Prayer. On this day millions of people may offer their prayers for guidance and leadership. As magickal people, the word *prayer* may not be a word we are comfortable using. However, the words *affirmation* and *incantation* carry the same intention. Some may find that using those words is a better fit for their practices.

Many of us, as magickal practitioners, embrace a higher power, contrary to what others may think it means to be "Pagan." As people who embrace and work with magickal spirituality, we too can use this day as a day to connect with our higher powers in whatever way is comfortable for us, for none need ever walk alone. To embrace the power of today, you may choose to light a candle, blow a kiss to the moon, or hug a tree.

Najah Lightfoot

May 3
Friday

4ℏ ♓

Color of the day: Coral
Incense of the day: Thyme

hawthorn Meditation

Hawthorn is one of the two flowers of May. It is a flower of hope and matters of the heart. Gather a handful of dried hawthorn flowers from your tree (if you're lucky enough to have one nearby) or from your magickal stash. Set aside.

Light a charcoal on a fireproof surface and let it turn white-hot. Place the dried flowers in your dominant hand. Thank your flowers for working with you today. Place your hands together in prayer pose. Rub them together vigorously and let the petals drop onto the charcoal slowly. As they drop, focus on three intentions that will make your heart happy and fill it with hope.

As the petals burn, watch as your wishes are consumed by fire and then released into the air, from whence they will manifest. This is elemental magick of the air, fire, and earth. Your elemental magick will ease your pain, and hawthorn itself will soon usher in fresh visions of hope as the universe answers your intentions.

Stephanie Rose Bird

 May 4
Saturday

4ℏ ♓
☽ v/c 3:06 pm
☽ → ♈ 4:41 pm

Color of the day: Blue
Incense of the day: Ivy

May the Force Be with You

It's not uncommon to hear "May the 4th be with you" every May 4th as people around the world celebrate Star Wars Day. The idea of the Force as a cosmic power that connects everything in the universe is an idea worth celebrating.

To connect to the greater universe, find a comfortable and quiet spot where you won't be disturbed. You can stand or sit. Begin by closing your eyes and taking a deep breath. As you exhale, push out any negative energy or thoughts inside of you. As you breathe, extend your consciousness up and out of your body. Visualize your essence rising above you, moving toward the sky. Feel yourself floating above the trees, the hills, and eventually the clouds and out into space. As your essence floats outside of our world, feel the energies of other planets, suns, and galaxies move through you and connect to them. Once you've connected to the greater universe, allow your essence to slowly drift back down into your body.

Amanda Lynn & Jason Mankey

May 5
Sunday

4th ♈

Color of the day: Orange
Incense of the day: Juniper

Cinco de Mayo

Praise the God and the Goddess

In May, the earth is a wealth of abundance. The God and the Goddess have blessed the earth with growth and lushness. Every growing thing is surging toward maturity and harvest. For this spell you will use your kitchen counter as your altar. On the counter, place a variety of salad vegetables, especially leafy greens. Wash and prep them so they are ready to go. As you work with the vegetables, say:

Every tree, every flower, every crop, and every herb

Is a gift of the God and the Goddess.

With shade, with beauty, with food they have blessed us,

Thanks to the God, thanks to the Goddess,

For the green world they have given us.

Serve the salad to yourself and any guests who may be present. Eat slowly and with purpose as you think of the God and the Goddess. Think about our beautiful green world that they have blessed us with.

James Kambos

May 6
Monday

4th ♈

☽ v/c 1:57 am
☽ → ♉ 5:42 pm

Color of the day: Ivory
Incense of the day: Clary sage

Matters of the heart

Spring is in the air, and it's only natural at this time that thoughts turn to love and romance. Whether you're currently in a good relationship and just want to grow closer or you're still searching for that special someone, this spell will help. You'll need a red candle, a knife or an athame, a lemon, a heatproof dish, and a box of matches.

Carve a heart into the candle, then cut the lemon in half. Rub half of the lemon up one side of the candle, and the other half up the other side of the candle. Put the candle safely on the heatproof dish and light it, saying:

As the flame glows, so does my heart. Share the fire with me.

Gaze into the candle flame until you know in your heart that love is near, then pinch out the flame or use a candle snuffer. Place the cold candle under your pillow. Discard the lemon.

Charlie Rainbow Wolf

 May 7
Tuesday

4th ♉

New Moon 11:22 pm

Color of the day: Gray
Incense of the day: Ylang-ylang

New Moon, New Start

The Wiccan and Neopagan sabbats that are not equinoxes and solstices occur on dates that are similar but not astrologically precise. We are currently in the midst of astrological Beltane.

Take a bottle of your favorite wine, kombucha, or other nonalcoholic beverage. With a flashlight in hand, safely travel to a calming, hidden place after nightfall. Using a black permanent marker, draw crescent moons on the bottle.

Meditate and then visualize the obscured moon enchanting the liquid. Once finished, give thanks and leave the bottle outside for thirteen days, at which time you can merrily consume it to invoke major lunar blessings!

Raven Digitalis

May 8
Wednesday

1st ♉

☽ v/c 5:55 pm
☽ → ♊ 7:20 pm

Color of the day: White
Incense of the day: Bay laurel

Travel Funds Spell

If you want to take a trip but lack the resources to do so, try this spell. Print a picture of the place you want to visit, and write on the image your full name and the name of the precise location of the destination. Take the Ace of Wands from a tarot deck and wrap around it a five dollar bill. Then place the card with the bill around it on top of the printed image of your travel destination. Keep this lucky stack somewhere safe in the east-facing side of your home. Cut back on unnecessary minor expenses and add any extra dollars to the stack as frequently as you can, even if it's only a single dollar. Each time you add money, say the place name and affirm:

I'm going there!

Your travel funds will manifest quickly in both expected and unexpected ways. New opportunities to earn additional income will likely come to you, so be prepared and alert.

Melanie Marquis

May 9
Thursday

1st ♊

Color of the day: Crimson
Incense of the day: Balsam

Anointed by Aphrodite

In the coastal city of Paphos lies an ancient sanctuary dedicated to Aphrodite where her devotees gave honey, fruits, flowers, cakes, and other decadent offerings. In her Homeric hymn, Aphrodite is said to have been bathed and anointed with fragrant oil by the Graces before being clad in shining robes. Such an evocative, luxurious scene, isn't it?

Align with the sensual, loving energy of Aphrodite through a ritual bath (or shower), slowing down to pay attention to the temperature and feel of the water on your skin. Sense all unwanted energy being washed away, dissolving down the drain, where it's neutralized and returned to the great cosmic cycle.

Then, holding a container of body oil, call upon the goddess:

Laughter-loving Aphrodite,

Gold-crowned goddess—

Please bless this oil

With your love and wisdom.

Thank you, queen of all creation!

Feel energy streaming from your hands, charging the oil with the power of the goddess. Then anoint yourself, taking your time as you revel in the sensation of the oil on your skin.

Melissa Tipton

NOTES:

May 10
Friday

1st ♊︎

☽ v/c 9:49 pm

☽ → ♋︎ 11:13 pm

Color of the day: Pink
Incense of the day: Rose

Energy-Changing Magic

Dion Fortune defined magic as "the art of changing consciousness [energy] at will." Today, can you consciously choose to change your energy in the moment?

Maybe you are running late and feel the mounting anxiety. Can you consciously shake your hands and release anxiety? What if there is a car trying to get into your lane? Instead of getting angry or feeling defensive, why not slow down a little, smile, and let the car squeeze in?

These small acts can literally change our personal energy at will.

The more we practice changing our energy, the easier it gets. Psychologist Rick Hanson believes we can "hardwire happiness" by practicing feeling happy. When something good happens or you see something nice, place all your attention on the situation. Smile and breathe in the happiness. Feel that tingling up your spine? That is the feeling of you changing your energy at will.

Dallas Jennifer Cobb

May 11
Saturday

1st ♋︎

Color of the day: Brown
Incense of the day: Rue

Success for All

This is Fair Trade Day. Fair trade aims to support success for all by ensuring that farmers, crafters, and other small producers make a living wage for their hard work. As part of that, this worthy cause also fights against poverty, exploitation, and climate change. You can support this endeavor by buying fair trade certified products or shopping at fair trade certified stores.

To celebrate Fair Trade Day, you'll need a fair trade chocolate bar (or other decadent food if you don't eat chocolate). Hold the chocolate in your hands and smell its rich scent. Visualize all the work that went into growing the cacao beans, processing them, and shipping the finished bar to you. Then say:

From earth to bean and over sea,

This cherished food has come to me.

Now I partake of this fine haul,

And with it wish success for all.

Eat the chocolate and savor its complex flavors. A higher price often means farmers can take better care of their crop, which improves quality.

Elizabeth Barrette

May 12
Sunday

1st ♋

Color of the day: Gold
Incense of the day: Hyacinth

Mother's Day

heart of the Empress

Mother's Day isn't just for those who have birthed children, but also for those who have been a caring guardian figure to others, giving them love, safety, and support. We can honor the living and remember those beloved mother figures who have passed on. We can also pay homage to the Earth in its creatrix energy through deities such as Demeter, Hathor, Pachamama, or Asherah—which can be especially healing for those who don't have a good or healthy relationship with the human mother figure in their lives.

The Empress card in the Tarot embodies mother-creatrix energy. She is all about supporting creativity, generating abundance, playing with sensuality, and recognizing sovereignty. Placing the Empress card upon the altar can aid us in that journey. To draw the essence of the Empress to you, make an offering of fruit, seeds, and/or spring flowers. Take a few moments each day for the next week to reflect upon the Empress, and keep the offerings fresh.

Laura Tempest Zakroff

May 13
Monday

1st ♋

☽ v/c 5:13 am

☽ → ♌ 6:36 am

Color of the day: White
Incense of the day: Lily

The Dreaming

Today we will be working with the Moon's energies and reaching out to Morpheus, the god of dreams. He can grant prophetic dreams, and to reach out to him you will need to create the right environment. Gather some incense, a feather, and a heat-safe vessel to burn the incense in or on. The incense will symbolize your request moving through the dreamscape and reaching Morpheus. Wings are symbolic of the god of dreams, so we will use a feather to establish a stronger connection. Move the feather through the smoke of the incense as you repeat aloud three times:

On swift wings shall I fly to land of lullaby. Let my dreams come and hear Morpheus's prophecy.

Place the feather on your altar to help facilitate your dreaming. Keep a small notebook near your bedside and write down what you remember upon waking so you can refer to it and see what was revealed.

Charlynn Walls

May 14
Tuesday

1st ♌

Color of the day: Scarlet
Incense of the day: Basil

Let's Go a-Maying

Time for romance! Consider this excerpt from the 1648 poem "Corinna's Going a Maying" by Robert Herrick:

See how Aurora throwes her faire

Fresh-quilted colours through the aire:

[...]

Our life is short; and our dayes run

As fast away as does the Sunne:

[...]

So when you or I are made

A fable, song, or fleeting shade;

All love, all liking, all delight

Lies drown'd with us in endlesse night.

*Then while time serves, and
we are but decaying;*

*Come, my Corinna, come,
let's go a-Maying.*

What else is there to do but to flirt and enjoy the delights of a May morning? Thinking of your own Corinna (male or female), invoke the powers of Aurora, Cupid, and Aphrodite. Read Herrick's poem aloud as you create a little pouch to hold clove, jasmine, and myrtle, moonstone, pearl, and amber, all of these intended to enhance your attractive parts. Tuck the pouch in your pocket and pick up your phone. Keep in mind that going a-Maying can lead to *anything*.

Barbara Ardinger

NOTES:

May 15
Wednesday

1st ♌

2nd Quarter 7:48 am

☽ v/c 12:41 pm

☽ → ♍ 5:33 pm

Color of the day: Brown
Incense of the day: Honeysuckle

Light a Flame!

My favorite day of the week is Wednesday. As a Gemini, which is ruled by the planet Mercury, I find Wednesdays are good days for doing business, communicating with others, and getting things done. Fueled by the power of Mercury and its lightness and swiftness of being, this day can give your works an additional boost. Of course, there is always the perpetual angst of Mercury retrograde occurring, but don't let that stop you. Just pay extra attention to what you need to do and get going!

For this spell you will need:

• Florida Water

• A red candle

• A fireproof candleholder

• A lighter or matches

• A Mercury dime (available online or through coin shops)

Wipe the candle upward and then downward with Florida Water. Allow it to dry and place it in the holder. Safely light the flame. Set the Mercury dime before the candle. Visualize the wings of Mercury effortlessly carrying you, helping you to succeed in your goals. Allow the candle to safely burn out.

Najah Lightfoot

NOTES:

May 16
Thursday

2nd ♍

Color of the day: Turquoise
Incense of the day: Myrrh

The Wave of Peace

According to the United Nations, International Day of Living Together in Peace aims "to uphold the desire to live and act together, united in differences and diversity, in order to build a sustainable world of peace, solidarity, and harmony."

Today, light a white candle for peace. Call on the Divine in any way you prefer, and request support in boosting the signal for peace. Close your eyes, breathe, and connect with a sense of inner tranquility. Think of a loved one: a partner, friend, or (human or animal) family member. Feel your heart open to this loved one. Wish them well and see them bathed in the light of your approval and positive regard. Then spread this light, approval, and positive regard across the surface of the planet. Visualize humans on every continent lighting up with this energy of love. Sense a wave of peaceful light encompassing the globe, increasing in momentum, and coming right back to you. When you feel ready, thank the Divine and extinguish the candle.

Tess Whitehurst

May 17
Friday

2nd ♍

Color of the day: Rose
Incense of the day: Mint

Lie on the Earth Spell

This simple spell can help you calm down, reconnect, and ground any energy that needs to be released. You will need to find a place outdoors where you can lie down comfortably undisturbed for at least fifteen minutes. You may want a blanket to put down on the ground. This can be in your own yard or in a public park or wild place.

If lying down for that long isn't possible, use a chair and take off your shoes, placing your bare feet on the ground.

When you find your spot, lie down and breathe. Set a timer for ten minutes, close your eyes, and breathe. As you do this, feel your connection to the earth. See if you can get your breathing in rhythm with the earth. Allow this to continue until the timer goes off.

After the timer goes off, release the connection you opened up to the earth. Open your eyes, slowly sit up, and take a look at the landscape around you.

Phoenix LeFae & Gwion Raven

May 18
Saturday

2nd ♍

☽ v/c 5:09 am

☽ → ♎ 6:23 am

Color of the day: Gray
Incense of the day: Patchouli

Spring Astronomy Day Spell

Today is Spring Astronomy Day. Sometimes we hold on to so much baggage that it clutters the mind and spirit. Today we will employ the powers of the universe to cleanse and clear. Astronomy Day is a perfect time for witches and magick makers to think beyond earthly parameters. Make a list of issues you want to be done with, using brown kraft paper (brown paper bag) and a regular pencil. Leave a good amount of space between each word. Cut out the words. Light a red candle on a fire-safe holder. As you set each word afire, recite:

> I draw on the powers of the universe. From the universe you came, to the universe you will go.

Gather the ashes with a silver spoon. Use them to write the words *thank you* on another piece of brown paper, adding an exclamation point. Your load should lighten over the next few weeks as your message is heard by the universe. Extinguish the candle.

Stephanie Rose Bird

May 19
Sunday

2nd ♎

☽ v/c 11:48 am

Color of the day: Amber
Incense of the day: Eucalyptus

Multiple Tarot Deck Spread

Like many witches, you probably have more than one tarot or oracle deck. Sometimes we like to put all our decks in a big bowl and mix up the cards. Then we do a spread using whichever cards we draw from our various decks. We love doing this because it is fun to see how the reading can be interpreted using different cards with different energies. It's also a good way to get in touch with your intuitive divination skills and see how the different decks can align with one another.

Draw some cards today and take a look at how the art, symbols, and colors from each deck create a unique reading for you. Write down anything interesting or special you notice while combining the different decks.

Amanda Lynn & Jason Mankey

May 20
Monday

2nd ♎

☉ → ♊ 8:59 am

☽ → ♏ 6:34 pm

Color of the day: Gray
Incense of the day: Neroli

Victoria Day (Canada)

Forging a New Path

The four suits of the tarot represent different areas of life, and you can use them not only as divination tools, but also to shift your energy within their respective domains. Choose a situation you'd like to change. Then separate out the minor arcana cards from the rest of your deck, shuffle, and draw a card. Based on the suit you've drawn, you'll focus on this dimension of your situation:

Pentacles: Actions and physical aspects

Swords: Thoughts and communication

Cups: Emotions and unconscious patterns

Wands: Desires and spiritual elements

Next, separate out all ten cards of the suit you've drawn. (For example, if you pulled the Two of Pentacles, separate out the rest of the pentacles, one through ten.) Shuffle this pile

and lay the cards out in a row. This sequence outlines the stepping stones you'll need to take to shift this aspect of your situation. Take a picture or record the order of the cards in your journal so you can refer back in the days to come.

Melissa Tipton

NOTES:

May 21
Tuesday

2nd ♏

Color of the day: Red
Incense of the day: Cinnamon

Pop That Corn!

Microwave popcorn is very popular these days, but when I was a kid, popping corn was a big event. Daddy would get out the old black skillet and the vegetable shortening and pop it on the stove. It was so exciting to hear it pop!

This spell can be done in the microwave, but I think it's more fun when done the old-fashioned way in a pan. Simply pop the corn, and as you hear the kernels explode, shout out aspects of your life that you're thankful for and that you'd like to see flourish and grow and prosper. As you eat the corn, think about those desires and what you can do to make them manifest.

This is a spell that can be done alone or in a group, with young and old alike. Corn brings prosperity and abundance into the home. Hung outside, it welcomes good energy. Eating corn is just plain delicious!

Charlie Rainbow Wolf

May 22
Wednesday

2nd ♏

Color of the day: Topaz
Incense of the day: Marjoram

A Rock in the Well Spell

This spell is based on old-time Appalachian folk magic. For some reason it was usually performed in May. Originally it was performed with a rock and a well. Since most of us don't have access to wells, you may also use a birdbath, a pond, a lake, or even a bowl of water for this spell.

Begin by finding a rock that appeals to you. Hold it near your heart and ask it a question that you need answered. Meditate on this question for a while as you hold your rock. When you feel ready, drop the rock into your chosen body of water. Observe the ripples in the water. Do you see any messages in them? Keep gazing at the water, and look for images that may help answer your question. Do this for no more than about fifteen minutes. When done, if you dropped the rock into a large body of water, simply leave the rock there and walk away. If you dropped the rock into a birdbath or a bowl of water, return it outside. If you failed to get results, wait about a week and try again with another rock.

James Kambos

May 23
Thursday

2nd ♏

☽ v/c 3:28 am

☽ → ♐ 4:24 am

Full Moon 9:53 am

Color of the day: White
Incense of the day: Carnation

Bodily Attuned

I am a dowser. I use pendulums and rods to attune to the electromagnetic energy of my environment and body. I have learned to use my body as a pendulum, and no longer need to have a tool.

We are, in essence, energy, and energy is affected by electromagnetism. Our body is an electromagnetic sensory tool, and we can learn how to "read" it.

Stand with your feet hip-distance apart. Feel balanced. Keep your knees soft.

Slow your breath, attuning to your body. Closing the eyes enables internal focus.

Ask your body to show you a "yes" response. Say something true: *My name is Dallas Jennifer Cobb.* (Use your own name.) Pay attention to any bodily response, like a sway or directional lean.

Now use an untrue statement to observe a "no" response: *I am 141 years old.*

Any time you need help choosing food or supplements, use this body pendulum technique to inform your decision.

Dallas Jennifer Cobb

NOTES:

May 24
Friday

3rd ♐

Color of the day: Coral
Incense of the day: Yarrow

Peaceful herb Blend

Use this herb blend to encourage a harmonious atmosphere of peace and positivity. It can be made in small amounts to use in the moment or in larger batches that can be kept for ongoing use.

Combine equal parts ground sage and lavender flowers. Conjure a feeling of peace and love in your heart, and envision the experiences of positivity and harmony you wish to create. Let the feeling in your heart radiate through the images you're seeing in your mind's eye. Project the energy of these emotionally charged visualizations into the herbs.

Use this blend to season dishes of buttered potatoes, roasted carrots, or sautéed mushrooms, or place in small bowls around the home to use as a potpourri. You can also sprinkle a line of the herb blend along the threshold of your home to welcome peaceful energies and encourage calm and cooperative behavior from all who enter.

Melanie Marquis

May 25
Saturday

3rd ♐

☽ v/c 10:47 am

☽ → ♑ 11:36 am

Color of the day: Black
Incense of the day: Magnolia

Slow Travel Spell

Slow travel refers to older and more leisurely modes of transportation, like taking a train, riding a horse, walking, biking, and boating. It also means taking your time as you go, enjoying the journey and not just the destination. It's about exploring a place in depth, rather than racing from one attraction to another. This fits well with the Pagan view of appreciating nature. For this spell you need a charm symbolizing slow travel, like a train engine, horse or horseshoe, boot, bicycle, or boat. Carry it on a short trip, such as walking around the block. Chant over it:

Travel safely and travel far,

Find adventure wherever you are.

Outward away and homeward bound,

Full of the stories that you have found.

Visualize all the excitement ahead of you, and watch for small discoveries along the way. When you get home, string the charm on your shoelace or a necklace or bracelet to carry it with you in your travels.

Elizabeth Barrette

May 26
Sunday

3rd ♑

Color of the day: Orange
Incense of the day: Marigold

Clear Quartz Protection Spell

Protect your mind, body, and spirit with this simple, all-purpose protection spell. Obtain a clear quartz point, which can be in the form of jewelry or not. Empower it by bathing it in bright outdoor sunlight (if available) or by holding it a safe but small distance from a candle flame. Either way, let it soak in the light for a minute or two. As you do so, say:

Spirit of the sun, I now invoke my divine right as a child of your light. Fill this stone with your fiery brightness and protection so that I may remain perfectly safe from both inner and outer dangers. Thank you.

Carry or wear the stone as needed, sensing yourself cloaked in a protective aura of light. If you want to employ this charm for an extended period of time, repeat the charging process once a week or so to keep the magic strong.

Tess Whitehurst

May 27
Monday

3rd ♑

☽ v/c 4:02 pm

☽ → ♒ 4:45 pm

Color of the day: Ivory
Incense of the day: Hyssop

Memorial Day

Honoring the Fallen

Today is Memorial Day in the United States, a time to remember those who fought and died while serving in the military. Today we can honor those who have passed on. You will need several flowers, either fresh, dried, artificial, or ones made from paper. (Check your local cemeteries' guidelines before leaving flowers.) You will also need a ribbon to tie your flowers together. You will use the flowers to create a tussie-mussie, or small bouquet of flowers, to honor their memory. When you tie up the flowers, use a ribbon with a message on it to the one who has passed on. This will let them know they are gone but not forgotten. Place the tussie-mussie on their grave with a moment of silence, and know that your message has been communicated to the deceased.

Charlynn Walls

May 28
Tuesday

3rd ≈≈

Color of the day: White
Incense of the day: Ginger

Rogue and Rebellious Christian Blessings

Whether or not you are a recovering Christian or perhaps even a Witch who honors Jesus, who was a teacher and healer, you can gift some Crafty blessings to those whose minds may be far from open. Taking a page from exciting free-form chaos magick, begin your walking, biking, or driving journey at 11:11 p.m., either by yourself or with others. Approach the closed doors of as many churches as you can find. Hold cut-and-dried or powdered eyebright and/or sage in your right hand. Forcefully blow the herb(s) at each door and declare:

Hateful eyes must open, as far as you can see. Only love can cross here, so mote it be!

Raven Digitalis

May 29
Wednesday

3rd ≈≈

☽ v/c 10:20 am

☽ → ♓ 8:33 pm

Color of the day: Brown
Incense of the day: Lavender

All Shall Be Well

Even on the sunshiniest days, some little bit of gloom can grab us. But it's not healthy to walk through our lives feeling depressed. Whenever that gloom gloms on to you, take a refreshing breath and speak this charm:

All is well.

All shall be well.

All can only be well.

Dear (name of goddess or god), I thank you for this day...

And I shall be happy today!

Declare your intention to stay cheerful. Wash your face, brush your teeth, and don your coolest outfit and most stylish shoes. Now take a walk, and as you stroll, sing the cheeriest song you know. Sing it loud. When you meet other people, smile and greet them. Wish them a good and safe day. Be cheerful and polite at home and at work. Tell people all shall be well.

Barbara Ardinger

May 30
Thursday

3rd ♓

4th Quarter 1:13 pm

Color of the day: Green
Incense of the day: Nutmeg

Words to Grow By

To boost the soil health (earthworms love this!) and the good vibes in your garden, break down cardboard boxes into flat sheets, choosing cardboard that isn't heavily printed or waxed and removing any tape or staples. Using a nontoxic marker or colored pencil, write positive intentions, words, and/or symbols on the cardboard. For instance, you could write "This garden is a temple of perfect love, will, and wisdom," or the word "love" or "harmony." You could also draw a reiki symbol, heart, or triskele. Focus on the energy of what you're writing, activating the power of these characters.

Place the cardboard on the soil writing-side down, and moisten it well. Layer mulch on top, making sure to cover the cardboard completely. Depending on how wet your climate is, the cardboard can take one to two years to break down, but you can use a utility knife to cut openings in which to plant any time you like. This method suppresses weeds, boosts soil nutrients, and provides earthworm habitat, while the words and symbols contribute positive energy to the land. It's a win-win!

Melissa Tipton

NOTES:

May 31
Friday

4th ♓

☽ v/c 10:55 pm

☽ → ♈ 11:28 pm

Color of the day: Purple
Incense of the day: Orchid

Spider Magic Blessing

May 31 is Web Designer Day, and as someone who has designed websites, I know it's a lot of hard work that few people understand or appreciate. At the same time, I can't help but muse about who the original web designers were—spiders and the deities associated with them, like Grandmother Spider and Arachne. While some may think Hermes is a good patron deity for the internet, both of these ladies bring some powerful magic to the table. In Navajo mythology, Spider Woman guides and protects humans. Arachne of Greek mythology reminds us to celebrate mastery of skill while keeping our ego in check. Whether you're making websites or crafting content for others, remember to be a guide for others and don't get caught up in your own hype.

To honor Grandmother Spider and Arachne, make an offering of sage, rosemary, flaxseed, and/or a spool of thread and recite this blessing:

Weaver women, thread spinners,
spin your web fine.

Grant me your wisdom
and elegant design.

Keeper of secrets, keen eye
and steady hand,

Goddess, help me stretch this
web across the land.

Laura Tempest Zakroff

NOTES:

June

The month of June is a time that inspires warmth, love, passion, and deep appreciation of beauty. Agricultural festivals in old Europe acknowledge and celebrate the many flowers and fruits that become abundant at this time. It is no coincidence that these plants—such as roses, raspberries, strawberries, wildflowers, and those that feature red or pink flowers or fruit—are associated with the planet Venus and the goddess Aphrodite. June is also the traditional month for weddings, and the term *honeymoon* refers to the beverage mead, made from fermented honey, that was traditionally given to the bride and groom as an aphrodisiac.

June brings the start of summer, and for thousands of years the summer solstice has been a prominent festival in many cultures. This celestial festival signifies the beginning of warm weather and abundant growth yet also reminds us of its opposite calendar festival: the winter solstice. All hail the Holly King! Spells done in June are often connected to love, romance, growth, health, and abundance.

Peg Aloi

June 1
Saturday

4th ♈

Color of the day: Blue
Incense of the day: Rue

Make a Bed for the Fairy Folk

The fairy folk are active during the magical month of June. This is a good time to let them know you care. For this spell you'll create a little bed for them, which they'll appreciate. You may create your bed in a wooded area or your yard. You'll need a fern leaf, a bit of soft grass, and a packet of California poppy seeds. Begin the spell when it's dark. Follow the instructions in this verse.

When the June dusk has turned to dark

And the only light is a firefly's spark,

Go to a quiet spot to make a fairy bed.

Here the little folk can rest their head.

Find a spot and lay a fern leaf
and a bit of grass so green,

Keep it hidden so it can't be seen.

Over it sprinkle your poppy
seeds to give sweet dreams.

Now the wee folk can sleep beneath
the stars and the moonbeams.

After you've made their little bed, quietly walk away. Don't try to see them. Soon you may receive some unexpected good luck.

James Kambos

June 2
Sunday

4th ♈

☽ v/c 6:04 pm

Color of the day: Gold
Incense of the day: Frankincense

Watch It Burn

To banish an unwanted condition, find a writing utensil and some paper. Draw a picture that symbolizes the situation. Don't worry about quality: a childlike rendering will work as well as a masterful sketch as long as it's meaningful to you. Even a word or phrase will do if it feels significant for you, like "anxiety," "abusive relationship," or "money fears." Loosely crumple the paper and safely light it on fire. You might place it in a fireplace or fire pit or burn it in a cauldron or cast-iron pot. As it burns, say:

Goddess of fire, thank you for
destroying this condition and
cleansing it from my experience
in all directions of time.

Feel the personal energy you've invested leaving the condition or situation and being reabsorbed into your energy field, as if the fire is healing your prior feelings of disempowerment by transferring your power directly back to you. Allow the fire to burn out completely (or safely extinguish it) and thank the Goddess.

Tess Whitehurst

June 3
Monday

4th ♈

☽ → ♉ 1:55 am

Color of the day: Gray
Incense of the day: Narcissus

Bug Off!

The goal of Insect Repellent Awareness Day, celebrated on June 3 every year, is to promote the use of insect repellents to prevent not only bites but also the spread of diseases that are carried by insects. A lot of insect repellents on the market, though, can be quite toxic not only to helpful bugs but to people and animals as well. Here are some more natural approaches to protect you from insect bites:

- *Lemon eucalyptus oil:* Mix 1 part lemon eucalyptus oil with 10 parts witch hazel and use in a spray bottle.

- *Lavender:* Use crushed fresh lavender flowers directly on the skin or apply lavender oil to both repel bugs and soothe bites.

- *Thyme:* If you're having a bonfire, add dried thyme to the fire to help keep bugs away. For a spray, mix 5 drops of thyme oil with 2 ounces of water.

- *Tea tree oil:* This oil has many great uses for skin conditions, but it can also deter bugs. Mix 1 part tea tree oil with 5 parts olive oil (or more if you have sensitive skin).

Laura Tempest Zakroff

NOTES:

June 4
Tuesday

4th ♉

Color of the day: Maroon
Incense of the day: Ylang-ylang

Working on This Year's Lessons

Because we never stop growing and learning, it's useful to have good tools to help us discover and learn our lessons. Do a Tarot reading for yourself today.

Get out your favorite deck and a few of your best Tarot books in case you want to augment what you already know as you read the cards. As you shuffle the deck, think about the four major elements of the human being, sometimes called the four bodies. Lay out a row of four cards:

1st card: Physical body

2nd card: Emotional body

3rd card: Mental body

4th card: Spiritual body

As you read the cards, think about which body you "live in" most of the time. Are you an athlete or regular exerciser? An actor or performer? An intellectual or scholar? A teacher or clergy or counselor? Do you easily move from body to body? What does the Tarot tell you are your four best lessons for this year?

Barbara Ardinger

June 5
Wednesday

4th ♉

☽ v/c 4:09 am

☽ → ♊ 4:36 am

Color of the day: Topaz
Incense of the day: Lilac

Citrus Salt Scrub

We are almost halfway through the year. Yay, we made it this far! As we prepare ourselves to keep moving forward, now is a good time to do some cleansing of our body and our senses. Use this citrus salt scrub as a way to get rid of any unwanted energies from the first half of the year and to make way for any new upcoming opportunities. You will need the following:

- ½ cup fine sea salt (for protection)

- ½ cup carrier oil of your choice

- 10 drops orange essential oil (for clearing energy and bringing happiness)

- A small glass jar with a lid

Mix the ingredients together in the jar and use in the bath or shower initially to create new energy to welcome in the second half of the year. Use the rest whenever you feel like you need a pick-me-up.

Amanda Lynn & Jason Mankey

 **June 6**
Thursday

4th ♊

New Moon 8:38 am

Color of the day: Crimson
Incense of the day: Clove

Strawberry New Moon Magick

We find ourselves in the new moon, of Strawberry Moon. Today, you can take some time to relax and dream up what it is you want to manifest. This is the time to look toward what is fresh and new, under the darkened sky. You are going to set an intention.

If you drink alcohol, grab a bottle of your favorite strawberry, rose or red wine. Wine with berry overtones works nicely, such as Meinklang Pinot Noir. Get your wine ready according to its needs, open it, and pour a glass before this rite. If you do not drink or prefer not to today, a strawberry or rose-scented incense will do the trick. Put your incense in a fire-safe incense holder and light it, keeping it nearby so you can reflect on the scent.

Get into a relaxed, meditative state by taking deep cleansing breaths. Sip the wine or enjoy your incense, watching its smoke; letting either touch the inner recesses of your mind. What is it you want in the world that doesn't currently exist? A poem, a decluttered room, a new

relationship, perhaps a painting or drawing? Think hard about what would fit your world and make it a better place. Continue to engage your mind. Make a mental note of what you want to do and how. When it's time, bring your intention to light!

Stephanie Rose Bird

NOTES:

 June 7
Friday

1st ♊

☽ v/c 8:16 am

☽ → ♋ 8:41 am

Color of the day: White
Incense of the day: Alder

Window Wash for Clarity

Use this window wash to clear away negative energies and bring clarity. In a glass pitcher or in an empty soda bottle or milk jug, mix one quart white vinegar with the juice and peel from one lemon. Add a large sprig of rosemary. Stir or shake the concoction vigorously to help distribute the lemon and rosemary throughout the vinegar. Let the mixture sit for a few hours, then strain out the lemon peel and rosemary. Pour the vinegar into a spray bottle.

Use the spray to clean all the windows and mirrors of your home. If you have a car, clean its mirrors and windows, too. As you spritz the spray, envision the cleansing, purifying power of the ingredients blasting away any murkiness or negativity. Imagine seeing the clearest blue sky in your mirrors or through your windows as you wipe each surface with a dry paper towel or piece of newspaper.

Melanie Marquis

June 8
Saturday

1st ♋

Color of the day: Black
Incense of the day: Sage

Karmic Lessons

Saturday is the perfect day of the week to work with the vibrations of the planet Saturn. One aspect of Saturn is the ability to deal with karma and its revelations. When we feel a block in our psyche, it can be due to a karmic entanglement. Karma can be a tricky thing, and it can entwine our past lives with our current one, leading to repercussions of which we are often unaware.

Create a space where you can meditate. You will need a quiet environment without distractions and a string (or ribbon) that is tangled up. As you clear your mind of the daily monotony of life, focus on untangling the knots in the string in front of you. As you do so, think to yourself:

As I untwine this string, so too do my issues in lives past and present unravel, freeing me to achieve my highest good.

Place the detangled string in a safe place or on your altar so you have a visual representation of your journey.

Charlynn Walls

June 9
Sunday

1st ♋

☽ v/c 3:05 pm

☽ → ♌ 3:29 pm

Color of the day: Yellow
Incense of the day: Hyacinth

Purifying Your Temple

A celebration honoring the Roman goddess Vesta was held between June 7 and June 15. The festival was known as Vestalia. During the week, the temple to Vesta was opened. Offerings were made to her, and the temple was cleaned and purified. Vesta is the goddess of hearth and home and is associated with the sacred flame that warmed homes, gave light, and cooked food.

Where is the sacred flame in your home? It could be an actual fireplace or a potbelly stove. Perhaps you associate your oven or stovetop with the sacred flame. Once you identify the place, mimic the rite of Vestalia. Open the door to the oven (while not in use) and clean it out and wipe it down. Take time to do this mindfully, remembering that this is the place where the food is cooked that nourishes you and your household. If you are working with a fireplace, do the same thing. Clean out any old ashes, redecorate the mantelpiece, and put fresh logs on the grate.

Phoenix LeFae & Gwion Raven

June 10
Monday

1st ♌

Color of the day: Lavender
Incense of the day: Neroli

hurray for herbs!

Today is Herb and Spices Day. Many staple foods taste bland by themselves. The flavor of dishes made with them comes from herbs and spices, from cooling mint to hot peppers. We also get many magical ingredients and medicines from them. Take time today to thank these plant allies for their help.

Summer is a fine time to walk in a garden, when the heat draws out the perfume of herbs, spices, and flowers. If you don't have a garden of your own, visit a botanical garden, park, or other place that grows such things. See how many you can recognize and identify. As you walk, say:

Herbs of earth and spice of flame,

Known by scent and taste and name,

Thanks for blessings you bestowed

As we've walked this mortal road.

Other ways to show your appreciation include learning about herbs and spices, planting new ones, cooking or crafting with them, and trying ones you haven't tasted before.

Elizabeth Barrette

June 11
Tuesday

1st ♌

☽ v/c 3:16 pm

Color of the day: Gray
Incense of the day: Basil

Shavuot begins at sundown

Column of Clarity

Sometimes it's hard to know where our own thoughts and feelings end and another's begin, but clear boundaries help us make clear decisions. To turn down the volume on outside influences and make space for your inner voice, start by releasing any energy that doesn't serve you in this moment. Close your eyes, bring your awareness to your breath, and imagine a column of light descending from the sky and moving through the crown of your head, down the center of your body, and into the earth. This column of light serves as a vacuum, attracting any unhelpful energy in your body and aura, sucking it down and out. Continue until you feel clear and grounded.

Then visualize this column of light expanding in diameter, first to the surface of your skin, then outward to encompass your aura. Really get a sense of this energetic container shielding you from outside energies. Within this space, bring to mind a situation or decision you'd like clarity on and allow your inner knowing to arise. When done, release the imagery.

Melissa Tipton

NOTES:

June 12
Wednesday

1st ♌ ♋

☽ → ♍ 1:39 am

Color of the day: White
Incense of the day: Marjoram

Simple Summer Lip Balm Spell

Making lip balm for the summer can save you money and ensure a high-quality product in your favorite flavor. Lip balm is easy to make. Gather these ingredients:

- 2 tablespoons beeswax
- 1 tablespoon coconut oil
- 1 teaspoon olive oil
- 1 teaspoon honey
- 4 drops peppermint essential oil
- 7 drops food-grade essential oil in your favorite flavor (I like grapefruit or orange.)

Add the ingredients to a small pot. Melt on low heat. As you stir, incant:

I make my own magic stuff,
I am magic, I am enough.

Intention sets this lip balm spell,
with every use I am well.

Pour into small containers. Cool. Add a lid and label. Coconut oil has a low level of natural SPF to protect your lips. As you use the balm, remember that you are enough and you are well.

Dallas Jennifer Cobb

June 13
Thursday

1st ♍

Color of the day: Turquoise
Incense of the day: Myrrh

Pride Month: A Light for All

Although it's often believed that LGBTQIA+ Pride Month is an exclusively queer celebration, the truth is that the celebratory rainbow also includes loving allies of the cause. You can send global blessings to those who are subject to prejudice simply for being who they are.

Buy or print out a Pride flag, ideally the updated version (called the Progress Pride Flag). With a permanent marker, draw two large hearts on the flag, one upright and one inverted. These should be drawn on top of each other in order to create a "double heart." After calling upon LGBTQIA+ ancestors in your own words, conclude by staring at the double heart for a number of minutes, with outstretched hands around the flag.

Speak affirmations intended to spread loving protection to all queer folks in need. Raising your arms above you and then to your sides, take deep breaths, and with each exhalation, see this light spreading to encircle the entire globe. Conclude with a big smile, then kiss the flag and leave it in a random public spot for someone to synchronistically find!

Raven Digitalis

June 14
Friday

1st ♍

2nd Quarter 1:18 am

☽ v/c 1:54 pm

☽ → ♎ 2:12 pm

Color of the day: Rose
Incense of the day: Cypress

Flag Day

Say It Loud!

Today is the day to let your flag fly! It can be your freak flag, your cultural flag, the flag of your home or country, or even your garden flag. The point is that this is a day of celebration. Flags have a long, rich symbolism. They make a statement. They are impactful. They announce an affiliation, an alignment, or a representation. They are a symbol of something that is important to you.

If you don't have a flag to fly, you can always wear jewelry or clothing that aligns with your intention to represent. Seize the power of this day! Fly your flag and make a statement. Reach out to others who support your cause or mission. Donate to an organization that is doing work that aligns with your beliefs, your desires, or what you would like to see recognized in the world.

Najah Lightfoot

June 15
Saturday

2nd ♎

Color of the day: Indigo
Incense of the day: Patchouli

Magically Charge a Garden Gazing Globe

Garden gazing globes were originally used to send back the evil eye and protect a home from jealous glances. This spell helps you charge your globe. First you'll need to buy a globe of your choice at a garden center if you don't have one. Next wipe the globe off with bottled water. Position the globe where it can be seen. You could put it on a stand in a flower bed, on a porch, or in a large flowerpot. Now say these words:

Send back the evil glare.

Send back the jealous stare.

This home is protected from all harm

Now that I have said this magical charm.

You may want to repeat this charm once a year.

James Kambos

♡ June 16
Sunday

2nd ♎

Color of the day: Orange
Incense of the day: Heliotrope

Father's Day

honoring the Ancestors

Your very existence means that someone fathered you. Whether you had a good relationship or a bad one with this person, whether you knew him or not, you had a father. This spell honors that connection, affirming what is good and helping to make what was bad less powerful.

You'll need a mirror on a wall. Gaze into it and really see yourself. Don't berate yourself. Don't judge yourself. Just look into the eyes of the person gazing back at you. It's not a reflection; it's a person who needs you.

Think about the life force that flows through your veins and all the ancestors that came before you so that you could exist. Thank the person in the mirror for being there for you when no one else is. Thank them for your life, and your breath, and your potential. Finally, high-five the mirror—a universal sign of support. You've got this!

Charlie Rainbow Wolf

⚠ June 17
Monday

2nd ♎

☽ v/c 2:05 am
☽ → ♏ 2:38 am

Color of the day: Silver
Incense of the day: Rosemary

Candle Blessing

There are times when we need to imbue our magickal working with a little extra *oomph*. One item we can charge ahead of time is a candle. You can charge one or more candles with this blessing.

Take the candles you have acquired and start by cleansing them with a sage smudge or salt water. Move the candles through the smoke from the sage or sprinkle them with the salt water to cleanse them of any prior residual energy. Once complete, place your hands over the candles, close your eyes, and take a deep inhale. Feel the energy come in as you take the breath. As you breathe out, feel the energy collected push out and into the candles. Push all the energy you can into them and say as you do so:

Bright these candles will burn, creating a beacon for our magick to follow.

After completing the spell, store the candles in a cool, dry place until you're ready to use them in ritual or other spellwork.

Charlynn Walls

▽ June 18
Tuesday

2nd ♏

Color of the day: Black
Incense of the day: Cedar

Water Protection Spell

Today is National Go Fishing Day, International Sushi Day, and Clean Your Aquarium Day—which definitely seems a bit fishy! Whether you happen to eat or keep fish (or neither!), I think we can all agree that it's vital to protect the water they live in. Here is a spell to help protect your favorite local body of water. When visiting, find a discreet place to draw a symbol, ideally directly in the sand or mud, but you can also draw it in the water itself with a stick. First draw a circle, saying:

I recognize the sovereign spirit of this water (name the body if you know it).

Draw three wavy lines through the circle and extending beyond it as you say:

May these waters flow free of pollution, free of contaminants, and free of harmful bodies.

Draw six points around the circle as you say:

May this water be protected at the north and the south, the east and the west, above and below. So mote it be.

Laura Tempest Zakroff

June 19
Wednesday

2nd ♏

☽ v/c 12:19 pm
☽ → ♐ 12:32 pm

Color of the day: Yellow
Incense of the day: Lavender

Juneteenth

Juneteenth Altar

Juneteenth is an emotionally charged celebration of freedom from enslavement. Understandably, it is a time when anger and other feelings may arise. With all that we hold inside, it is a great day to get busy and manifest something with meaning, like an altar.

Start by laying a red (for our blood), black (for the Black people) and green (for Mother Nature) cloth(s) on a table or mantel. Then collect the Earth's gifts respectfully and with great care:

* 5 pink carnations (for healing and self-love)

* 4 red roses (a symbol of quiet strength)

* 3 oak leaf branches (to symbolize African American strength, endurance, and cultural continuity)

* 1 orange, peeled and separated (to symbolize the release of trauma)

• 9 cracked hazelnuts (the Celtic tree of justice and wisdom)

Put the flowers and oak branches in a vase of water and place on the cloth(s). Arrange the other items artfully. Go to this altar three times today for prayer and reflection.

Stephanie Rose Bird

NOTES:

June 20
Thursday

2nd ♐

☉ → ♋ 4:51 pm

Color of the day: Green
Incense of the day: Jasmine

Litha – Summer Solstice

Quick Money Ritual

If you need to call in some money fast, try this simple ritual. Add a few drops of eucalyptus oil to a small bottle of unscented lotion. Shake to combine. Alternatively, purchase lotion already scented with eucalyptus. (It's okay if it contains other fragrances as well.) Or, if necessary, use unscented lotion that won't irritate, but keep some eucalyptus oil nearby.

Wash and dry your hands. Safely light a white or green candle and sit in front of it. Close your eyes, take some deep breaths, and relax. Rub a small amount of the lotion into your hands while mindfully inhaling the scent. (If the lotion isn't scented, first rub in the lotion, then open the bottle of eucalyptus and inhale.) Hold your palms up like you are ready to receive bundles of cash. Imagine the energy of wealth and abundance being drawn irresistibly toward your palms. Breathe it into your body. Smile and anticipate receiving wealth swiftly and in both expected and unexpected ways. Extinguish the candle.

Tess Whitehurst

June 21
Friday

2nd ♐

☽ v/c 6:58 pm

☽ → ♑ 7:08 pm

Full Moon 9:08 pm

Color of the day: Pink

Incense of the day: Violet

Full Moon Spell for Awareness

This full moon spell will help boost your psychic awareness and magickal power. Using a marker or eyeliner, draw a circle to represent the moon on your forehead and on the back of each of your hands. Anoint your pulse points with coconut oil or olive oil. Bask outside in the moonlight in a comfortable position. Invite the moon's energy to enter your body. Envision the circles you drew on your body opening up like gateways to let in the lunar tide. Feel the moon's power within your body, and envision this power literally fusing with the neural networks that run throughout your form. Say:

Mother moon, share your light!
Mother moon, share your sight!
Show me all that I should know.
Share with me your magick glow!

Notice any images or insights that come to mind. Pay attention to your intuition over the next few days and weeks.

Melanie Marquis

June 22
Saturday

3rd ♑

Color of the day: Gray

Incense of the day: Ivy

Herbal Sun Tea for Peace and Clarity

It's the height of summer and the perfect time to make some sun tea. Take advantage of the mighty summer sun to brew your intentions into a delicious concoction.

Gather a sun tea container or large Mason jar, fresh water, fresh mint, and fresh chamomile. (Dried herbs will work as well.) Place the herbs in the container and then fill with fresh water. Now let the sunshine work its magic. As the tea brews throughout the day, allow the herbs to infuse it with clarity and peace. When it's time to enjoy your delicious beverage, feel the cooling flavors as they bring a sense of calm over your whole being. Refrigerate and enjoy your sun tea over the next few days.

Amanda Lynn & Jason Mankey

June 23
Sunday

3rd ♑

☽ v/c 11:05 pm

☽ → ♒ 11:14 pm

Color of the day: Amber
Incense of the day: Almond

Protect Our Children

Here is a spell to protect our children from hate speech and crimes. Gather your coven (or work alone). Bring your children's favorite stuffed animals and a package of confetti. Cast your circle. Set a chair in the center, and as you place each stuffed animal on the chair, speak the child's name and your intention to protect the child with divine love and blessings. Sprinkle confetti over the stuffed animals and say:

> Let this confetti be blessed.
>
> Let it be strong.
>
> Let it touch our children
> with safety and strength.
>
> Let its blessed power protect our
> children wherever they go.

Raise your phone and play the aria "O Isis and Osiris," a prayer of protection, as sung by the high priest Sarastro in the opera *The Magic Flute*. (Find it on YouTube.) Note that while Sarastro is blessing a marriage here, this prayer can protect us all.

Barbara Ardinger

June 24
Monday

3rd ♒

Color of the day: Ivory
Incense of the day: Lily

Saint John's Day Cleansing Spell

Saint John the Baptist's feast day is celebrated on this day by people of different religions all over the world. Many believe that this holiday is an evolution of Summer Solstice celebrations from pre-Christian people. This may be the case, but there is one religion that has fully embraced the celebration of Saint John's Day, and that is Vodoun.

On Saint John's Day in New Orleans, people gather and celebrate John the Baptist by performing head-washing rituals, which is a traditional cleansing practice performed in the Vodoun religion.

If there is a Vodoun house near you, they often open up their services and offer community head washes for Saint John's Day. If that isn't possible, consider performing a cleansing of your own.

The whole point of the story of Saint John revolves around the concept of baptism. For cleansing on this holy day, go to a body of water and fully immerse yourself as an act of cleansing and devotion to the spiritual world.

Phoenix LeFae & Gwion Raven

June 25
Tuesday

3rd ♒

☽ v/c 6:30 pm

Color of the day: Maroon
Incense of the day: Geranium

Sun Flowers

Many flowers that enjoy full sunlight also resist heat and drought. They are often associated with the sun and the element of fire. Examples include sunflowers, sunchokes, black-eyed Susans, daisies, Indian blankets, marigolds, Mexican hats, yellow coneflowers, and zinnias. Sunflowers and some others are heliotropic, leaning toward the sun.

You can pick these flowers and preserve them to save the sun's energy for the darker parts of the year. Small, soft flowers like marigolds may be pressed whole. For larger ones, like sunflowers, pick off the petals and press them. Those with a big center, like coneflowers, may be dried as seedheads for interesting texture in flower arrangements. As you harvest the flowers, visualize the sunlight going into them and filling them with the power of fire. Once preserved, you can use these spell components in many ways. Add petals to incense or use them to cast a circle. Toss dried seedpods into a ritual fire. They're especially useful at Yule and Beltane.

Elizabeth Barrette

June 26
Wednesday

3rd ♒

☽ → ♓ 2:08 am

Color of the day: White
Incense of the day: Bay laurel

Self Celebration Day Spell

Guess what? Today is my birthday. So I'm inviting you to my party, a self celebration party.

I have struggled with low self-esteem, fears, phobias, and regular self-sabotage for years. As I have actively sought recovery, these symptoms have lessened. Now I can see the good qualities I possess and recognize the evidence of my recovery in changed behaviors and shifted feelings.

Look in a mirror, asking: *What do I like the most about physical me?*

Place a hand on your heart, asking: *What do I love the most about emotional me?*

Lightly touch your third eye, asking: *How do I honor spiritual me?*

Place a hand on top of your head, asking: *What do I admire about intellectual/mental me?*

Place a hand on your belly, asking: *How do I take care of all of me?*

Wrapped in the knowledge of physical, mental, emotional, spiritual, and self-care value, celebrate your innate goodness today.

Dallas Jennifer Cobb

June 27
Thursday

3rd ♓

Color of the day: Crimson
Incense of the day: Mulberry

We Are the Universe Experiencing Itself

An ancient, widespread mystical belief is that everyone and everything is, in fact, the universe, God, or (insert your own term here) experiencing itself.

To more deeply experience this reality, visit your favorite sacred space and meditate until all the cares of yesterday, tomorrow, and today seem to fade away.

Anoint your third eye (brow chakra) with either sandalwood paste or powder, turmeric powder, eyebright powder, or honey. Declare:

I am all Oneness, I am all Being.
Enlighten my life as holy eyes seeing!

Throughout the day and beyond, pay close attention to synchronicities and remember that you, yourself, are existence experiencing itself in every moment. It's time to take a step back to more deeply listen, learn, and love.

Raven Digitalis

June 28
Friday

3rd ♓

☽ v/c 4:45 am

☽ → ♈ 4:52 am

4th Quarter 5:53 pm

Color of the day: Purple
Incense of the day: Vanilla

Declaration of My Independence

On this day in 1776, the final draft of the Declaration of Independence was submitted to the Continental Congress. It is a good day to channel those energies into your own life. Creating your own independence will allow you to follow your dreams.

Determine who or what you feel is holding you back from achieving your full potential. You will need a piece of paper and a pen. You are going to write your own declaration. Title your work "Declaration of My Independence." Write down who or what you are declaring your independence from, and establish your goals or your "unalienable rights." List everything, and if you need to recopy the final draft on a new piece of paper, feel free to do so. You will want your document organized and legible. Once your document is complete, write "So Mote It Be" at the bottom and sign it to seal in your intention.

Charlynn Walls

 June 29
Saturday

4th ♈

Color of the day: Blue
Incense of the day: Pine

Summertime Bliss

It's summertime, it's Saturday, and it's the period of the waning moon, so today is a good day to kick back and spend some time relaxing. During the summer we feel energized, and many of us make plans to go here, there, and everywhere. Our schedules get loaded up with people to see, places to go, trips to take, and adventures that must happen! But with all those plans can come chaos, so sometimes it's good to bring balance to a summer day by carving out a moment in time when you can just *be*.

For this spell you will need your favorite summertime libation, your favorite drinking glass, comfy clothes, and your favorite song.

Pour yourself a drink, get comfy, and listen to your favorite piece of music. Bask in the moment, stare at the sky or the stars, and appreciate the moments of summertime bliss.

Najah Lightfoot

June 30
Sunday

4th ♈

☽ v/c 12:56 am
☽ → ♉ 8:00 am

Color of the day: Gold
Incense of the day: Juniper

Begin Anew

The last day of any month is always a good time to bring things to a close. This spell will help to end what needs to finish so the new month might start anew. Of course, it's not without responsibility; the spell will help, but you still have to do the work! You'll need a piece of paper, a black pen or pencil, a small cardboard box (it doesn't have to be new), and some tape.

Write down what needs to be finished. This may be a relationship that has run its course, a project that is lingering, or a habit you want to get rid of. Put the paper in the box and tape it shut. As you are closing the box, say:

I close this door, to open more. I have finished with thee, so mote it be.

Tape the box securely closed and take it out to the trash. Let the obstacles go so you can start afresh tomorrow.

Charlie Rainbow Wolf

July

In 46 BCE, when Julius Caesar decided to reform the Roman lunar calendar, the names of the months were numbers. He moved the first of the year back to January, and, being the egoist he was, he renamed the fifth month (the month of his birth) for himself: Iulius (Julius, today's July). He also gave it a thirty-first day. (Then he named the next month after his heir, Augustus.)

July (the month of my birth, too) is high summer. In many places, it's the hottest month of the year. It's the month in which everything blooms until the heat of the sun makes flowers—and people—wilt and nearly melt.

What do I remember from my childhood Julys? Rereading my favorite books. Dragging the big old washtub out on the side lawn, filling it with cold water, and splashing all afternoon. Helping my father tend his flowers—roses, columbines, tulips, and hydrangeas. Climbing to the very top of our neighbor's huge weeping willow tree. Chasing fireflies before bedtime and putting them in jars to glitter and wink throughout the night. Sleeping in the screened porch with all the windows open to catch every possible breeze. What are your favorite July memories?

Barbara Ardinger

July 1
Monday

4th ♉

Color of the day: Lavender
Incense of the day: Hyssop

Canada Day

Belonging

I am Canadian, but for years I didn't identify with my national identity. When I began to travel and live abroad for work, I quickly became aware of what being Canadian meant. I became a passionate patriot. I love my country.

This year I drove across two-thirds of Canada and was astonished by the regional differences. We are not homogenous, though we are all Canadian.

Regardless of where you live, let's use the occasion of the birthday of Canada to celebrate our respective countries and recognize the mosaic of differences that make up our national identity. Let's conjure what "All Are Welcome Here" looks and feels like.

Envision the map of your country. See its dimensions. Pay attention to the variety of races, colors, languages, and cultures present. Conjure an image of this diversity coming together harmoniously, finding belonging, peace, and identity within your beloved country.

Dallas Jennifer Cobb

July 2
Tuesday

4th ♉

☽ v/c 11:43 am
☽ → ♊ 11:50 am

Color of the day: Gray
Incense of the day: Bayberry

Loving Reflection

Insecurity can lead to feeling that we're in competition with others, like there's a finite supply of love and acceptance to go around. Learning how to give ourselves this love and acceptance uncouples our self-worth from externals, allowing us to enjoy connection with others without the need to compare and compete.

Using a dry erase marker, write on a mirror that you use daily, choosing from the following affirmations (or create one of your own). You can add hearts and other symbols if you like!

My worth is an unshakeable fact.

Today, I feel loved for who I am.

I see myself through the eyes of love.

Today, I learn to love myself in new ways.

Every day, spend a few moments in the mirror, basking in these loving words and allowing their energy to ignite your inner stores of love and acceptance. When done, clean the mirror with a soft cloth.

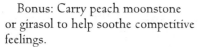

Bonus: Carry peach moonstone or girasol to help soothe competitive feelings.

Melissa Tipton

NOTES:

July 3
Wednesday

4th ♊

Color of the day: Brown
Incense of the day: Honeysuckle

A harvest of Color

The fruit and crop harvests are still weeks away, but now is the time for the harvest of color in the flower garden. It is the power and the glory of nature's color spectrum. Daisies are sparkling white, zinnias are blooming in every sun-kissed color you can think of, and impatiens are red, pink, white, and salmon. There is a color for everybody.

For this beautiful spell you'll need a pair of sharp scissors. Go into the garden, if you have one, and begin cutting bouquets. (If you don't have your own garden, buy a couple of bouquets.) As you do this, be mindful. These flowers are gifts to us from Mother Earth. You should feel yourself calm down.

When done, take your flowers inside. Arrange them in vases, cups, or jars and fill with cool water. Place one container on your altar. Place the others around your home. Sit at your altar and thank nature for its harvest of color.

James Kambos

 ## July 4
Thursday

4th ♊

☽ v/c 4:44 pm

☽ → ♋ 4:51 pm

Color of the day: Turquoise
Incense of the day: Balsam

Independence Day

Developing Independence

On Independence Day, think of ways to develop your independence. Where do you go, and where haven't you gone that you would like to visit? Consider your current limits and take one step further. This expands what you can do for yourself, rather than relying on others.

For this spell you'll need the edge of a map. This can be an old map or just a printout. Tear off a large corner, about hand-size. In the middle, write some places to which you go. Along the edge, off the map, write places—local or distant—to which you haven't gone. Visualize the journey. Tuck the map into your pocket.

Then go visit one new place locally. If that's unfeasible, research travel to a distant location, not just pretty pictures but concrete steps of how to get there and what to do on location, including any precautions. Keep the map scrap as a reminder to expand the range of where you can go and what you can do.

Elizabeth Barrette

 ## July 5
Friday

4th ♋

New Moon 6:57 pm

Color of the day: Rose
Incense of the day: Mint

Clearing the Way

Today is a new moon, an excellent time for cleansing magic. If you wear ritual jewelry or use tools on a regular basis as part of your practice, you will want to cleanse them from time to time. These items are particularly sensitive to our energies, and we want to make sure they do not hold any residual negative energy when they are being used so it does not negatively impact our practice.

Gather the items that need cleansing and place them in a small basin. If the items are okay to soak in water, you can submerge them. If not, you can use incense to cleanse them. After choosing your method, focus and center yourself by concentrating on cleansing your tools. Say the following three times:

Remove negativity so the way is clear.

Charlynn Walls

July 6
Saturday

1st ♋

☽ v/c 11:47 pm

☽ → ♌ 11:56 pm

Color of the day: Black
Incense of the day: Patchouli

Eye Amulet Painted Rocks

Eyes have been symbolic in magic since the beginning of time. Whether it's known as the all-seeing eye or the evil eye, the idea of protecting yourself from the harmful gaze of others has been part of global traditions for centuries, if not longer.

Today, get crafty and create your own amulets for protection by painting eyes on rocks and placing them in any space that you feel needs a little extra guardianship. Not only will they add a little extra pop and decoration to your space but they will also protect it. You will need the following:

- Unpolished river rocks
- Acrylic paint
- Paintbrushes

Create sacred space however you choose, then start painting eyes on the rocks. While doing so, put into the rocks the energy that they will guard and protect wherever you place them from any negativity and harm. Set them out in the sun to charge and dry, and when you are ready, place them around your home and garden.

Amanda Lynn & Jason Mankey

NOTES:

July 7
Sunday

1st ♌

Color of the day: Yellow
Incense of the day: Almond

Islamic New Year begins at sundown

One Plant to Rule Them All

Gardening just ain't my thang. As Witches, however, we choose to honor the planet by way of harvest festivals, recycling, elemental magick, ethical purchasing, volunteerism, and other ways. It is our responsibility to be as mindful as possible when it comes to recognizing our imprint on the planet. Whenever and however we can connect with and honor Mother Nature, we are performing a sacred act.

To successfully experience and align with the planet's abundance of flora, purchase a basic potted plant designed to remain in its container. This could be bamboo, aloe, a cactus, or anything else. Research how to take care of the plant, including its ideal type of sunlight and amount of water. Every time you water it, say:

With this water I honor the
Mother. I also grow in wisdom
and gift this to others.

Raven Digitalis

July 8
Monday

1st ♌

Color of the day: White
Incense of the day: Clary sage

Carry On!

A new week brings the energy of getting back out into the world and engaging with people. Some of us may have lots of emails to answer, appointments to keep, or business to attend to. Many of us may feel overwhelmed or have anxiety with all the things we need to do in the upcoming week. A spell of protection is in order! You will need:

- A white candle
- A fireproof candleholder
- Florida Water (to cleanse your candle)
- Olive oil or a blessing oil of your choice
- A sharp point (A pushpin, a nail, or even the end of a paper clip will do.)

Wipe the candle upward and then downward with Florida Water and allow it to dry. Carve a pentagram (a five-pointed star enclosed in a circle) into the candle. Anoint the candle with the oil and place it in the holder.

Say:

By the light of the day, by the light of the sun, I am protected wherever I am, wherever I go. I accomplish with ease all that I must do! Blessed be. So mote it be.

Allow the candle to safely burn down.

Najah Lightfoot

NOTES:

July 9
Tuesday

1st ♌

☽ v/c 2:04 am

☽ → ♍ 9:48 am

Color of the day: Red
Incense of the day: Cinnamon

Walk into Good Fortune

For this spell you will need two bay leaves and a cinnamon scroll, both available from the spice section of the supermarket. Bay keeps bad luck at bay (see what I did there?), while cinnamon is appealing to the gods.

Stand barefoot and put the bay and the cinnamon between the palms of your hands. Rub them together briskly until you start to feel heat from the friction. Part your hands and let the leaves and cinnamon fall to the floor.

Wipe the palm of your right hand onto the sole of your left foot, then wipe the palm of your left hand onto the sole of your right foot. Now step into the residue of bay and cinnamon that is on the floor. Envision the herbs and spices leading you forward to your luck and abundance. When you have that image firmly in your mind, you can wash your hands and feet.

Charlie Rainbow Wolf

July 10
Wednesday

1st ♍

Color of the day: Topaz
Incense of the day: Lilac

Abundance Charm

Craft this charm to draw abundance into your life. Cut out a circle of dark green fabric. With a green pen or marker, write the word "abundance" on the fabric three times. Lay the fabric in front of you, with the side that you wrote on facing up. Place in the middle of the circle three acorns and two shiny pennies. Touch the acorns and pennies as you imagine experiencing the abundance you seek. Sprinkle the acorns and coins generously with cinnamon and basil, envisioning more and more abundant blessings. Gather the fabric around the mixture, twist the top, and tie it off with a red string. Carry the bundle with you or put it in a special place in your home or business to help draw in abundance and magnify good fortune.

Melanie Marquis

July 11
Thursday

1st ♍

☽ v/c 9:55 pm

☽ → ♎ 10:06 pm

Color of the day: Purple
Incense of the day: Apricot

Mint Magic

It's National Mojito Day, which is of course a great day to enjoy one of these tasty drinks. But it's also a great opportunity to highlight some of the magical properties of one of its key ingredients—mint! Easy to grow and wonderfully aromatic, this versatile herb has a reputation for keeping the peace, aiding in memory and communication, calming the mind, and providing protection.

A fresh sprig of mint placed on your altar or hung by your doorway can aid in protecting your home.

A cup of mint tea shared with someone you're disagreeing with can help calm an argument and lead to a resolution. You can also anoint yourself with mint oil or tincture before going into a difficult situation.

A little satchel of dried mint carried on the body can help stimulate the memory while keeping you calm.

If you decide to grow mint, be sure to keep it in a container or someplace you're okay with it spreading—because it will. No arguments there!

Laura Tempest Zakroff

▽ **July 12**
Friday

1st ♎

Color of the day: Coral
Incense of the day: Thyme

Time to Get Outdoors

Most of us work indoors nearly all the time. It's summertime. Time to get outdoors. Find a private place and visualize it as a magical island. Read aloud Caliban's speech from Shakespeare's *The Tempest*:

> *Be not afeard; the isle is full of noises,*
>
> *Sounds and sweet airs, that give delight, and hurt not.*
>
> *Sometimes a thousand twangling instruments*
>
> *Will hum about mine ears; and sometime voices,*
>
> *That, if I then had waked after long sleep,*
>
> *Will make me sleep again: and then, in dreaming,*
>
> *The clouds methought would open, and show riches*
>
> *Ready to drop upon me; that, when I waked,*
>
> *I cried to dream again.*

Let yourself sink into a dream and see the twangling instruments. Hear their music and other sounds of nature. Pull the music into your body and let it heal whatever is unwell in you.

Receive the riches dropping from the clouds: healthy breathing, happy inner organs, overall good health. When you awaken, stretch and explore your magical island.

                    Barbara Ardinger

NOTES:

 July 13
Saturday

1st ♎

☽ v/c 6:49 pm

2nd Quarter 6:49 pm

Color of the day: Blue
Incense of the day: Rue

Wind Chime Blessing

Today, obtain some wind chimes with a sound you love. If it's sunny out, spread a white cloth outdoors in sunlight and place your chimes on top. Allow them to soak in the power of the sun for a minute or two. Otherwise, cleanse them by bathing them in incense or herbal smoke or by misting them with rose water. Hold the chimes to your heart. Feel grateful for all the many blessings you already have. Let this gratitude carry over as you visualize and expect waves of wealth and prosperity to pour in, followed by waves of success, harmony, health, friendship, and love. Call on the Divine and say:

> Thank you for my abundant riches, glorious success, inner peace, radiant wellness, stellar support system, and divine romance.

Feel even more gratitude. Hang the chimes outside your front door. Whenever you notice their mellifluous sound, sense abundant blessings flowing into your life.

Tess Whitehurst

July 14
Sunday

2nd ♎

☽ → ♏ 10:53 am

Color of the day: Amber
Incense of the day: Eucalyptus

Bastille Day Justice Spell

Bastille Day in France is the celebration of the people overcoming the status quo of the ruling classes. It is a day of remembering that the people are the true body of power and not those that hold the money or assumed power.

As a way to honor that fight and add power and energy to the people in our world fighting fascism right now, perform this spell. You will need a glass-encased yellow candle and a bay leaf.

Start by using felt markers or paint to decorate the glass of the candle with words, letters, symbols, and images that represent justice to you. When you feel complete with this process, light the candle. Use a felt marker to write the word JUSTICE on the bay leaf and burn it in the candle flame, being careful not to burn your fingers.

Leave the burnt leaf on the top of the candle wax. Let the candle burn down completely.

Phoenix LeFae & Gwion Raven

July 15
Monday

2nd ♏

Color of the day: Gray
Incense of the day: Lily

horse Spirit Meditation

Today is National I Love Horses Day, a time to celebrate the economic, military, agricultural, historical, and cultural contributions of horses. As witches, let's delve into horse spirit and how it can enhance our spiritual lives.

Horses represent many things, but today let's focus on the freedom they symbolize. On a piece of paper, use vine or compressed charcoal to draw several horses running. Don't be shy. Draw in your own way. Use your imagination. Then wash your hands and tape the drawing to a wall.

After sunset, safely light a red pillar candle on a table in the room with the drawing. Imagine the ways that horses transported your ancestors to the place where they lived a hundred years ago. Clap three times loudly to praise them and the horses that brought them to their home. Extinguish the candle.

Stephanie Rose Bird

July 16
Tuesday

2nd ♏

☽ v/c 9:10 pm
☽ → ♐ 9:25 pm

Color of the day: Scarlet
Incense of the day: Ginger

Consistent Success

How many times have you heard the advice that if you want to succeed at something, consistency is key? While regular effort can, indeed, be a crucial part of reaching our goals, it's also important to assess whether what we're doing is truly effective, because simply doing an ineffective thing harder won't lead to success.

In these situations, we might question whether we're "good enough" or deserving of success, perhaps experiencing self-blame and shame. But if a task calls for a hammer and we're using a spoon, it's unlikely to work, simply because the tool isn't matched to the task. In life, it can be trickier to tell when we're using a metaphorical spoon instead of a hammer. This petition spell helps shed light on mismatched "tools" so we can focus on approaches that work.

Guides, I ask for your guidance and aid with (describe what you want). Please help me focus my time and energy on what is most effective. So mote it be!

Melissa Tipton

 ## July 17
Wednesday

2nd ♐

Color of the day: Yellow
Incense of the day: Lavender

Emergency Preparedness

It's the height of summer in the Northern Hemisphere, with abundant energy, warmth, and light. Now is a great time to think about emergency preparedness.

I'm not a survivalist or a "doom and gloom" person, but I like to be prepared for whatever may come. The pandemic and subsequent lockdowns added another layer of preparedness. I got into the practice of keeping a cash stash in addition to my usual emergency preparedness setup of first-aid and camping gear, water, and food.

Money is stored energy. Beginning today, conserve some energy in the form of a stash of cash. Tell yourself it's for a rainy day or just in case. Each time you add to it, invoke:

I conserve some energy to sustain me.

I am ready to face emergency.

While I hope for the best, I'm prepared for the worst, and with this magical conserving of energy, I'm prepared for any emergency.

Dallas Jennifer Cobb

July 18
Thursday

2nd ♐

Color of the day: Turquoise
Incense of the day: Carnation

Time for a Pause Spell

We are about a month after the summer solstice. Now nature begins to take a pause. You can just feel it. The rush of spring growth is over and the climb begins toward the harvest. Even weeds seem to grow more slowly now. Take a tip from nature and take a pause yourself.

For this spell you'll need a clock or watch and a piece of fabric. Perform this spell when you won't be disturbed. Shut off your phone. Place the clock or watch and the fabric on your altar. Cover the clock with the fabric. Say these words:

Stop the clock and pause all time.

Now is the time to relax my mind.

As you sit before your altar, close your eyes. Do a short meditation. Think of ways you could take a pause. For example, you could take a walk, read, or sit on your porch. Now open your eyes and go do one of those relaxing activities—without guilt. When you return to your normal routine, think of how you could work a pause into your life on a regular basis.

James Kambos

☽ July 19
Friday

2nd ♐

☽ v/c 3:58 am

☽ → ♑ 4:14 am

Color of the day: White
Incense of the day: Rose

honoring the End of Life

Life is a cycle of birth, death, and rebirth. The process, though it may seem frightening, is a natural part of life. When we have a loved one who is dying, it can be overwhelming because of our strong emotional attachment. We must set aside our own feelings to be able to honor our loved one in their final stage of life. One way we can do that is by doing a simple spell to help them during that final stage.

You will need an item that has meaning for you related to the person who is nearing the end of their life. As you hold the item in your hands, you are also holding this person in your heart. Feel the love you have toward them welling up and say:

All my love to you. May your journey be swift so we can meet again in the next life.

Now visualize yourself being in an emotionally better place than you are now. You have honored your loved one and your grief and are now ready to move past it.

Charlynn Walls

 ♡ July 20
Saturday

2nd ♑

Color of the day: Indigo
Incense of the day: Sandalwood

heart Scrying

Above all else, it is important to know yourself, your strengths and weaknesses. Understand the marks that time has left upon you. Scars show that you survived.

For this spell you'll need a translucent heart, such as a large bead, ornament, or paperweight. Hold it in the sun and see how the light shines through it. Contemplate your own heart. What tragedies or hardships have you survived? What scars have they left behind? How can you take care of those? Visualize your heart, and all its scars, illuminated by the sun. Pour your energy into it for self-love and healing.

Then choose one thing to work on today. You could try a new coping skill or read a self-care book. You could meditate on a past challenge and what you might do differently now. You could focus positive affirmations on one area of scar tissue. Do whatever works for you. Love your heart the way it is, even as you work to heal it.

Elizabeth Barrette

☺ July 21
Sunday

2nd ♑

☽ Full Moon 6:17 am

☽ v/c 7:26 am

☽ → ♒ 7:43 am

Color of the day: Orange
Incense of the day: Frankincense

Full Moon Spell for Love

Try this full moon spell to attract more love and happiness into your life. You'll need a moonstone or quartz crystal and a handful of rose petals. Go outside on the night of the full moon, and raise the moonstone or crystal toward the sky. Invite the lunar energies to fill the stone or crystal. Place the stone or crystal on the ground and surround it with a ring of rose petals. Hold your hands over this arrangement as you imagine experiencing greater love and happiness. Conjure those feelings as strongly as you can, then project the energy into the moonstone or crystal. Leave this all outside overnight. The next day, retrieve the moonstone or crystal to carry with you as a talisman to attract more love and joy. Leave the rose petals in place to be naturally scattered by the wind.

Melanie Marquis

⚥ July 22
Monday

3rd ♒

☉ → ♌ 3:44 am

Color of the day: Silver
Incense of the day: Narcissus

The Leonid Flame of Transformation

It's that fabulous time of year again when—according to tropical astrology—the Sun enters Leo! Being a Sun sign Leo myself, I couldn't not make mention of this miraculous period.

To take advantage of Leo's abundant, generous blessings at any time while the Sun is in Leo (until August 22), simply go outside holding a small offering such as a stone, a leaf, a flower, or some herbs. Face the Sun and take six very deep breaths. Afterward, declare:

Mighty Leo, shining Sun, I bless your light; please gift me some!

For the next thirty-one days, keep an eye out for signs from Leo, including your own shining personality shifts.

Raven Digitalis

 **July 23**
Tuesday

3rd ♒

☽ v/c 5:58 am

☽ → ♓ 9:23 am

Color of the day: Maroon
Incense of the day: Cedar

Nature Bliss

One of the best things about summer is the plethora of plants growing everywhere. The scent of flowers permeates the air, as well as the scents from flowering trees and herbal gardens. A stroll through your neighborhood or your local botanical garden can do wonders for witchy senses, for at our core we are nature people. Nature is who we turn to for inspiration, guidance, and creativity. Nature fuels our imagination and connects us to the power of the Earth.

For this spell you will need a flower, a plant, an herb, or a tree that calls to you.

Hold the flower, plant, or herb in your hand. If it is a tree, give it a hug. Breathe in the essence of the plant, flower, herb, or tree. Take a moment to connect with its Earth essence. Allow yourself to be one with its earthly goodness. Blessed be!

Najah Lightfoot

 **July 24**
Wednesday

3rd ♓

Color of the day: White
Incense of the day: Marjoram

A Pop of Protection

This is a good protection spell, and it's also fun to do! You'll need an empty toilet roll, a pen or Sharpie, two pieces of tissue paper, some corn flour, and some salt. The spell is finished outdoors, so make sure you have somewhere you can safely go and make a bit of an environmentally friendly mess!

Draw a square on the toilet roll. Put one piece of tissue paper in one end, and fill the toilet roll with a mixture of corn flour and salt. Put the second piece of tissue into the other end of the toilet roll.

Take the filled toilet roll outside. Turn around clockwise four times while holding it. As you do this, repeat:

You can't touch me.
I was born to be free.

On the last "free," clap your hands together onto the toilet roll. This will loosen the tissue and the contents should come spilling out! Dispose of the empty toilet roll in a suitable receptacle.

Charlie Rainbow Wolf

July 25
Thursday

3rd ♓

☽ v/c 10:31 am

☽ → ♈ 10:52 am

Color of the day: Crimson
Incense of the day: Mulberry

Common Threads Spell

Today is known as Thread the Needle Day, which celebrates the idea of successfully navigating a difficult situation or limited window of opportunity in order to resolve a conflict. If you've ever tried to thread an actual needle, you'll understand how the expression came to be. Figuratively or physically, threading a needle takes patience, skill, and good (in)sight. If you're trying to bring two or more opposing sides or viewpoints together to end a dispute or promote community, here's a handy spell to try.

For each person or side, assign them a three-inch square piece of cotton cloth. (Your choice of color or pattern—you can get creative if you'd like!) Write their name or opinion on one side. Next stack the squares of cloth so the names/issues face inward. Then using black thread, either by hand or by machine, sew them together along the sides, focusing on unity and resolution. Finally stitch an X from corner to corner across the squares, fully uniting them. Place the sewn square on your altar or in a place where these folks will meet up next.

Laura Tempest Zakroff

NOTES:

 July 26
Friday

3rd ♈

☽ v/c 6:14 pm

Color of the day: Pink
Incense of the day: Orchid

Melt Away Chocolate Bar Spell

Need to get rid of something in a hurry? This spell will do just that, and all it requires is a pin and a bar of chocolate. Start by using a pin to write what you want to get rid of on the chocolate bar. This could be a bad habit or a friendship that has reached its end. You don't have to be super detailed, but write enough to make your intention clear.

When you are done writing, take your chocolate and set it outside in the sun away from your home if possible. Set the bar in a place where it won't be disturbed and animals won't be able to eat it, and say:

I now rid myself of what
I no longer need.

As this chocolate melts I shall be freed!

The spell is done when your chocolate has melted and you can no longer read the words you wrote on it. Ideally you want to work this spell on a warm, sunny, dry day. Dispose of the chocolate in a trash can.

Amanda Lynn & Jason Mankey

July 27
Saturday

3rd ♈

☽ → ♉ 1:23 pm

4th Quarter 10:52 pm

Color of the day: Gray
Incense of the day: Ivy

Clutter Clearing

Clearing clutter gets energy moving, dissolves blocks, and clears the way for beautiful new conditions and ideas to flow in. And today's a great day for it. Diffuse some essential oil or light some incense (or skip this step). Play some music that matches your mood. (Music moves your energy through your emotions, so when you choose music that matches your mood, it strikes the chord that will most effectively help get your personal energy flowing.)

Now go through a particular finite area, such as your refrigerator, dresser, closet, or medicine cabinet. Make separate piles for things you want to recycle, donate, throw away, give away, or place elsewhere in your home. When you're finished with this area, close your eyes, breathe, and notice the energy you've activated within your body and emotions. Repeat with another area or call it a day. When you're finished, turn off the music and make sure the incense or oil burner is extinguished.

Tess Whitehurst

July 28
Sunday

♃ ☿

Color of the day: Gold
Incense of the day: Marigold

Ask the Three Fates for Advice

When our lives get too complicated, it's time to ask the Three Fates for advice. Plato's account of the Fates tells us that they sing to us. Lachesis sings about the past, Clotho sings about the present, and Atropos sings about the future. Choose three questions to ask the Fates, such as:

- What in your past should you dismiss or forgive?

- What in your present can be trimmed and/or set aside?

- What are you facing that you may need advice to deal with?

Instead of casting a circle, cast a triangle, one point of which faces where you were born. Draw the triangle with strong purple thread and anchor the thread with river rocks. Lay a moonstone or black tourmaline at each point, encircling each stone with the thread.

Stand or sit in the middle of the triangle and appeal to the Fates:

Sagacious Singers of Life—

*Speak to me of past,
present, and future.*

Where am I going?

*What elements of my life are
best cleansed or changed?*

Barbara Ardinger

NOTES:

July 29
Monday

4th ♉

☽ v/c 4:59 pm

☽ → ♊ 5:28 pm

Color of the day: Ivory
Incense of the day: Hyssop

Finding Inner Peace

We live in a fast-paced world where we are constantly bombarded with information and always on the go, which can be overwhelming. Working with energies from the moon on this Monday, we will attempt to find calm and peace within ourselves so we are better equipped to deal with the world.

You will need a white votive candle to represent the inner peace you desire. Make sure you place the candle in a fire-safe container and light it only if it is safe to do so. If you are in a dorm room or a space where fire is not acceptable, you could use a battery-powered candle. As you light or turn on the candle, repeat the following as long as you feel it is necessary:

Peace within, peace without.

When you feel the power well up and reach its peak, push it out into the universe (through visualization and/or gestures) and conclude with:

So mote it be!

Charlynn Walls

July 30
Tuesday

4th ♊

Color of the day: Gray
Incense of the day: Basil

Stone and Tech Protection Spell

There are several stones dedicated to July. As this month comes to a close, let's turn our attention to one of them: onyx. I wear onyx every day and have done so for decades. Wearing this stone makes me feel empowered, grounded, protected, and stronger. This is an often overlooked stone, but through its connection to July and the many qualities it has, such as protection from online psychic vampires, negativity, and haters, you will come to appreciate it.

Gather nine onyx beads and a thin red cord that can pass through them. Make a knot and then push the first stone onto the cord. Make another knot and repeat until all the onyx beads are on the red knotted cord. Place this magickal tool outside for a fortnight to charge the stones, or bury it under salt for two weeks. Then blow off the salt or dust and place the cord in a circle on your desk where you work. This will provide protection in the cyber world.

Stephanie Rose Bird

July 31
Wednesday

4th ♊

☽ v/c 10:46 pm

☽ → ♋ 11:19 pm

Color of the day: Topaz
Incense of the day: Bay laurel

Freeze That Drama Spell

If you find yourself in a tricky situation where you are being gossiped about or have some interpersonal drama that you can't seem to shake, perform this spell to make it stop.

Make a perfect square piece of paper. This should be no bigger than three inches on each side. Write down the names of the people who are gossiping about you or causing you trouble three times in a row. If there isn't a specific person but rather a situation, write down the situation with as few words as possible.

With a red pen, write the word *STOP* in big bold letters on top of the names.

Fold the paper three times. Create each fold by pointing the paper's edge away from you. When this is complete, place the paper in a container filled with water. This will need to be a container that you won't need going forward.

Place this container with the paper submersed in the water in the back of your freezer. As you do so, say these words:

Stop your tongue of speaking ill,

Hear my words, my wish fulfill.

No more harsh words, gossip, trouble.

Whatever you say returns to you double.

Phoenix LeFae & Gwion Raven

NOTES:

August

S ummer is at its height of power when August rolls in, bringing with it the first of the harvest festivals, Lughnasadh (or Lammas), on the first of the month. Lughnasadh is a festival of strength and abundance, a reflection of August itself. Lugh and the Corn God are highly celebrated during this month and are particularly good to work with in spells or rituals for abundance, prosperity, agriculture, marriage, or strength. The Earth Mother in her many forms is ripening and overflowing with abundance. While we often see the first harvest as being associated with corn, there is much more that has been harvested by this point. We must remember not to overlook anything or take anything for granted in our lives, and the harvest is an excellent reminder of that. It is a time to begin focusing on expressing appreciation and giving thanks for all that we have.

The full moon this month is most often called the Corn Moon, but also goes by the Wyrt Moon, Barley Moon, or Harvest Moon. The stones carnelian, fire agate, cat's eye, and jasper will add extra power to your spells and rituals at this time. Use the herbs chamomile, St. John's wort, bay, angelica, fennel, rue, barley, wheat, marigold, or sunflowers in your spells. The colors for August are yellow, gold, and the rich green of the grass and leaves.

Kerri Connor

August 1
Thursday

4th ♋

Color of the day: Green
Incense of the day: Myrrh

Lammas

Unblocking the Path to Abundance

This simple harvesting spell really packs a punch when done on the first day of the first harvest! You'll need a glass jar, a cup of vinegar, a teaspoon of salt, and an old penny (one that isn't bright and shiny). Half-fill the glass jar with vinegar and dissolve the salt in it. Put the penny in the water, and as you do so, say:

*I call upon Lugh to fight for me
and remove all obstacles standing
in the way of my abundance.*

Leave the penny in the solution and give it another stir. Leave it in the moonlight for three nights. Then remove the penny and pour the vinegar down the drain—it won't hurt anything. Envision anything blocking the flow of abundance going down the drain with the vinegar. Keep the penny in your purse or wallet, but make sure you don't spend it—it is your money draw!

Charlie Rainbow Wolf

August 2
Friday

4th ♋

Color of the day: Rose
Incense of the day: Cypress

Continuing the harvest

As we continue to celebrate the Northern Hemisphere's harvest season, we can draw upon its life-giving, abundant energy with little effort. What's more, we can share that abundance with others near and far. After all, what on earth are we here to do but to help make it a better place?

Wanna be a better Witch? I've learned that the secret to this is giving—within our means, of course, and not only financially. Every time you decide to gift something, be it a plant, fruit, veggies, money, clothing, a meal, or anything else, first enchant the offering by saying:

*Power of the harvest, power
of the gift, I offer this to others
to nourish and uplift!*

Raven Digitalis

 August 3
Saturday

4℔ ♋

☽ v/c 6:31 am

☽ → ♌ 7:10 am

Color of the day: Black
Incense of the day: Rue

Mustard Magic

Today is National Mustard Day, which pays tribute to one of the world's most popular condiments. Not only is mustard tasty and easily accessible in most places, but it has many magical uses as well, depending upon the variety.

Common mustard has been connected with magically protecting the voice. To aid those who sing or engage in public discourse, an amulet can be made of the dried roots or flowers to be worn on those occasions. But if you are in a pinch and need to have your voice heard, a little taste from a handy mustard packet can do the trick! (A good reason to keep a couple of packets in your glove box or desk drawer.)

Black mustard seed is used in banishing and protection workings to ward off harmful spirits and people. Add it to protection amulets, sprinkle seeds around your house or along the perimeter of your property, or hang in satchels by your main entry doors.

Laura Tempest Zakroff

☽* **August 4**
Sunday

4℔ ♌

New Moon 7:13 am

Color of the day: Yellow
Incense of the day: Juniper

Riding the New Moon

It's unlikely that you'll get outside at the exact moment the moon is new, but you can go out tonight and gaze up at that crescent in the sky. Wearing turquoise jewelry (courage, protection), call out to Selene, whom you see riding the crescent moon, to fly down to you.

Entering your deepest mystical state, visualize yourself meeting the goddess and climbing aboard the new moon. Rise with her and gaze down at your home, neighborhood, city. Ride the moon across the night sky with Selene. As you soar, notice new beginnings of magic, pleasure, and work, things you never saw before.

In your mind's eye, dawn comes. Selene gently steers the new moon down to where your physical body is waiting. As you dismount, the moon slips below the horizon. When you open your eyes, you understand that time was compressed. Look around. What new "real" things are you seeing now? What new beginnings are now open to you? Give thanks to Selene and step into a new beginning.

Barbara Ardinger

August 5
Monday

1st ♌

☽ v/c 11:16 am

☽ → ♍ 5:17 pm

Color of the day: Gray
Incense of the day: Neroli

Dog Days of Summer

In some locations, August can be so hot that we pine for the cold days of winter. And with climate change bringing hotter temps, August can be a brutal month. But today is one for the dogs! Today we honor Sirius, in the constellation Canis Major. Sirius is the big dog in the night sky and the brightest star. During the hottest time of summer, the Dog Star appears to rise alongside the sun, and we experience the "dog days of summer." Watching the stars on a summer night is a truly magical experience.

Today, if you share your home with a dog, give your pup some love. Some dogs love frozen treats, others like to lie in a backyard pool, and some just want to be petted. As an alternative, consider donating to a shelter that provides care to animals who need a loving home. Tonight, gaze upon the Dog Star Sirius. Think about the millions of years it has lit up our night skies, and give thanks for dogs!

Najah Lightfoot

 ## August 6
Tuesday

1st ♍

Color of the day: Black
Incense of the day: Ylang-ylang

Best Choice Divination

Use this divination to illuminate the path most likely to lead to success. Place a cupcake (or a thick slice of cake or dense bread) on a fireproof dish. Insert into it a series of birthday candles, choosing a different candle to represent each option you are contemplating. Light the candles quickly and as simultaneously as possible. Let them burn down completely, and notice which one melts down the fastest. The choice represented by this fastest-burning candle is your best option. Act swiftly.

Did any of the candles fizzle out before burning down past the halfway mark? The option represented by a candle that goes out prematurely will likely fail to get off the ground. Did any of the candles spark? The choice represented by such a candle carries a volatile energy that could be either an asset or a hindrance.

Make sure all the candles are out and cooled down before disposing of any remnants. You can eat the cupcake if you like, but you'll definitely want to scrape off the top layer where all the melted wax has dripped.

Melanie Marquis

August 7
Wednesday

1st ♍

Color of the day: White
Incense of the day: Lilac

Navigate Straight to Your Goal

A lighthouse, a literal beacon in a storm, is a powerful symbol of hope and successful navigation toward a desired outcome or goal. Today, create or obtain a simple likeness of a lighthouse, such as a figurine or framed postcard. Place it on your altar and light a candle. On a small piece of paper, write out your intention. The intention can be general, such as "I am fulfilled and joyful," or it can be more focused and specific, such as "I land the perfect job."

Place the paper under the lighthouse. Invoke the Divine in any way you prefer. Close your eyes and imagine you are sailing in a foggy sea at night and you see the illuminated lighthouse appear. As you move toward it, feel joy knowing that the lighthouse holds the energy of your manifested intention. Feel grateful to the Divine for steering you toward your perfect outcome. Extinguish the candle. Repeat this process daily until the candle burns down or your intention is manifested.

Tess Whitehurst

August 8
Thursday

1st ♍

☽ v/c 4:40 am
☽ → ♎ 5:31 am

Color of the day: Purple
Incense of the day: Nutmeg

An herbal harvest Spell

Warm, sunny August mornings are a perfect time to harvest your herbs. For this spell you'll need a small sharp knife, some paper towels, string, and a place away from direct sun to hang your herbs for drying. Begin by cutting the herbs you wish to dry. Rinse them in cold water. Next place them on paper towels near an open kitchen window to absorb excess water. Hold your hands above your herbs and say:

Basil, mint, oregano, and dill [or say the names of the herbs you're drying],

You've perfumed my garden well.

I've raised you from plant and seed.

Now I ask that you fulfill my culinary needs.

Now tie the herbs in small bunches of no more than six stems. Hang only one type of herb per bunch. Then hang the herbs in an airy spot away from direct sunlight to dry completely. On a chilly day, remember the blessing you said and let the herbs help you flavor your favorite recipes.

James Kambos

August 9
Friday

1st ♎︎

☽ v/c 5:45 pm

Color of the day: Pink
Incense of the day: Violet

heart healing Bath Spell

Sometimes the weight of the world can start to impact the flow and energy of our hearts. It's easy to have a broken heart from the troubles around us, whether they affect us personally or not. Taking some time to clear out our heart's energy and offer ourselves comfort and healing can be a powerful process.

For this spell you will need access to a bathtub and the following ingredients:

- 1 cup salt
- ½ cup milk (or milk alternative)
- A pinch of dried damiana
- A bag or stocking
- A handful of fresh rose petals

Start the water to fill the bathtub. Make the water as warm as you like, and adorn the bathroom as you see fit. You might want to bring flowers, candles, aromatherapy, or music into the room with you. Whatever you do, keep it soft, inviting, and calming.

As the water fills, add in the salt and milk. Put the damiana in a bag or stocking before adding it to the water to keep it from making a mess in your tub. Sprinkle the rose petals on top of the water.

Allow yourself to slowly immerse in the tub and sink in so your heart is under the water. Breathe deeply and envision a rose gold light glowing from your heart space. Allow this rose gold light to clear out negative energy, soften hard edges, and heal wounds. Allow this process to go on for as long as you need.

Phoenix LeFae & Gwion Raven

NOTES:

August 10
Saturday

1st ♎

☽ → ♏ 6:34 pm

Color of the day: Brown
Incense of the day: Ivy

Spirit-Cleaning Bath

As the wheel of the year continues to turn ever so rapidly toward a new year, let's take a breather today and slow things down. The goal is to move forward these next few months with greater intent and purpose. It is time to create a potion to add to your bath.

First, take a small piece of aquamarine and let it sit in a bowl of spring water under the moonlight for three hours. Aquamarine ushers in peace, instills courage, and purifies. It is a symbol of sea goddesses from across the globe. It will also enhance your psychic powers.

Pulverize ⅓ cup sea kelp and ¼ cup lavender buds with a mortar and pestle. Add this to a bowl containing 1½ cups fine sea salt. Mix well. At midnight, add this blend to a shallow, warm (but not hot) bath. Then pour in your Aquamarine Moon Water.

Lay your head back on a sea sponge. Listen and watch as you receive messages from the intuitive realm to help improve and empower your life as you move forward.

Stephanie Rose Bird

August 11
Sunday

1st ♏

Color of the day: Amber
Incense of the day: Heliotrope

Strength of the Mountains

In Japan, August 11 is Mountain Day, a public holiday established to celebrate and appreciate the blessings the mountains provide. Today we will tap into the strength of the earth and mountains to bring stability to our lives. Go outside if possible or bring a small amount of soil indoors in a container. If you are outside and able to put your bare feet on the earth, do so. Otherwise, set the container of soil on a table and place your hand in the dirt. Feel the connection between you and the element of earth. As you connect with the earth element, say aloud three times:

May the mountains of the
earth strengthen me so I may
be able to serve others.

Charlynn Walls

August 12
Monday

1st ♏︎

2nd Quarter 11:19 am

Color of the day: Silver
Incense of the day: Clary sage

Walking with Intention

It's a great feeling when you can actually walk your talk. This spell calls for walking our intention into reality by placing our petition into our shoe. For this spell you will need a piece of paper, a pen, and your shoes. Take a moment to write down what it is that you want. You can even draw a symbol or sigil. When you have decided on your intention, fold up the paper and place it under the inner sole of one of your shoes. As you do so, recite this chant:

I cast this magic with my feet.

With each step it is complete.

I put my spell inside my shoe.

I walk with magic through and through.

Feel your magic working as you walk throughout the day. Keep the spell inside your shoe for as long as you desire or until your spell is complete.

Amanda Lynn & Jason Mankey

August 13
Tuesday

2nd ♏︎

☽ v/c 5:01 am

☽ → ♐︎ 6:01 am

Color of the day: White
Incense of the day: Bayberry

Armchair Travels

When you're not able to physically travel, engage in a little magical travel instead. Start by generating your astrocartography chart, which you can do for free by googling the term. Your chart will show you different areas of the globe that correspond to different planetary energies. Choose a location you want to "travel" to, and for the next week, spend time each day engaging with that place by looking at photos, reading about it, listening to its local music, cooking its cuisine, imagining the place in meditation, etc.

As you do so, open to lessons of that location and its ruling planet. For instance, perhaps as you're meditating on Maine, which is on your Moon line, you get the urge to start journaling your dreams. (Dreams are ruled by the Moon.) Or maybe you've been looking at photos of Egypt, which is on your Pluto line, and you notice yourself wanting to research Egyptian mythology of the underworld. (Pluto rules the underworld.) Follow the magical breadcrumbs!

Melissa Tipton

August 14
Wednesday

2nd ♐

Color of the day: Yellow
Incense of the day: Lavender

Deepening Meditation

Meditation is a skill of the mind that lays a foundation for many other skills. When you learn to control your mind, you can use more of your brain consciously. You can also control aspects of your body that are not usually voluntary, like turning down pain signals or turning up heat when you feel cold.

To deepen your meditation practice, sit or lie in a comfortable position. Go down into your thoughts as far as you usually can. Then feel for the edges. What can you do here, and what can you not do? Try to recall more details of a distant memory; they're in there somewhere. Think about speeding up or slowing your heart rate by will; your brain is driving that. Visualize a dial to turn your senses up and down or to increase or decrease a personality trait. It's all part of you, and you can learn to control it.

Take your time coming back up to everyday awareness. Remember what you have learned.

Elizabeth Barrette

August 15
Thursday

2nd ♐
☽ v/c 12:52 pm
☽ → ♑ 1:51 pm

Color of the day: Crimson
Incense of the day: Apricot

Come to Me

Thursday is ruled by Jupiter, the planet of expansion, luck, and good fortune, healing, prosperity, and miracles. Use the energy of Jupiter for a drawing spell.

You will need:

• A 24-inch string (A shoelace will do in a pinch.)

• A piece of paper and a pen

Quietly focus on what you seek to draw to you. Whether it is love, money, healing, or luck, engage Jupiter's energy. When you know what you seek to attract, write your desire on the paper. Fold the paper in half, and tie one end of the string around it. Holding the other end of the string, sit at a table and throw the paper over the edge, out of sight.

Now pull the string to you, repeatedly saying "_____, come to me," inserting the name of a person, a sum of money, or a specific healing. As you draw the paper to you, envision your good fortune arriving.

Dallas Jennifer Cobb

August 16
Friday

2nd ♑

Color of the day: Coral
Incense of the day: Rose

Sweet Dreams

This spell ensures a good night's sleep, one that is full of good dreams. You'll need a whole nutmeg, some dried oregano, and a piece of cheesecloth or butter muslin (usually available from fabric shops). Nutmeg has a reputation for bringing dreams and visions when ingested—a little goes a long way! Oregano is protective and brings calm and relaxation. Together, they help to protect against nightmares.

To do this spell, simply wrap the nutmeg and oregano in the fabric, and place under your pillow. This will help your sleep to be sound and your dreams to be pleasant. To remember your dreams, write the word "remember" on a bottle of water and place it next to your bed, last thing before you close your eyes. In the morning, as soon as you awaken, take a drink from the bottle. You should be able to remember your dreams.

Charlie Rainbow Wolf

August 17
Saturday

2nd ♑
☽ v/c 4:43 pm
☽ → ♒ 5:45 pm

Color of the day: Gray
Incense of the day: Magnolia

Blessings of Bast & the Black Cat

Did you know that today is Black Cat Appreciation Day in the US? How cozy and witchy is that! One dark and dreadful thing to be aware of, however, is that European Christians murdered, brutalized, and tortured thousands upon thousands of pure-black cats during the European witch craze, believing them to be shapeshifting familiars, demons, and devils.

Today, you can honor all beloved felines by researching and calling upon the ancient Egyptian goddess Bast (Bastet). With a good quantity of unopened dry or wet cat food before you, dedicate the food to her, give her thanks, and donate it to your local animal shelter.

Raven Digitalis

August 18
Sunday

2nd ♒

Color of the day: Orange
Incense of the day: Frankincense

Nature's Altar

To honor nature's beauty and strengthen your magickal connection to the Earth, try setting up this nature altar using resources provided by your local ecosystem. Begin by arranging a small handful of pebbles or stones in a circle to delineate the space you want to make into an altar. Next, gather other items from the environment that appeal to you. Use only things provided by the immediate ecosystem. Arrange these items artfully within the altar space. You might make a spiral of leaves, a stack of stones, a sculpture of twigs, or a mosaic of varying shades of dirt. Observe how your human touch has connected with nature's inherent beauty and rearranged its aspects to form something new, just as we do through the process of making magick. Place your palms flat on the ground in the altar space as you say:

*Nature do I serve, and nature do
I wield! With nature, I destroy!
With nature, do I build!*

Leave a piece of your hair or a small piece of your fingernail within the space. Let the altar arrangement naturally scatter and return to the earth.

Melanie Marquis

NOTES:

August 19
Monday

2nd ♒

☽ v/c 2:26 pm

☽ Full Moon 2:26 pm

☽ → ♓ 6:52 pm

Color of the day: Lavender
Incense of the day: Lily

Empower Your Mission

B usinesses write mission statements to illuminate the positive
intentions behind their actions as
well as to inform the choices that
forge their path. On this Aquarius
full moon, write a personal mission
statement for the same reasons.

Light a candle on your altar or go
outside and gaze at the full moon.
Invoke the power of the moon by saying something like, "Divine Mother
Moon, hail and welcome." Then
patiently craft a statement in the
present tense. Include the positive
changes you are choosing to make
in the world, as well as the concrete
action steps that are helping you
make them. State the beliefs that
explain why these gifts and actions
are important to you, and clarify what
makes your offerings unique. Play
around with the wording until your
statement feels just right. Then read
it aloud to the moon. Feel and sense
the moon empowering your mission.
Give thanks to the moon.

Place your mission statement on
your altar or someplace else where
you'll see it daily. Extinguish the
candle.

Tess Whitehurst

Notes:

August 20
Tuesday

3rd ♓

Color of the day: Maroon
Incense of the day: Geranium

When It's Time to Move On

Yes, it happens: jealousy and witch wars arise in our Neo-Pagan communities. When people just can't get along anymore, it's time to move on, to find a new organization or coven where it's peaceful. In Shakespeare's *As You Like It*, the exiled Duke Senior finds peace in the Forest of Arden.

Go outside, find a shady spot, wrap yourself in protective energy, and declare your intention to find your own Forest of Arden where you can restore friendships and spirituality to your life. Contemplate this speech (excerpted) by Duke Senior:

> Hath not old custom made
> this life more sweet
>
> Than that of painted pomp?
> Are not these woods
>
> More free from peril than
> the envious court?
>
> [...]
>
> And this our life exempt
> from public haunt
>
> Finds tongues in trees, books
> in the running brooks,

> Sermons in stones and
> good in every thing.
>
> I would not change it.

Visit meetings and rituals. Revive old friendships. Make new friends. Don't gossip! Contribute meaningfully to your new community.

                    Barbara Ardinger

NOTES:

August 21
Wednesday

3rd ♓

☽ v/c 5:54 pm

☽ → ♈ 7:02 pm

Color of the day: Topaz
Incense of the day: Honeysuckle

Safe Travels, Safe home

Getting there is only half the equation. This spell reminds you to come home safely, too.

Here is what you'll need:

- 2 pieces of paper, two inches by two inches each

- An item representing your destination (a coin, a picture, or anything you like)

- An item representing your home (such as soil from your yard, your cat's whisker, or a loose thread from your favorite blanket)

- A drawstring bag

On one piece of paper, write:

I arrived safely at _____
on _____.

Fill in your destination and the date you'll be arriving there. Be as specific as space allows. Include the address, or hotel name, or city you're traveling to. Fold the paper three times.

On the other piece of paper, write:

I arrived safely home on _____.

Fill in the date you'll be arriving back home. It's best not to use your full address. Put your street name or number or just the town. Fold the paper three times.

Place all the items in the draw-string bag and keep them with you at all times while traveling.

Phoenix LeFae & Gwion Raven

NOTES:

August 22
Thursday

3rd ♈

☉ → ♍ 10:55 am

Color of the day: White
Incense of the day: Balsam

A Golden Grain Spell

In most regions, the golden grains are beginning to be harvested now. Grains such as corn, wheat, and oats have fueled civilizations for centuries, and without them human civilization would not exist. This is a spell giving thanks to the abundance and quality of life grains have given us. You'll need only a small dish containing a few grains. Even a few kernels of corn will do. Place the dish of grain upon your altar. Sit before the dish and say these words:

Golden grains, you have sustained kingdoms and nations.

Without you there would be no civilization.

You have been raised in many lands

Since before recorded time began.

Carry the dish outside and respectfully scatter the grains on the earth.

James Kambos

August 23
Friday

3rd ♈

☽ v/c 8:44 am

☽ → ♉ 8:00 pm

Color of the day: Purple
Incense of the day: Yarrow

Raise It Up!

National Ride the Wind Day is a time to marvel at not only the magic of flight but also the power of wind to create energy and help us travel—and you don't even have to fly in a plane, jump from a helicopter, or windsurf to partake in the fun! One of the simplest ways to celebrate is to fly a kite, and you can easily add a little more magic to it as well.

The magic is simply adding some written intentions or symbols to your kite so that as it rises, so does your intent. You can write on the body of the kite and also attach streaming ribbons of colors that coordinate with your working. If you're worried about the kite flying away, use symbols or hidden code to describe your goals.

You can of course take a store-bought kite and augment it, but if you have the time, making a kite with friends or family can be a fantastic activity and learning exercise.

Laura Tempest Zakroff

August 24
Saturday

3rd ♉

Color of the day: Indigo
Incense of the day: Patchouli

Fructify Yourself!

Oh, for the love of fruit! Summer brings delicious, delightful, cooling fruits to our tables. We love to incorporate juicy, ice-cold watermelons, cucumber water, and fresh tomatoes from the garden into our meals. Equally delightful is the sound of ice shaken in a tumbler to make a quenching gin and tonic with a slice of cooling lime, or the increasingly popular sour ales made from fruit flowing from the tap at your favorite brewery.

For this spell you will need:

- Your favorite fruit
- A strainer
- A glass of water

Place the fruit in the strainer. Hold the glass of water and say:

Blessed be, element of water.

Pour the water over the fruit and gently shake the strainer. Place the fruit in the refrigerator and allow it to chill. Then enjoy the fruit with your favorite summer meal. Thank the Goddess for providing us with an abundance of fruit!

Najah Lightfoot

August 25
Sunday

3rd ♉

☽ v/c 9:40 pm

☽ → ♊ 11:04 pm

Color of the day: Yellow
Incense of the day: Almond

Athena Back to School Spell

Olive oil is a very versatile oil. It can be used for cooking or burned in an oil lamp for light. The manufacture of olive oil also requires ingenuity and cooperation, and the olive tree is sacred to Athena, the goddess of civilization and learning. For these reasons, olive oil is a great tool for blessing both school supplies and any tools you might be using when seeking new knowledge (such as books, notebooks, pens, etc.).

For this spell you will need a few drops of olive oil in a small bowl and any items you want to bless. Lightly dip your index finger into the bowl of oil and then draw an invoking pentagram (or other symbol that resonates with you) on your item while saying:

Bring to me knowledge and light.

May all I wish to learn be in sight.

Bless the journey I undertake

And the choices I will make.

Athena, hear my plea.

Let wisdom be all that I see.

As you place the olive oil on your items, visualize them glowing with Athena's knowledge and light.

Amanda Lynn & Jason Mankey

NOTES:

August 26
Monday

3rd ♊

4th Quarter 5:26 am

Color of the day: White
Incense of the day: Rosemary

New Beginnings

For many, this day marks the return to school or college. For others, the idea of signing up for self-improvement, skill-building, informational, and fun workshops comes to mind. The beginning of the academic year is a time of fresh hopes and embarking on dreams.

There are many offerings for pagans, witches, and magick workers. Today, take a moment to ask your inner self these questions: What do you need or want to learn? How will you make it possible? What can you do right now to ensure success?

The ritual for success is simple. Smudge your entire naked body as you focus on these questions. Take a relaxing bath to which you have added a cup of rose water and a half cup of lavender water.

Recite the following affirmation:

I am open.

I invite the help of good spirit.

I am a seeker, ready and willing to do what it takes to meet my goals.

Blessed be!

Stephanie Rose Bird

August 27
Tuesday

4th ♊

Color of the day: Gray
Incense of the day: Cedar

Portal to the Future

Activating dormant qualities within ourselves, developing new skills, and embodying more of the whole Self is the journey of life. When we need a boost, visualizing the future version of ourselves that we wish to embody can help clarify where we're headed.

Spend some time in meditation fleshing out your future self, choosing something that feels outside of your comfort zone yet doable within the next three to six months. What qualities do you possess and how do you express them? How and where do you spend your time and with whom?

Once the image feels vibrantly alive, light a stick of incense (bonus: choose an incense that coordinates with the vibe of your future vision) and use it to draw a doorway in the air. As you step through this door, you are stepping into your future self. In the days and weeks to come, listen to your intuition as it guides your next steps, bringing you into full embodiment of this expanded version of Self.

Melissa Tipton

August 28
Wednesday

4th ♊

☽ v/c 3:14 am

☽ → ♋ 4:47 am

Color of the day: Brown
Incense of the day: Marjoram

Put Away Summer

As the growing season draws to a close, it's time to put away your summer things and clear out the old energy. This makes way for new fall things and fresh energy. Begin by brushing your hands or a fan over your body to clear your aura. Then sweep the floor from the edges toward the door and out over the threshold, or into a dustpan at the threshold. Visualize negativity leaving with it.

Look at your summer things. Do you have outdoor toys that will need replacing in the spring or that have been outgrown? Discard worn-out ones, or donate those that are still good. Check your clothes. Will you or your kids be the same size in the spring? If not, then discard, repurpose, or give away clothes you won't wear again. Swap out any towels, sheets, tablecloths, decorations, or other thematic items for fall ones.

Finally, concentrate on the spiritual energies of summer and tuck them away. Think of fall and bring those energies forward as the seasons turn.

Elizabeth Barrette

August 29
Thursday

4th ♋

Color of the day: Purple
Incense of the day: Jasmine

Feel-Good Nettle Magic

Stinging nettle (*Urtica dioica*) has many uses. An adaptogen, it is great for treating exhaustion, stress, and adrenal fatigue. It enhances growth, stimulates immunity, and is effective against bacterial infection. Eaten as seeds, nettle stimulates feel-good energy. Nettle grows throughout North and South America, Europe, and Asia and prefers stream banks and damp and disturbed land. Now is the time to harvest it. Be sure to first properly identify nettle.

You will need a small paper bag on which you have written "Nettle Seeds." Look for brown, ripe seeds, which contain the most concentrated medicinal qualities. Gently pluck the seeds and tuck them in your bag, removing any prickly fiber.

Eat a teaspoon of nettle seeds a day, sprinkled on salads, baked into bread and crackers, or eaten with a teaspoon of honey. Ingestion stimulates increased energy and the feel-good neurotransmitters acetylcholine and serotonin. When you need to magically upgrade your energy, reach for "good feeling" nettle seeds.

Dallas Jennifer Cobb

August 30
Friday

4th ♋

☽ v/c 11:24 am
☽ → ♌ 1:09 pm

Color of the day: White
Incense of the day: Alder

Get Rid of Guilt Spell

Sometimes we have no real reason to feel guilty, and sometimes we do. But after carrying it around for a while, there comes a time to get rid of guilt. This spell will help with that.

Perform this spell on a sunny day. You'll need a stick. Go to a rural or secluded spot. A dirt road or a field would be good. Stand so you are looking at your shadow. Bend down, and with the stick, write the word *guilt* across your shadow. Then say:

Guilt, we are done.

Dissolve into the earth.

Burn into dust by the heat of the sun.

Now scratch the word *guilt* away using the stick. Break the stick and toss it into the weeds. You should feel like a weight has been lifted from your shoulders. Walk away.

James Kambos

August 31
Saturday

4th ♌

Color of the day: Blue
Incense of the day: Sandalwood

Banishing the Negative

Each day we brush up against the negativity of others, and we often take on that emotional residue. To maintain our focus and resolve, it is necessary to banish the negative from our lives.

For this spell you will need a small bowl of salt and a small black or white candle. You will need enough salt so that the candle will stand up in it. As always, when using an open flame, be sure you do not leave it unattended and use caution.

Light the candle, and as it drips its wax into the salt, say:

*Drip, drip, drip. Let the
negative flow away.*

Once the candle has finished burning and has gone out, take the melted wax and salt out of the bowl and safely dispose of it. The act of throwing it out will eliminate the negative from your life.

Charlynn Walls

September

The equinox happens toward the end of this month, heralding the beginning of autumn in the Northern Hemisphere and the start of spring in the Southern Hemisphere. An equinox happens when the sun crosses the celestial equator, an imaginary line in the sky not unlike our Earth's own equator. It's on the equinox that the sun rises due east and sets due west. This is why people often go to famous landmarks to watch the rising or setting of the sun on the equinoxes and solstices. In our ever-changing world, it's nice to know there are at least some constants!

Astrologically, the autumnal equinox is when the sun sign of Libra begins. It's fitting, as this is the time when day and night are of equal length, and Libra is the sign of the scales. The full moon that corresponds with this event is called the Harvest Moon or the Corn Moon. The few days around the equinox and the full moon bring a period in which everything is ripening and full of energy. It all seems to be coming into fullness, preparing either for the coming of winter or the start of the growing season.

Charlie Rainbow Wolf

▽ September 1
Sunday

4th ♌

☽ v/c 8:25 pm

☽ → ♍ 11:48 pm

Color of the day: Gold
Incense of the day: Heliotrope

Refreshing Autumn Rain

In many areas, summers run hot and dry. Moving into autumn, however, the rains return to water the dry ground. Welcome them back with this ritual, which can be performed in wet or dry weather.

Dress in shades of blue and gray to honor the fall rains. Fabric printed with water or clouds also works well. Stand tall and raise your arms to salute the sky. Then say:

Clouds come and rain fall,

Send your water over all.

Sky breathe and wind blow,

Bring your blessings, down they go.

Storm dance and rain pour,

Banish drought forevermore.

Grass bend and trees strain,

Welcome back the autumn rain!

If the rain has not yet arrived, then you can take a bowl of water and sprinkle it around the four quarters of your space in an act of sympathetic magic. On a rainy day, you can do the welcome chant from the safety of a porch or other sheltered spot.

Elizabeth Barrette

NOTES:

September 2
Monday

4th ♏︎

New Moon 9:56 pm

Color of the day: Lavender
Incense of the day: Neroli

Labor Day (US) –
Labour Day (Canada)

Economic Justice Spell

Many of us work far too hard for not enough pay, and many women and people of color are paid less than white males for the same amount of work. Economic justice is something worth fighting for!

For this spell you will need a coin and access to a fountain or wishing well. Start by taking your coin, holding it in your dominant hand, and reflecting on a more fair and balanced world. Imagine all people being treated with dignity and respect and getting paid a fair amount for their hard work. Pour the energy of economic justice into your coin and place it in your pocket.

As you go about your day, take out your coin and put more energy into it when you encounter someone working or you have thoughts about economic justice. You can carry your coin with you for several days or weeks until you come across a fountain or well, or you can put it in a well or fountain at the end of the day.

As you flip your coin into the water, say:

Fairness and justice for everyone!
Amanda Lynn & Jason Mankey

NOTES:

September 3
Tuesday

1st ♍

Color of the day: Black
Incense of the day: Ylang-ylang

Charge Your Wallet with Money Spell

For this working you will need a money-drawing magickal oil or a kitchen oil that you have charged with prosperity energy. Sit down with your wallet in a place where you will be undisturbed. Take everything out of your wallet—everything. Remove pictures, cards, cash, change, trinkets, and anything else that is in your wallet, then set it down in front of you.

Go through all of these items and make sure they belong in your wallet. Does each item fill you with feelings of abundance and prosperity? If not, set it aside, or if possible, throw it away. Anoint any cash, change, credit card, or money in any form with the money-drawing oil. Just put a small dot of oil on the tip of your finger and rub this on each of the items. Repeat this process with your empty wallet.

When complete, slowly and intentionally return all of the items to your wallet and say this:

My life is filled with riches.
My life is filled with wealth.

My wallet overflows with money,
Money beyond just for myself.

Phoenix LeFae & Gwion Raven

 September 4
Wednesday

1st ♍

☽ v/c 12:06 pm
☽ → ♎ 12:12 pm

Color of the day: White
Incense of the day: Lavender

Magical Anti-Germ Potion

With kids back in school, we're in the midst of germ season. Children exchange germs quickly and efficiently while playing, touching, sharing erasers, and trading lunch items. It is time for a Magical Anti-Germ Potion.

Tea tree oil, made from *Melaleuca alternifolia*, is the perfect ally, with antiviral, antibacterial, and antifungal qualities. It's also good for the treatment of psoriasis, acne, and eczema. That means you can spray Magical Anti-Germ Potion on any germ-infested item and on skin. Never spray tea tree oil in anyone's eyes. You can use this to make hand sanitizers by soaking paper towels in it.

In a large spray bottle, combine 2 teaspoons tea tree oil and 2 cups water. As you shake the liquid thoroughly before spraying, remind it of its magical purpose, chanting:

Anti-this and anti-that,
help me if you please

To keep us well and happy
and free of all dis-ease.

Every evening, use the potion to treat your kids' shoes, lunch boxes, pencil cases, and markers.

Dallas Jennifer Cobb

NOTES:

September 5
Thursday

1st ♎

Color of the day: Green
Incense of the day: Clove

Money Manifestation

Jupiter presides over this day of the week. We can utilize the energies of the planet of abundance to work on bringing prosperity into our lives.

Sprinkle cinnamon in the bottom of a small bowl and then place several pennies inside. Cinnamon will attract success and prosperity to you. The pennies represent your desire to attract and manifest money in your life. Find a spot in your home where you can see the bowl and walk by it often. After you have set the dish in the desired location, say:

Copper pieces dropped in again and again, bring me financial gain.

Each time you pass the bowl, add a penny to it to renew the spell and continue to bring prosperity into your life.

Charlynn Walls

September 6
Friday

1st ♎

Color of the day: Pink
Incense of the day: Vanilla

Lights Out

When a situation or person dominates our thoughts, it's hard to get perspective. This spell helps you create space, opening your mind to creative solutions and new possibilities. Fire requires oxygen to burn, and this spell temporarily cuts off the supply to a situation that's been getting too much airtime in your mind. You'll need a small votive candle, a glass jar, and a heatproof surface.

Start by charging the candle with the energy of the situation you wish to step back from. Hold the candle in both hands as you envision the situation, feeling its energy ebbing out of your body, mind, and soul and into the candle. Set the candle on a heatproof surface and light it. As you place the glass jar over the candle, upside down, chant the following incantation:

As this flame winks out,

My thoughts grow calm and still.

This situation I surrender

To divine wisdom and highest will.

If you find yourself mulling over the situation in the future, repeat the process, allowing yourself to release what no longer serves and return to center.

Melissa Tipton

NOTES:

⬟ September 7
Saturday

1st ♎︎

☽ v/c 1:08 am

☽ → ♏︎ 1:18 am

Color of the day: Gray
Incense of the day: Sage

A Scarecrow Protection Spell

The scarecrow decorations you see now at garden centers can be magically charged to make great protective charms for home and garden. The great thing is no one needs to know that they're magical.

You'll need a scarecrow decoration that you can stick into the ground. You'll also need a square piece of fabric about the size of a handkerchief, garden twine, and some protective herbs. I use one peeled clove of garlic, a dash of black pepper, and at least two basil leaves.

First, position your scarecrow where it can be seen from the street. If you wish, surround it with an autumn theme. A pot of mums, a hay bale, and some pumpkins look great together. Place your herbs in the center of the fabric and tie up the corners with garden twine. Now attach the herb bundle to the scarecrow however you wish. You could tie it onto an arm or tuck it into the shirt.

When everything is ready, charge your scarecrow with these words:

Scarecrow so brave, standing guard,

Protecting my home and my yard,

Protect with garlic, pepper,
and basil leaves.

Any scoundrel who crosses
here shall know grief.

As the scarecrow weathers and fades, respectfully dispose of it and the herb bundle. Repeat next year.

James Kambos

NOTES:

September 8
Sunday

1st ♏

Color of the day: Yellow
Incense of the day: Marigold

Summon a Muse

Modern Witches and Pagans are drawn to a variety of ancient gods, ancestors, and pantheons. The Greco-Roman myths hold a special place for many of us.

Mnemosyne, the goddess of memory, is the mother of the nine Muses in ancient Greek mythology. They are as follows:

Calliope: Epic poetry

Clio: History

Erato: Erotic and choral poetry

Euterpe: Music and song

Melpomene: Tragedy and performance art

Polyhymnia: Hymns, religious poetry, and miming

Terpsichore: Light verse and dance

Thalia: Comedy and epic poetry

Urania: Astronomy and astrology

Before beginning a creative endeavor, meditate and speak to a Muse. Create your own spell by offering them something, such a song, a piece of writing, or a work of art. This will help start the communication process.

Whomever you feel "called upon to call," their assistance may very well prove invaluable, and even long-lasting, in your life's creative journey.

Raven Digitalis

NOTES:

September 9
Monday

1st ♏︎

☽ v/c 1:11 pm

☽ → ♐︎ 1:26 pm

Color of the day: Ivory
Incense of the day: Narcissus

Chrysanthemum Money Spell

Chrysanthemum literally translates to "gold flower," and these cheerful flowers begin to bloom when they sense the daylight beginning to wane. So work some chrysanthemum magic today to replenish a waning bank balance or simply to expand and bless your finances.

Purchase a pot of chrysanthemums (of any size and color). Set it outside by your front door or in a sunny windowsill. Relax and gaze at the flowers. Appreciate their appearance and inhale their hearty scent. Patiently stay with this until you feel your energy merging with the energy of the flowers. Sense the vibration of the blooms opening up channels of receptivity to wealth within you. Feel yourself becoming a money magnet. Imagine golden sparkles of light filling your wallet, purse, or bank account. Feel grateful for this financial boost, knowing it has already been set in motion.

Give the flowers a little water and perhaps set a crystal on the soil as a reciprocal gesture of thanks. Continue to lovingly care for the chrysanthemums throughout their life cycle.

Tess Whitehurst

NOTES:

▽ September 10
Tuesday

1st ♐

Color of the day: White
Incense of the day: Cedar

Mutable Earth

What do you know about the land you live and walk on? We Neo-Pagans follow an earth-based religion, so let's get down to earth—literally—so we know what we're grounding ourselves in.

Dig up a handful of dirt in your yard and hold it in your hand. Notice that it's not the same as potting soil. It's natural dirt. Feel its texture. Is it solid? Muddy? Sandy? Poke around in it. Do you find tiny rocks? Worms or insects? (Let them go.) We like to think of Mother Earth—Gaia—as unchanging, but she's always been mutable.

Recognize that all who live on earth—all plants, animals, even minerals—are our kin and it's their dirt, too. Honor Gaia by taking care of the dirt where you live. Don't drop trash on it. Place your handful of dirt in a dish in the north corner of your altar. Ground yourself in the mutable earth and link your magic with the power of Gaia.

Barbara Ardinger

💲 September 11
Wednesday

1st ♐

2nd Quarter 2:06 am
☽ v/c 8:21 pm
☽ → ♑ 10:38 pm

Color of the day: Brown
Incense of the day: Bay laurel

Prosperity Charm

Use this spell to bring more money into your bank account. On the inside of an envelope, write your bank account number. Put a few dollars into the envelope along with some shiny coins. In a small bowl, mix together some powdered cinnamon, basil, and oregano. Envision the spices as thousands of dollars as you mix them together. Every night for seven days in a row, sprinkle a generous amount of the spice mix into the envelope as you say:

> More money to me, by all good
> means, may it come my way,
> in hand the next day!

On the seventh night, add the rest of the spice mix and seal the envelope. Keep it with your checkbook or bank statements, or tuck it in your purse or wallet. Refresh the charm every month or so, or whenever you feel the power of the magick has waned.

Melanie Marquis

September 12
Thursday

2nd ♑

Color of the day: Turquoise
Incense of the day: Carnation

Kick the habit

For this spell you'll need a pen and paper, a jar with a lid, about a cup of coffee beans, and a nail. Write down what habit you want to break on the paper, then add it to the jar. Put the coffee beans in one at a time, saying:

Counting beans makes you history.

When all the beans are in the jar, insert the nail (point down) into the beans and put on the lid. Any time you feel the habit you want to break starting to overcome you, grab the jar and shake it, saying:

*I counted the beans. You no
longer have a hold over me.*

Remember, just doing the spell will not suddenly banish the habit. It will take diligence and determined work on your part, but you can do this. It just takes the desire to succeed and a commitment to see things through to their completion.

Charlie Rainbow Wolf

September 13
Friday

2nd ♑

Color of the day: Rose
Incense of the day: Thyme

Freya the 13th Altar

Many people fear Friday the 13th, but when you consider that Friday is named for the goddess Freya and 13 is her number, it's easier to enjoy the day. Freya is a complex Nordic goddess of many things, including love, sex, fertility, battle, death, magic, and witchcraft. As the goddess of witches, she and her day should be heralded and embraced. One of the ways you can do that is to make this altar today.

Lay out a flax and hemp cloth on a small table. (Any natural or mostly natural textured cloth will work.) Put a small bowl of honey in the center. Put out a nice piece of jewelry for Freya to wear in her world and some perfume that is decadent and luxurious. Add a pig or boar, a horse, and two gray cat toys or statuary. If you have a piece of amber, she would also love that. Go to this altar for any of Freya's attributes. Reflect on her beauty and her beautiful things and ask for her blessings.

Stephanie Rose Bird

September 14
Saturday

2nd ♑

☽ v/c 3:35 am

☽ → ♒ 3:53 am

Color of the day: Blue
Incense of the day: Pine

Blessed Bees

September is National Honey Month, an opportune time to recognize the importance of bees in our lives. Without our pollinators, the whole planet's ecosystem would be in trouble. While most of us can't become beekeepers, we can help bees in several easy ways:

- Fall is a great time to plan your garden for the following spring. Choose bee-friendly plants that are native to your region. Some of my favorites include sunflowers, basil, lavender, calendula, clary sage, hyssop, and verbena.

- To treat pests, use organic products and natural solutions rather than harmful sprays and chemical fertilizers.

- Create mini bee baths—which are just like a bird bath, but shallow, with stones that bees can rest on to refresh themselves.

- Buy local. Support your local beekeepers by keeping an eye out for them in local shops and at farmers' markets. Many people find that consuming locally produced honey also reduces their allergies!

- Research the kinds of bees in your area so you can recognize them on sight—and know what they need to thrive.

Laura Tempest Zakroff

NOTES:

September 15
Sunday

2nd ≈≈

Color of the day: Orange
Incense of the day: Eucalyptus

Show Me Tarot Spell

When you find yourself at a crossroads or need to make a decision, asking for a little help or a sign can show you which path to take. Any time you feel stuck or uncertain, you can use this tarot reading to give you the direction you need.

Take out any tarot deck you like or feel would best serve you in this question. Shuffle the cards three times. As you shuffle, say this:

Show me, show me the path to take.

Show me, show me the move to make.

Show me, show me what I seek.

*Show me, show me, it's
now time to speak.*

Take the first four cards off the top of the deck and set them aside. Each of these cards represents one path of the four roads of the crossroads. Flip over the fifth card to represent the center of the crossroads. This is the answer to the question you seek.

Don't look at the four discarded cards; focus only on the fifth. The answer is here.

Phoenix LeFae & Gwion Raven

September 16
Monday

2nd ≈≈

☽ v/c 1:04 am
☽ → ♓ 5:39 am

Color of the day: Silver
Incense of the day: Clary sage

Rock On

This is Collect Rocks Day, a wonderful opportunity to honor the earth element. Most of the planet consists of stone, although much of it is covered by a comparatively thin layer of water.

Before you start, take a moment to thank the Earth for her gifts. If you're looking for anything special, meditate on that to improve your chances of finding it. There are many ways to collect rocks. If you live near a rockhound shop or Pagan store, you can buy some. Quarry yards are great places to look for larger landscaping stones. If you have a yard, you can walk around and search for interesting pebbles—near your driveway is a good place. You can even visit rockhound sites where you pay a small fee to dig for quartz, agate, or other semiprecious stones.

When you get home, thank the Earth for sharing its stones with you. Clean them up and store them with labels of their type, because different ones have different magical properties.

Elizabeth Barrette

September 17
Tuesday

2nd ♓

Full Moon 10:34 pm

Color of the day: Gray
Incense of the day: Ginger

Lunar Eclipse

Full Moon Release Spell

Tonight we have a full harvest moon with a lunar eclipse. When these occur together, it is the perfect time to do some type of release spell. This could include any number of release situations. Perhaps you wish to release a person, job, or some type of negative situation from your life. With a regular full moon, it is usually a good time to try to work some type of magic that will bring something to you. Now, with a full moon/lunar eclipse combination, the opposite is true: this is the time to release something from your life. First think of what it is you wish to release. Then let's begin.

This spell is best done in a darkened room. Sit on the floor in a comfortable position. Ground and center. I recommend using no candles or incense—just you and the dark and the quiet. Breathe steadily.

In a calm voice, state what it is you wish to release. If it's a person, wish them well. You may say their name. Then say something like, "They are released." If it is a situation, then say, "It's released." You may also add phrases such as "with harm to none."

Do this release spell for about fifteen minutes. When done, slowly return to a regular state of mind. Turn on dim lights, play soft music, or take a bath. Do anything to help you focus calmly. You are done.

James Kambos

NOTES:

September 18
Wednesday

3rd ♓

☽ v/c 5:02 am

☽ → ♈ 5:24 am

Color of the day: Topaz
Incense of the day: Honeysuckle

Acorn Protection Spell

O ak is a strong and water-resistant wood, which is why it's used to make whisky barrels, boats, and flooring. The powers of the oak tree are easily harnessed in magical work because of the abundance of acorns—which are, of course, oak seeds! This spell utilizes the power of the oak to protect your home.

Start by collecting four acorns near your home. (If you live in a zone with no oak trees, collect four tree seeds native to your area.) Once you have gathered the acorns, hold them in your hand and feel the protective energy that radiates from them. Let that energy mingle with your own. When you are done, the acorns should be warm to the touch.

Place an acorn on each side of your home. You can bury each acorn or simply set it next to your house. (Alternatively, if you don't have a yard, simply place each acorn in an out-of-the-way space in your home.) As you set down each acorn, say:

Mighty oak, protect this space.

Share with us your power of place.

Keep our home safe from harm

With this acorn, the oak tree's charm!

Repeat this spell every year for maximum effect.

Amanda Lynn & Jason Mankey

NOTES:

September 19
Thursday

3rd ♈

Color of the day: Crimson
Incense of the day: Jasmine

Return to Me Spell

I once left an event wearing someone else's boots, the same size and color as mine. They didn't feel quite right, so I returned to the venue and found a woman at the door, searching.

When my daughter was small, I made tiny labels that were sewn into all her clothes, so they always made their way home. With my own back-country camping gear, I have carefully written my name in indelible ink, so ownership is clear. Sometimes magic is disguised as common sense.

We can assume our stuff is safe, but too often it can be lost by being confused with other people's things. Use a Sharpie marker and practice a "Return to me" spell.

Write your name, or a symbol that you can use consistently, on all your favorite jackets, hats, boots, and shoes. As you write, whisper to them:

Always, always return to me.

Blessed be.

                  Dallas Jennifer Cobb

September 20
Friday

3rd ♈

☽ v/c 4:39 am

☽ → ♉ 5:03 am

Color of the day: Coral
Incense of the day: Mint

Steeped in Good Vibes

When you wish to do a spell, you can use an herbal reference book or internet search to find a tea aligned with your spell's intention. For instance, you might use rooibos for a spell requiring strength or determination or hibiscus for love or dream work. Place four bags of your chosen tea in a two-quart lidded glass container filled with water.

Place the tea in a sunny spot and use the following evocation before letting the tea steep for three to five hours:

Power of the Sun,

Power of (type of tea),

Please lend your energy to my aim:

(State your spell's purpose.)

Thank you!

Place the tea in the fridge until chilled. (You can leave the tea bags in the water for a more full-bodied flavor.) When you're ready to cast your spell, hold a cup of tea in both hands, sending the energy into the liquid, where it's magnified by the power of sunlight

and your herbal allies. Drink, focusing on your desired outcome. Leftover tea is best used within two days.

Melissa Tipton

NOTES:

September 21
Saturday

3rd ♉

Color of the day: Black
Incense of the day: Patchouli

UN International Day of Peace

hail and Farewell

Depending on where you live, this is the last day of summer. It's time to say hail and farewell to the season that brings us picnics, butterflies, long lazy afternoons, and warm nights. Although summer may have been fun, many of us can hardly contain our anticipation for the upcoming autumn season. Sometimes we get giddy thinking about it. But before we welcome the season of fall, we need to give summer a proper farewell.

For this spell you will need:

• A yellow candle

• A fireproof candleholder

• Your favorite summer food

Light your candle and place your favorite food next to it. Gaze lovingly into the flame. Thank the season of summer for its blessings. Share a piece of your food with the earth. You can allow the candle to safely burn down, or snuff or pinch it out.

Najah Lightfoot

September 22
Sunday

3rd ☿

☽ v/c 6:14 am

☽ → ♊ 6:24 am

☉ → ♎ 8:44 am

Color of the day: Gold
Incense of the day: Hyacinth

Mabon – Fall Equinox

Back to Base Spell

Cast this spell whenever you find yourself overwhelmed by worldly concerns and mundane obligations. It will help you regain a sense of balance and joy and strengthen your sense of self, reminding you of your core being and essence.

Light a candle in a holder, and stand with the candle in front of a mirror. Take some deep breaths as you look at your reflection. Then bring your focus deeper within, to the core of who you are. Close your eyes and see in your mind's eye the very essence of your being. Let the image form as it will, wherever your vision and emotions lead you. Imagine the image you see reflected in the mirror before you. Open your eyes and visualize this reflection of your essence stepping into you and meshing with your outward form. If you like, you can say:

I call back to myself all that I
am and all that I will be.

I reclaim the totality of my power!
I reclaim the totality of me!

When you're ready, take a slow, deep breath, then blow out the candle. You'll be able to get back to your day feeling more balanced and back to center.

Melanie Marquis

Notes:

September 23
Monday

3rd ♊

Color of the day: Gray
Incense of the day: Hyssop

Just Leaf That Stuff Behind

Still being in the throes of the Fall Equinox in the Northern Hemisphere, we can draw upon this seasonal energy to continue releasing those things that no longer serve our lives. Additionally, we can extend this releasing energy out into the world. As Witches and workers of magick, it is our duty and privilege to ride the Wheel of the Year and make the most of the turning tides. As we help ourselves, we help the world.

If available, get some dried and fallen autumn leaves. If not, substitute another type of dried leaf, such as bay.

Use a marker to carefully write words on the leaves, for yourself, for others, and for the world at large. Suggestions include *protection, clarity, world peace,* or anything else your intuition guides. This type of spell helps get or keep the ball rolling in the right direction. Carefully and privately burn all of the leaves outside while repeating:

> *Great Burning Season now at play, these now are banished forever and a day!*

Raven Digitalis

September 24
Tuesday

3rd ♊
☽ v/c 7:59 am
☽ → ♋ 10:50 am
4th Quarter 2:50 pm

Color of the day: Scarlet
Incense of the day: Cinnamon

Emotional Healing Bath

We can't magically erase painful emotions, but we can invoke divine support for healing them and letting them go. Do this today by safely lighting a white candle and drawing a warm bath. Dissolve one cup Epsom salt and ¼ cup sea salt in the water, and scatter the petals of one white rose across the surface of the water.

Stand outside the bath and direct your open palms toward the water. Imagine healing white light moving up from the core of the earth, through your feet, and into your heart. Also imagine white light moving down from the cosmos, entering the crown of your head, and moving down to your heart. From your heart, channel this light down your arms and out your hands into the water. Say:

> *Great Goddess, help me feel and heal my emotions so I can let them go at the perfect time and in the perfect way. Thank you.*

Then soak. Extinguish the candle when done.

Tess Whitehurst

September 25
Wednesday

4th ♋

Color of the day: Yellow
Incense of the day: Lilac

Instant Messaging

Today is Wednesday, a great day to work with the energies of Mercury. In this day and age, delivering messages happens at the click of a few buttons. When communicating with spirits, it can be a little trickier, so we will want to work with Mercury to make sure our messages are delivered with efficiency and clarity.

You will need a piece of paper and a pen to write down a message to someone who has passed on. To deliver it, you will need a fireproof vessel to place the message in and a lighter or matches to set the message aflame. Make sure to watch the flame as it catches and make sure that it burns out completely. You can then scatter the ashes in the wind and the message will be delivered.

Charlynn Walls

September 26
Thursday

4th ♋

☽ v/c 6:12 pm
☽ → ♌ 6:47 pm

Color of the day: White
Incense of the day: Mulberry

Shake Away the Attachment

This spell removes unwanted attachments from others. It's a great way to get an ex to stop pestering you, to get coworkers to stop harassing you, or just to shake off a lingering memory that is no longer appropriate for you to carry. You'll need a jar of cayenne pepper, a pen and paper, thirteen matches, some sea salt crystals, and lavender oil.

Empty the cayenne pepper into another receptacle. Write the person's name on the paper and put it in the empty pepper jar. Add the matches, then pour in some sea salt until the jar is nearly full. Finally, fill the jar with whatever cayenne pepper will fit into it. Keep tapping the sides of the jar so the pepper settles.

For the next five days, shake the jar. On the sixth day, shake the jar, rub the outside of it with the lavender oil, and then—keeping the jar closed—dispose of it off your property. Know that the person in question no longer has power over you, and celebrate!

Charlie Rainbow Wolf

 September 27
Friday

4th ♌

Color of the day: Purple
Incense of the day: Cypress

Time to Declutter and Share

How much *stuff* do we collect as we wander through our lives? We love each item when we first buy it, but then what? Look in your desk drawers, in all your drawers. Do you even recognize everything in there? Look in your closets. When did you last wear some of those clothes? Look on shelves. Do you even have enough shelves? It's time to neaten your home and share the excess. If you haven't used or worn or read or watched an item, give it to people who need these things. Open some windows to let in cleansing breezes and appeal to Hestia for guidance:

Helpful Hestia—

*Lead me through my home
as I declutter my space.*

*Show me what I don't notice.
Show me what to toss.*

*Show me what to share and where
or with whom to share it.*

*Show me what to keep and
what to move and rearrange.*

*Help me tidy my home
and simplify my life.*

Barbara Ardinger

September 28
Saturday

☽ v/c 11:36 pm

Color of the day: Indigo
Incense of the day: Ivy

Bounty of Fall Altar

Fall is a time of quick changes and bright colors. In temperate zones, the temperature drops and witches know the harvest is almost complete. On this early fall day, it's time for deep engagement with the lively and colorful side of nature.

Go outside and collect elements of fall that call to you. Please take your time! These may be maple, elm, birch, hawthorn, oak, hickory, or hazel leaves. You may be drawn to pine cones, nuts, rose hips, fallen branches, gourds, or the last vestiges of life in the garden. Collect these items and take them inside.

Once you return indoors, arrange your items artfully on a table that has been set with a gold, yellow, or orange tablecloth. Put out a bowl of water as well. This will be inviting to the spirits, and many travel across water quite well. Sit down with your grimoire or journal and an ink pen. Take several deep cleansing breaths, and as you look at your fall altar, write down all the wisdom you hear, smell, and see. This is your time, and now you have brought the bounty of nature into your space.

Stephanie Rose Bird

▽ September 29
Sunday

4th ♌

☽ → ♍ 5:42 am

Color of the day: Amber
Incense of the day: Juniper

Glorious Autumn!

In many cities and towns, autumn leaves are at their peak. Social media abounds with pictures and photographs of trees in their autumn glory. The colors of gold, yellow, vibrant orange, and chartreuse pierce our visions and bring the promise of magickal wishes made manifest. In Colorado, where I live, people travel to the high country to behold the beauty of the changing aspen trees. For this spell you will need:

• A gathering of autumn leaves

• A piece of bread

• A cup of water

Arrange the leaves around the bread. Hold the cup of water in your hand and say:

Blessed be, water that falls from the sky.

As you pour water over the bread and leaves, say:

Thank you, Mother Earth, for your abundance and the season of fall.
May we be blessed, one and all!

Najah Lightfoot

September 30
Monday

4th ♍

Color of the day: White
Incense of the day: Lily

EVOO, Oh Yes!

What better day to appreciate the versatility of olive oil than on National Extra Virgin Olive Oil Day? With a history that can be traced back over five thousand years, olive oil not only is appreciated by chefs and culinary experts around the world but also has a multitude of uses, from health and beauty to religious and spiritual applications.

EVOO is my go-to for anointing, especially when working with folks who have allergies to strong scents and manufactured essential oils. Because I use it a lot in my cooking, it's always fresh and at the ready in my kitchen for whatever I need. It's easy to infuse herbs into olive oil, whether you wish to add flavor or use the oil for non-culinary metaphysical purposes.

Olive oil is also a primary tool in Italian folk practices for determining whether someone has had the evil eye (*malocchio*) cast upon them. Water is placed in a dish and some oil is poured on top of it. If the oil stays separate, there's no curse. If it mixes with the water, then evil is afoot and blessings must be done to remove the curse.

Laura Tempest Zakroff

October

Days that turn on a breath into rapidly waning light. Wispy, high dark clouds in an orange and turquoise sky. Bright orange pumpkins carved into beautiful art and lit from inside. The eerie music of screeching cats. These fond images of October burn at a Witch's heart, calling to her even across the seasons where she's busy setting up her tent for festival. By the time October finally arrives, Witches and other magic users have already had discussions about costumes and parties, rituals and celebrations, and we look forward with happiness to the whole month of both poignantly somber and brightly playful activities.

In Celtic Europe, our ancestors acknowledged October as the last month of the summer season, with winter officially beginning on Samhain. They carved slits in squashes to keep light in the fields so they could finish their day's work, and when the custom came to America, it eventually evolved into the tradition of carving jack-o'-lanterns. American Witches often use magical symbols to carve their pumpkins, creating beacons for their Beloved Dead. In the spirit of the turn of energies at this time, we give candy to children to ensure that they, our future, will remember the sweetness inside and be good leaders when their turn comes. May we all be so blessed.

Thuri Calafia

October 1
Tuesday

4th ♏

☽ v/c 5:39 pm

☽ → ♎ 6:20 pm

Color of the day: Red
Incense of the day: Basil

'Tis the Season of the Witch!

It's here, it's here! It's officially
Witch season, although for many
of us, our practices are not a hobby
or only honored during one season of
the year. For many of us, we Witch
proud every day! However, one can't
help but get caught up in the vibes of
October. I always say, "We Witches
kick it off!"

On this day, honor a Witch who
has gone before you or influenced you
in a positive way. For this spell you
will need:

• A white candle

• A fireproof candleholder

• A red rose

• Salt

Place the candle in the holder and
lay the red rose before the candle.
Pour a ring of salt around the candle
and the rose.

Light the candle and gaze at the
flame. Think of your favorite Witch,
wish them well, and tell them in a
whisper that they are never forgotten.
Allow the candle to safely burn down,
or pinch or snuff it out. The rose can
be dried and placed upon your altar
along with the salt.

Najah Lightfoot

NOTES:

 October 2
Wednesday

4th ♎

New Moon 2:49 pm

Color of the day: Brown
Incense of the day: Marjoram

Solar Eclipse – Rosh hashanah
begins at sundown

A Book of Shadows Meditation

Today we have a new moon with a solar eclipse. Most occultists agree this is not a good time to work magic or cast a spell because the Earth is in the "shadow" of the eclipse. However, this is a time of swift changes and a perfect time to work in your Book of Shadows.

For this activity get out your Book of Shadows and sit at your altar. Clear your mind and think of three things you wish to change about yourself or your life. Next, on a blank page in your book, write down those things you wish to change. Meditate on them. Now one by one, go over them in your mind. Ask yourself about these changes: "Why do I want to make these changes? Are these changes realistic, and should I set time limits to make these changes?" Change your list if you wish, and think about it some more.

When you feel done, put your Book of Shadows away. Begin planning how you're going to make these changes. After the Earth is out of the "shadow" of the eclipse (in about three days), get to work. From time to time refer to your Book of Shadows and make any new changes you need.

James Kambos

NOTES:

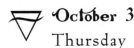

October 3
Thursday

1st ♎

Color of the day: Turquoise
Incense of the day: Balsam

Completing the Magical Circuit

In Qabalistic thought, Malkuth is the plane of form where energies coalesce into material substance. Occultist Dion Fortune taught that bringing your magic into Malkuth helps to ground the energy, completing a circuit, if you will, that might otherwise be left to dissipate and cause unwanted side effects, such as "bad luck" or strange occurrences.

Your body is a wonderful vehicle for grounding energy in Malkuth, and this can be as simple as making ritual gestures in the air with your hand or writing a spell on paper rather than completing the steps in your mind.

Let's do this now: Write down something you want on a piece of paper. Imagine that you already have it—what does it look, sound, smell, feel, and perhaps even taste like?—and send that imaginative energy into the paper. Now light a candle on a heatproof surface or use a bonfire and burn the paper safely, wafting the smoke up into the cosmos with your hands, sending forth the energy of your spell. Then put out the candle or bonfire.

Melissa Tipton

October 4
Friday

1st ♎

☽ v/c 6:40 am
☽ → ♏ 7:22 am

Color of the day: Coral
Incense of the day: Orchid

Entering the Mysteries

This is the perfect time to honor the Eleusinian Mysteries, which were celebrated at this time of year in ancient Greece. These initiatory rites were dedicated to the goddesses Demeter and Persephone. If you feel the call of self-initiation, here is a simple spell that can help you on your path.

You will need a piece of paper, a pen, an envelope, and six pomegranate seeds (or juice if you cannot get the fruit). Ground yourself by closing your eyes and taking several deep breaths. Focus on your desire to go further along your path. Open your eyes and write your intentions and what you want out of your path on the paper. Fold the paper into thirds and place it in the envelope and seal it.

To complete your self-initiation, eat six pomegranate seeds or drink a small amount of juice. The seeds are symbolic of the balance that was achieved when Persephone consumed six pomegranate seeds binding her to the Underworld for half the year.

Recite aloud:

I know the journey is difficult, but I accept that it is my path to tread.

Charlynn Walls

NOTES:

October 5
Saturday

1st ♏

Color of the day: Gray
Incense of the day: Pine

Altar to Your Beloved Dead

Throughout October, the veil between this world and the next will become continually thinner. Honor your loved ones on the other side today by setting up an altar for them. Include an image of each deceased loved one (human or otherwise). Place at least one candle near each image, along with an offering of one or more items this loved one appreciated while they were alive, such as a nonperishable food or beverage, fruit, flower, small potted plant, book, poem, perfume, or anything else that feels right. Further decorate your altar with fall flowers, such as chrysanthemums and marigolds, and fall produce, such as apples and pumpkins. An incense holder and incense would also be a nice addition, as sweet-smelling smoke is a traditional offering for the spirits.

Light the candles and sit in quiet communion with your loved ones for at least a minute or two once a day until Samhain. Also, see if you can notice the subtle changes in the ether that correspond with the thinning of the veil. Can you hear the spirits? Can you sense eternity?

Tess Whitehurst

October 6
Sunday

1st ♏

☽ v/c 6:52 pm

☽ → ♐ 7:34 pm

Color of the day: Orange
Incense of the day: Almond

Smoke Signals

D ivination comes in many forms. One especially well suited for autumn use is capnomancy, or divination based on smoke patterns. The color, shape, and behavior of the smoke send messages.

You can do this type of divination with incense, a pile of burning leaves, a bonfire, or whatever you prefer. (Take standard precautions for working with fire.) Once the flames die down, examine the smoke. Watch how it flows through the air, forming shapes. Smoke that rises smoothly predicts easy times ahead, while smoke that sputters or boils without obvious wind is a warning of turmoil. You might see a snake (rebirth), a sphere (perfection), a figure eight (infinity), a spiral (magic), or other symbols. If the smoke "follows" you as you move, especially against the wind, it means that elemental air and fire like you.

Write down the date and a description of what you see in the smoke. Later you can return to check if the predictions came true.

Elizabeth Barrette

Notes:

October 7
Monday

1st ♐

Color of the day: Ivory
Incense of the day: Narcissus

Fire Spell for Success

Cast this spell to bring success. Using the head of a pin or sewing needle, carefully engrave along the length of an orange taper candle a word, phrase, or symbol to express your wish. Cut off the very bottom of a whole, unpeeled orange so it can sit flat. Place the orange on a fireproof dish and set it on a stable surface. Poke a hole into the center of the curved top portion of the orange, and insert the candle into it, twisting the candle until you achieve a tight fit. Light the candle and envision your wish coming true as the candle burns. You can either use a small candle so that you can watch it burn down completely in one session, or put out the candle after a few minutes of visualizing, repeating the spell each night for several nights until the candle has entirely melted away. Scatter the edible flesh of the orange outside, removing any wax.

Melanie Marquis

October 8
Tuesday

1st ♐

Color of the day: White
Incense of the day: Ylang-ylang

Banishing with Bay

This spell helps you get rid of inhibitions. You'll need a bay leaf and a fine point marker, both available from grocery stores. You'll also need a green or black jar candle, a heatproof surface, and a box of matches. Write what you feel is impeding your progress on the bay leaf. If you feel you need to elaborate for clarity, use more than one leaf. This is acceptable, but remember the order in which you wrote on them. Light the candle. Then light the bay leaf with the candle flame, saying:

I burn thee to stop thee burning me.

When the bay leaf gets too hot to handle, drop it into the jar candle. Repeat with as many leaves as you used, keeping them in order (so the spell maintains its clarity of intent). When you are finished, pinch out the candle or use a candle snuffer, and put the lid on the candle. Save this candle to repeat the spell for new situations in the future.

Charlie Rainbow Wolf

October 9
Wednesday

1st ♐

☽ v/c 1:54 am

☽ → ♑ 5:38 am

Color of the day: Topaz
Incense of the day: Bay laurel

Fire-Safe Witch

It's Fire Prevention Day. Let's face it—most magical folks love setting things on fire! But nothing ruins a spell or ritual faster than a fire hazard. Here are some handy tips to be aware of when burning things and a little blessing to keep things safe:

- While candles that have lots of herbs, crystals, and other interesting bits in them look cool, they can be a serious fire hazard. These are best burned in larger cauldrons, away from any flammable materials.

- Those little charcoal tablets get surprisingly hot! Nestle them in a bed of sand or salt in a fireproof container and then place everything on a tile or trivet for added security.

- When burning anything in your cauldron, keep a lid handy. If your cauldron didn't come with a lid, find a plate or other suitable cover that can be used to snuff out the flame in case of an emergency.

- Fire charm:
  O bright flame, charming spark,
  bring forth your good light and
  illuminate the dark.

  Laura Tempest Zakroff

NOTES:

October 10
Thursday

1st ♑

2nd Quarter 2:55 pm

Color of the day: Purple
Incense of the day: Apricot

Money Is Arriving

There's nothing ambiguous about this spell. We're not talking about substituting the word *abundance* for what you really want. It's about money.

There is one tricky part to this spell. You have to give some money away to get your money. Also note the name of this spell. The money is coming. Believe that. This spell is best performed during a waxing or full moon or whenever you need money. Here is what you'll need:

- A small bowl
- ½ cup rice
- A 4-inch gold candle
- A 4-inch green candle
- 2 cinnamon sticks
- 2 small pieces of pyrite
- 2 small pieces of malachite
- Coins or paper money (You choose the denominations.)

Fill the bowl with rice. Set the candles in the rice upright. Place the cinnamon sticks upright next to the candles. Put the stones next to the candles. Bury the money in the rice.

Safely light the candles and say as many times as possible before the candles burn down:

Money is arriving.

Never leave the candles unattended. When the candles are fully burned, fetch out the money and give it away the same day.

Phoenix LeFae & Gwion Raven

NOTES:

October 11
Friday

2nd ♑

☽ v/c 11:53 am

☽ → ♒ 12:31 pm

Color of the day: White
Incense of the day: Mint

Yom Kippur begins at sundown

The Magickal Number 11

For many people, the number 11 holds psychic, divinatory, mystical symbolism. When the clock strikes 11:11, many sense it to be a positive sign from the universe or the divine mysteries. Use this October portal to boost your prosperity magick! For this spell you will need:

- A green taper candle
- Florida Water
- A tool to carve words or symbols into your candle
- Blessing oil or prosperity oil
- Gold glitter
- A fireproof candleholder
- Coins of different denominations

Wipe the candle upward and then downward with Florida Water and allow it to dry. Carve words or symbols of prosperity into your candle. Anoint the candle with the blessing or prosperity oil, then sprinkle gold glitter over it. Set the candle in the holder, and arrange the coins around the base of the candleholder.

During the 11 o'clock hour, light your candle. Visualize abundance and prosperity flowing effortlessly, seamlessly, and continually to you. Allow your candle to safely burn down. Carry the coins in your pocket or place them in a sacred space.

Najah Lightfoot

NOTES:

October 12
Saturday

2nd ≈≈

Color of the day: Brown
Incense of the day: Sandalwood

Create Your Porta-Witch

Back when I was creating and leading rituals all over Southern California, I soon discovered it was best to take my sacred tools with me instead of borrowing or making do. I made myself a Porta-Witch, which is what I called the picnic basket with my altar supplies in it. You can make one, too.

First, buy a lidded picnic basket. Clean it carefully and bless it as you bless your tools. Now start filling your basket:

1. A compass (You need to know where the directions are.)

2. Your symbols of the elemental powers (Make them personal but still obvious to others.)

3. A small goddess figure or two

4. Plastic bags of matches, charcoal, sacred oils, incense, etc.

5. Small clay saucers in which to burn incense

6. Candles and four candleholders

7. Your ritual knife and wand

8. An altar cloth

Bless each object as you place it in the basket, then surround the basket with a sphere of protective light. See magic happening as you work with your Porta-Witch.

Barbara Ardinger

NOTES:

October 13
Sunday

2nd ♒

☽ v/c 10:11 am

☽ → ♓ 3:55 pm

Color of the day: Gold
Incense of the day: Marigold

Journey into the Self

As the veil continues to thin and we move ever closer to Samhain, it is the perfect time for journeying deeper into yourself. Don't be afraid. Finding what lurks beneath your surface may seem daunting if it's not the type of thing you do regularly. Clearly, this is where your imagination, creativity, memories, sensuality, spirituality, and ancestors are most accessible. You need only three things for this work: a piece of copal, a lighter, and charcoal, which will be put into a censer or on a fire-proof plate. Copal is a visionary tool used for shapeshifting, vision quests, and more.

You need to go outside. Make sure you're dressed comfortably. Wear a ceremonial robe or relaxed clothing. Stand or sit, whichever you prefer. Light the charcoal, and once it is white-hot, add the copal. Copal lets out plumes of copious smoke. The smoke will tell you stories. It will open up your mind, challenging your perceptions along the way. Listen closely and watch even more closely.

Take this journey into yourself with the aid of this mystical, compelling, truthful, and powerful herb.

Stephanie Rose Bird

NOTES:

October 14
Monday

2nd ♓

Color of the day: Silver
Incense of the day: Hyssop

Indigenous Peoples' Day –
Thanksgiving Day (Canada)

Giving Thanks

As a Canadian, I have much to give thanks for: democracy, socialized medicine and education, and a relatively good standard of living. Where I place my attention, the energy grows. So today, on Canadian Thanksgiving Day, let's undertake a gratitude spell.

On a piece of paper, write:

1. *Thank you, thank you, thank you for _____.*

Fill in the blank. Then write:

2. *I am pleased by _____.*

Complete the phrase and continue:

3. *I am happy about _____.*

4. *I am glad that _____.*

5. *I am thankful for _____.*

6. *I am appreciative of _____.*

7. *I am blessed by _____.*

8. *I am delighted by _____.*

9. *I am grateful for _____.*

Lucky, lucky me.

This simple gratitude spell can be used nightly to shift your energy and attention, releasing stress and stimulating feel-good hormones throughout your body before sleep. Realistically, you can use this spell to change your outlook any time you need.

Dallas Jennifer Cobb

NOTES:

☉ October 15
Tuesday

2nd ♓

☽ v/c 4:00 pm

☽ → ♈ 4:34 pm

Color of the day: Gray

Incense of the day: Bayberry

Pennies Against Poverty

Nobody wants nor deserves to feel the struggle of poverty financially or on any other level. Whether today, tomorrow, or any time the opportunity presents itself, this simple spell can bring abundant energy into one's own life and the lives of others. When you encounter a dark, dirty, or otherwise icky-feeling penny, take it to a secluded spot. After ensuring you don't have an audience, spit at the penny, then toss it away from you and declare any variation of the following:

I banish poverty in my life!

Naturally, you can change the wording to say "_____'s life" (insert name) or anything else that comes to mind.

Remember that banishing must conclude with an invocation of the opposite. The final step of the spell is to quickly inhale and see financial abundance entering yourself or the other(s) you have chosen to magickally assist.

Raven Digitalis

☉ October 16
Wednesday

2nd ♈

Color of the day: White

Incense of the day: Lilac

Sukkot begins at sundown

Illuminating Perspective

To shed light on an issue that's causing confusion or a feeling of stuckness, write a description of the issue on a piece of paper, ideally one that, if held up to the light, you can see through partially. Regular printer paper is fine; just avoid anything heavy like card stock or construction paper. Be sure to write down any aspects of the situation that feel particularly confusing or obstructed.

Tape the paper onto an eastern- or southern-facing window of your home that receives sunlight for at least part of the day, and activate the spell with the following incantation:

Outer light and inner sight,

Wisdom will the Sun ignite.

Show me what I need to see,

To align this issue with harmony.

Let the paper absorb light through the window for as long as feels needed, paying attention to any intuitive guidance that arises regarding your situation.

Melissa Tipton

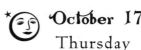 **October 17**
Thursday

2nd ♈

☽ull Moon 7:26 am

☽ v/c 3:26 pm

☽ → ♉ 4:00 pm

Color of the day: Green
Incense of the day: Carnation

Full Moon Samhain herb Bundle

It is the last full moon before Samhain. The veil is thin and we are able to feel the presence of our beloved dead more than ever. Tonight would be perfect for charging a bundle of herbs dedicated to communicating with the ancestors.

The following herbs have associations with protection, divination, and the sacred dead: apple leaves, cinnamon, mugwort, eucalyptus, bay laurel, willow, rosemary, mullein, lavender, clove, and marigold. Gather what you can find (fresh or dried is fine) and wrap them with twine. If you are only able to find your herbs in chopped or powdered form, you can make an herbal pouch instead. Place the bundle or pouch under the full moon and recite the following chant:

Under the moon I charge these herbs and open the door of Samhain.

I call to my beloved dead and sacred spiritual kin.

You are welcome to this place of remembrance and communication,

But only those who come with love and trust may join herein.

Sit with your herbs for a moment before you leave them under the moon for the night and allow them to do their work. In the morning, place your herbs on your altar, in a doorway, or in any spot you feel is appropriate for welcoming in your beloved dead.

Amanda Lynn & Jason Mankey

NOTES:

October 18
Friday

3rd ♉

Color of the day: Rose
Incense of the day: Vanilla

Get Rid of a Lover Spell

If it is time to get rid of the creep in your life, try this spell. You'll need one apple and a paring knife. Wash and dry the apple. Dry it vigorously, like you're rubbing the louse out of your life. Next, with the knife, carve your soon-to-be ex's initials into the apple's skin. Now peel the apple. In your mind, see your lover getting smaller and smaller. Let the peel drop to the floor. You should eat the remainder of the apple. Enjoy every bite of it. When done, say these words:

No more lies, no more cheating, no more strife.

Now you're out of my life.

Pick up the peel and get rid of it. You may compost it and let it rot, or throw it deep into a wooded area, or toss it in a trash container away from your home. There, you got rid of the peel—and the heel!

James Kambos

October 19
Saturday

3rd ♉

☽ v/c 3:33 pm

☽ → ♊ 4:07 pm

Color of the day: Blue
Incense of the day: Magnolia

Garage or Storage Clean-Out

Not everyone has a garage, but almost everyone has a storage area containing at least a few items that walk the line between treasure and junk. Creating order in such an area can boost your clarity, mitigate overwhelm, and even make you feel like there's more time in the day.

So today, choose one of these areas: a garage, closet, or something smaller like a junk drawer or toolbox. Light a candle and possibly some incense. Call on the Divine to help you shift your energy in a positive way. Then clean that sucker out!

If it's a smaller area, you can pull everything out of it to start. If it's a larger space, you can pull everything out of one general area at a time. Clean the inside of the space you've cleared by sweeping, vacuuming, and/or wiping it down. Then look at each item and put it back only if you love it, use it, or need it. Otherwise give it away, recycle it, or (if necessary) throw it out. Extinguish the candle and incense when done.

Tess Whitehurst

October 20
Sunday

3rd ♊

Color of the day: Yellow
Incense of the day: Hyacinth

Spirit Sight

In every moment, we're viewing ourselves and the world through a particular lens. Like a pair of glasses, our lens can become smudged by family patterns, cultural conditioning, and other biases. Regularly "cleaning our glasses" aligns our individual sight with a more expansive spirit point of view. With spirit sight, we're able to see previously hidden options in life, free ourselves from the harsh perspective of the inner critic, and more.

Sit comfortably where you won't be disturbed. Close your eyes and focus on your breathing until you feel centered. Imagine a brilliant star descending from the heavens, hovering a few feet above you. Envision its cleansing energy entering your crown chakra, filling your body and aura with light.

Rub your hands together rapidly, letting heat and energy build, then place your palms over your closed eyes, allowing the starlit energy to stream from your hands, thoroughly cleansing your vision. Release the image of the star from your mind and place your hands on the ground, letting any excess energy flow into the earth.

Melissa Tipton

October 21
Monday

3rd ♊

☽ v/c 5:00 pm

☽ → ♋ 6:50 pm

Color of the day: White
Incense of the day: Rosemary

Apple a Day

Today is National Apple Day. This beautiful fruit is sacred in some Pagan traditions. It represents magic, the five elements, and the mysteries of life and death.

Celebrate this holiday by doing something with apples. If you don't have your own apple tree, the best way is to visit an orchard where you can pick your own apples and enjoy products such as apple cider. Give thanks to the Earth and the apple trees for their abundance. In many areas, fall weather supports planting apple trees in your yard. Choose trees suited to your environment; planting two different varieties gives better pollination. In case of inclement weather, you may prefer working indoors. Read about the sacred and magical uses of apples, or study heirloom apple cultivars. You could also cook with apples. Take time to cut one in half, between the stem end and the blossom end, to observe the pentacle inside its core. Invite your friends over for an apple ritual!

Elizabeth Barrette

October 22
Tuesday

3rd ♋

☉ → ♏ 6:15 pm

Color of the day: Maroon
Incense of the day: Geranium

Leaf Gold

National Color Day celebrates the wonderful diversity of color in the world. Whether by playing with paints, taking a hike in nature, or making a playlist of "colorful" songs, there are a lot of fun ways to appreciate the hues in your life.

One of my favorite things to do is watch the leaves changing color where I live. No matter where I have resided, there's always a shift. In some places the change is subtle, and other places it's a riot of color, like in New England. I hand-collect the fallen leaves for spell projects and especially for decorating altars. There are so many different shapes and colors— all free and on my doorstep!

Here are some ideas for using some of that leaf gold for your magic:

- Collect all one kind of leaf (such as oak or maple), then search for the subtle variations. Display them fanned out chromatically or make a garland out of them.

- Collect one color of leaf but from different varieties, and do the same as above.

- Connect with a favorite tree and gather a leaf fallen to write an intention on. Release it to the wind when you're done.

Laura Tempest Zakroff

NOTES:

October 23
Wednesday

3rd ♋

Color of the day: Brown
Incense of the day: Lavender

Sukkot ends

Water Blessing

Use this spell to express gratitude for your blessings and welcome in more blessings. Fill a cup with water and take it outside along with a selection of quartz crystals and a small pitcher of water to refill the cup. Drink the water slowly, savoring it as you think about the blessings that water brings and the necessity of water for our very survival. Then fill the cup again, nearly to the brim. Place the cup on the ground near the base of a tree or other plant. Turn your attention to the quartz crystals as you begin to think of your blessings. Place the crystals in the cup of water one by one as you fill your heart with gratitude and name each blessing. Keep adding crystals until the water spills over the brim of the cup. Say:

> My cup runneth over!
> I welcome more blessings!

Pour out the remaining water and leave the crystals as an expression of thankfulness.

Melanie Marquis

October 24
Thursday

3rd ♋

☽ v/c 12:47 am

☽ → ♌ 1:24 am

4th Quarter 4:03 am

Color of the day: Crimson
Incense of the day: Nutmeg

An Apple a Day

It's harvest time, and what fruit is more magical than the beloved apple? Even the seeds are arranged in a pentagram when the apple is cut across its width—the apple itself knows it's magical! Apples are associated with many deities and are said to be the favored fruit of the deceased. This spell to promote good health deals with the living, though! Simply obtain an apple of your choice, cut it in half width-wise, and eat it! Between bites, recite these words:

> The apple tastes sweet. I honor the deities who give me my health.

There's a reason the words are arranged like this, so please don't paraphrase. You want to maintain the pure intent of the spell. When you have eaten the apple, take the core outside and say:

> The fruit is in me. I give to those around me. I share my being.

This spell can be done at any time, but it is best done on a Friday.

Charlie Rainbow Wolf

October 25
Friday

Color of the day: Pink
Incense of the day: Thyme

Talk to Me Spell

There are times when we need clear communication and can't get it. If you are being iced out by someone or are getting the silent treatment, this spell can help you open up communication and get things moving.

You will need the following items:

- A glass-encased white candle
- A felt tip pen (for writing on the candle's glass)
- A small bowl of olive oil
- A pinch of dried deer's-tongue or peppermint
- A pinch of dried rose petals

Using the felt tip pen, write the word *Communication* around the top of the candle's glass. Repeat this as many times as it will fit. Around the bottom of the candle's glass, write the words *Talk to me*. Repeat this as many times as it will fit.

In the middle of the glass, write the name of the person you want to communicate with you. If you have their birthdate, write this under their name.

Dip your finger in the olive oil and rub this on the top of the wax to lubricate the situation. Sprinkle the top of the candle with the herbs. Say this:

(Name of person), come and talk to me.

*Communication is open
and flowing, I see.*

Let's go to the heart,

Stop being apart.

Communication is easy and free.

Light the candle and let it burn safely to completion.

Phoenix LeFae & Gwion Raven

NOTES:

October 26
Saturday

4th ♌

☽ v/c 4:04 am

☽ → ♍ 11:47 am

Color of the day: Indigo
Incense of the day: Rue

The Power of Marigold

Flowers come in a stunning variety of shapes, sizes, scents, colors, and textures. They have a language all their own, and they can speak to you deeply, uplifting and touching your soul.

Flowers can be employed to treat various spiritual and physical ills. They brighten the spirit and speak to the spirits. This becomes very evident in Mexican and Mexican American culture in the fall. Marigolds, the flower of October, become a bright beacon for the spirits. Pathways are created from them that lead deceased family members from the cemetery back home.

Calendula is a particularly healthful and attractive type of marigold, especially selected for its ability to speak to ghosts and spirits. Mundanely, it's used in soothing herbal skin preparations. Today, purchase or pick a dozen calendula flowers. If they are freshly picked, gently rinse them off with soapy water before bringing them inside. Add these spirit guides to your family altar or living room

mantel. Let your family know, whichever realm they are in, that they are loved and remembered.

Stephanie Rose Bird

NOTES:

October 27
Sunday

4th ♏

Color of the day: Amber
Incense of the day: Frankincense

Tra-la-la DI-DAAA!

W here are you? Oh, there you are. Under the bed. A drab, insignificant human being, depressed, stupid, and afraid. Your life is yucky.

Say the Sacred Magic Word (the title of this spell). Again. One more time. There you are! You're out! You're a magnificent technicolor superhero or superhera. As wise as Apollo or Athena. As powerful as Thor or Brunhilda. As compassionate as Osiris or Isis. You're ready to do good in the world.

You can do more than battle against hostile aliens from outer space. You can do battle right here against liars and thieves, against evil landlords and corrupt politicians. You can defend the defenseless. You can defang and declaw members of gangs and take their weapons away.

Look around your neighborhood, your city. Who needs help? How can you help them? What good and useful organizations can you work with? Where can you march? Say the magic word. Go into action to help the ordinary people on earth.

Barbara Ardinger

October 28
Monday

4th ♏

☽ v/c 11:54 pm

Color of the day: Gray
Incense of the day: Neroli

A Fivefold Kiss of Loving Bliss

I f you are unfamiliar with the traditional Wiccan Fivefold Kiss, I encourage you to research this blessing and modify it for our purpose.

Instead of giving the Kiss to another person, change every spoken instance of "your" to "my."

Before reciting each line, kiss the tips of the middle finger and pointer finger of your right hand at the same time. The other fingers should be tucked in, so that these two fingers act as one. This method of pointing directs energy from within and is also a common method of casting a circle without using an athame or wand. You can carry the blessing of the sacred smooch to each part of your body named in the chant. While giving the Kiss to these five parts of the body, envision each part surrounded by peaceful white light. Inhale deeply after each kiss.

This is an especially powerful daily mini-ritual for those of us who struggle with loving ourselves.

Raven Digitalis

October 29
Tuesday

4th ♍

☽ → ♎ 12:30 am

Color of the day: Scarlet
Incense of the day: Ginger

Bless My Creativity

As we move indoors in the Northern Hemisphere, we can spend more time doing creative activities. I do more collaging, crafting, and knitting in the dark months.

Today, set up a small creativity altar. It can be anywhere. Mine is on the shelf near where my boxes and bins of crafty supplies reside.

A creativity altar can include craft supplies of paper, ribbons, wool, and beads; bright colors to stimulate and inspire; and clipped pictures of artists or artwork that you love and admire.

The colors of green (for new beginnings), red, gold, or silver (for luck and prosperity), and blue (for a zen-like calm) always work for me.

You may want to make and place a vision board collage on the altar to anchor and inspire creativity.

Through the dark months ahead, let your creativity altar be the gateway to slipping into a timeless state, fully engaged with your artistic desires.

Dallas Jennifer Cobb

October 30
Wednesday

4th ♎

Color of the day: White
Incense of the day: Honeysuckle

Dress Up for Your Beloved Dead

In our experience, the night before Samhain is often less busy than the day of the sabbat. Take advantage of this quieter energy by spending time with your beloved dead without worrying about trick-or-treaters or coven experiences. For this spell you will want to spend a few minutes dressing up. This doesn't mean you have to wear your finest clothes, but you should dress in a way that feels special, or in a way in which your beloved dead might best remember you. If your deceased grandma bought you a sweater she absolutely loved, put it on to make her happy! As you get dressed, think of the memories associated with your clothes and the dead you hope to connect with.

Once you are dressed up, light a candle and invite your beloved dead to join you. Say their names, feel their energy around you, and share whatever is on your mind with them. The veil between the worlds is thin for only a brief time each year, so what better way to make it special than by dressing up! When your time is done, extinguish your candle and thank your beloved dead for visiting.

Amanda Lynn & Jason Mankey

October 31
Thursday

4th ♎

☽ v/c 12:57 pm
☽ → ♏ 1:29 pm

Color of the day: Purple
Incense of the day: Clove

Samhain – halloween

Pendulum Divination

S amhain is when the veil is the thinnest between our world and the spirit realm. It is a particularly suitable time to get answers to questions. To do that you will want to use a pendulum, which is typically an oblong object attached to a chain that is held by the practitioner. Many of today's pendulums are crystals that are suspended by a chain. If you do not have a pendulum, you can tie a ring to the end of a chain to accomplish the same task. The pendulum board can be a simple piece of paper where you write that the north-south axis is labeled "yes" and the east-west axis is labeled "no."

Once you are ready to begin, focus on the question you need an answer to or a loved one you are trying to connect with on this day. Hold the pendulum above the board and say, "So I seek, so I will find." Ask your question and let the pendulum guide you to the answer.

Charlynn Walls

NOTES:

November

The sounds of nature begin to quiet down in November, but this
month is far from silent. Yes, the cheery morning birdsong of spring
is gone, and crickets are no longer fiddling on warm summer afternoons,
but November has its own "voices." On a frosty November morning, you'll
hear a faint, faraway gabble. Raise your eyes toward the sky, and coming
over the horizon, in a V formation heading south, is a flock of wild geese.
The sound makes you pause and wonder: how do they know it's time to
migrate? As you rake leaves, the late autumn breeze stirs them, and they
softly rustle as they click and swirl up the street. Few sounds say November
like the wind. It may be as gentle as a baby's breath or it may roar, carrying
the weight of the coming winter as it howls in the night. During the night
you can also hear November's most haunting voice: the lone hooting of an
owl. Yes, this month has many voices, but every evening I hear the most
comforting voice of all. That voice belongs to the crackling of burning logs
as my hearth fire wards off the chill of a dark November night.

During this mysterious month, let the voices of November speak to you,
igniting your imagination and your magic.

James Kambos

November 1
Friday

4th ♏

New Moon 8:47 am

Color of the day: Coral

Incense of the day: Cypress

All Saints' Day

Portal to a New You

Talk about a liminal time! Not only is it All Saints' Day and the Witches' New Year, but it's a new moon as well. Plus, both the sun and the moon are in Scorpio, the sign of alchemy, secrets, and desires.

Today is a portal to a new way of being, so light a black candle, invoke the Divine, and answer the following questions in a journal. (Don't think too much beforehand. Just write and let your feelings flow.) What conditions would you like to let go of forever, and which would you like to invoke? What world are you leaving? What world are you stepping into? Who are you in this new cycle of time?

Now find or create a symbol that serves as a powerful representation of this transformation for you. This could be a character from a film, a painting, a picture, a rune, or anything else that feels right. Place the symbol (drawing, statue, printout, whatever) on your altar and hold a vision of it daily for the next thirty days.

Tess Whitehurst

November 2
Saturday

1st ♏

Color of the day: Black

Incense of the day: Ivy

Poetic, Musical Love

In one of the subplots of *The Merchant of Venice*, Jessica (Shylock's daughter) elopes with Lorenzo. It's true love. In act 5, they are sitting together and gazing up at the sky. Lorenzo's speech is one of Shakespeare's most evocative:

> How sweet the moonlight
> sleeps upon this bank!
>
> Here will we sit and let
> the sounds of music
>
> Creep in our ears: soft
> stillness and the night
>
> Become the touches of sweet harmony.
>
> Sit, Jessica. Look how
> the floor of heaven
>
> Is thick inlaid with patines
> of bright gold:
>
> [...]
>
> Such harmony is in immortal souls;
>
> [...]
>
> Come, [musicians] ho! and
> wake Diana with a hymn!
>
> With sweetest touches pierce
> your mistress' ear,
>
> And draw her home with music.

Set your intention to reach that level of poetic love. Choose a moonlit night, sit somewhere romantic and beautiful with the one you love, and gaze up at the sky. Play romantic music. Recite Lorenzo's speech. Draw poetry, music, and love down from heaven.

Barbara Ardinger

NOTES:

November 3
Sunday

1st ♏

☽ v/c 12:51 am

☽ → ♐ 1:19 am

Color of the day: Yellow
Incense of the day: Heliotrope

Daylight Saving Time
ends at 2:00 a.m.

Rue Altar/Table Wash

Rue is an especially useful herb, particularly when cleaning your magical space or trying to keep negativity out of your mundane spaces. For this spell you will need some dried rue, a pitcher of water with a lid, and a towel. Simply add the dried rue to your pitcher of water and let it steep for twenty-four hours. Strain the rue from the water and use your rue-infused wash for cleaning. Post-Samhain, we recommend using this rue wash to cleanse your altar. Remove your altar items and wash away any lingering traces of death.

With the holidays coming up, use your rue water to wipe down your kitchen table and floors. The energy of the rue will keep everyone who visits your home in good spirits and will help stop nasty arguments before they get started. When you are done cleaning indoors, dispose of the rue water outside near your front door to keep out unwanted visitors.

Amanda Lynn & Jason Mankey

November 4
Monday

1st ♐

Color of the day: Ivory
Incense of the day: Lily

Persephone Blessing

November is National
Pomegranate Month. Whenever I see or taste a pomegranate, I instantly think of the Greek goddess Persephone. When she was taken to the Underworld, she ate six pomegranate seeds, which tied her to staying there for half the year. As the fruit often shows up in markets in late fall, it's another reminder of Persephone's journey to the Underworld. Soon winter will be upon us, but life will return in the spring.

I always purchase a couple of pomegranates—one to eat and one for my altar in honor of Persephone. Amazingly, the altar fruits never rot or go bad; they simple dry out. So I have a small collection from previous years. Here is a blessing to honor Persephone with if you'd like to place a pomegranate on your altar too:

Persephone, Kore, Maiden Goddess,

Daughter of Earth and Queen of the Underworld,

Guide to spirits and the season-changer,

I honor your mysteries!

Laura Tempest Zakroff

November 5
Tuesday

1st ♐

☽ v/c 5:23 am
☽ → ♑ 10:17 am

Color of the day: White
Incense of the day: Cedar

Election Day

Bring Out the Vote Spell

Cast this spell on the morning of Election Day to help remove any barriers to voting that might occur. Write the word "voters" on a piece of paper, or be more specific and name the particular voters you wish your spell to help, such as "young voters" or "voters in New York State." Place a yellow candle in a secure holder on a heatproof surface. Surround the paper and candle with a ring of orange zest. Light the candle and envision droves of voters freely making their way to the polls to cast their votes. Say:

May the roads be open, may the roads be clear! May the voters come out and bring victory here!

Let the candle burn out safely in its holder. This spell can be adapted to open roads in any situation. Just write down a description of the desired situation instead of the word "voters" and adapt the visualization to fit your specific goal.

Melanie Marquis

 November 6
Wednesday

1st ♑

Color of the day: Topaz
Incense of the day: Bay laurel

The Day After

Good morning, United States of America! Today, many people will be either happy or sad, elated or pissed off, celebrating or lamenting. Some may feel indifferent. Lots of us will be happy that the campaign season, with its endless ads, is over.

There is sure to be a combination of feelings and emotions swirling around us, for yesterday was Election Day in the US. I am writing this on September 20, 2022. As I cast my eye to the future, I realize that you will be reading these words in 2024. Know that we have made it to this day, however you feel. Do something nice for yourself. Take it easy. Take a breather. You deserve it!

Najah Lightfoot

November 7
Thursday

1st ♑

☽ v/c 5:38 pm
☽ → ♒ 5:58 pm

Color of the day: Green
Incense of the day: Apricot

Save Me Spell

November is the hardest month for me. The decline in sunshine can leave me feeling sad and depleted. When the darkness begins to wear on me and I start to feel hopeless, helpless, and depressed, I know it's time for a "Save me" spell.

There are two essential ingredients for this spell: vitamin D and conscious breathing. You can use either one, or both, for positive effect. Find a good-quality vitamin D supplement with minimal additives that is easily consumed. I use a liquid supplement and drop it in my morning coffee—easy and repeatable magic.

Breathing? There are many breath techniques used in yoga to affect energy. Try sniffing in four times, followed by one long exhale, to energize and uplift yourself. On really bad days, I've heard the voice in my head say, "Help, save, save, save, meeeeeee," with "me" being the long exhale.

Dallas Jennifer Cobb

November 8
Friday

1st ♒

Color of the day: Rose
Incense of the day: Rose

Ask Your Dream Team

When you're in need of guidance beyond what the ego can offer, tap into the power of your dreams. Before bed, state your request:

In my dreams tonight, please show me what I need to know regarding (briefly describe your situation).

The next morning, before doing anything else, journal everything you remember from your dream, even if a detail seems irrelevant. If you can't recall the entire dream, that's okay; capture what you can. Once you start writing, previously forgotten aspects of the dream will often emerge. Journal your interpretations, keeping in mind that, like a tarot card, there isn't one right way to understand your dream.

If you're feeling stuck, ask yourself:

- What are you trying to do in the dream, and who or what helps or hinders you?

- What insights arise if you view every character in the dream as an aspect of yourself?

- How do you feel about the different characters or situations in the dream? When have you felt this way before in waking life?

- Choose one character, symbol, or setting in the dream and free-associate. What does it make you think of?

Melissa Tipton

Notes:

November 9
Saturday

1st ≈

2nd Quarter 12:55 am

☽ v/c 7:23 pm

☽ → ♓ 11:00 pm

Color of the day: Gray
Incense of the day: Sage

A November Fire Scrying Spell

There was a time when fire scrying in a fireplace was a popular fall and winter activity for families as they sat in their parlors in the evening. This spell takes us back to those times. To go about fire scrying, just follow the suggestions in the verse below. You may also use your cauldron or a small heatproof container. In whatever container you choose, start your fire carefully and never leave it unattended.

*To read your fate in the November
fire as it crackles and blazes,*

*Look into the fire and upon
the flames set your gaze.*

*Feed the fire with the holy
herbs of basil and thyme.*

*In the smoke and fire you'll
see a message or a sign.*

*Perhaps you'll see a face, a
number, or a name.*

*A sign of your destiny will
arise from the flames.*

*And when the November fire
dwindles to one ember,*

*Thank the sacred flame for a prophecy
you shall always remember.*

Let the fire cool for at least three days. Check to be sure the ashes are completely cool before you dispose of them. You may also wish to keep some of the ashes in a small container as a keepsake. If you don't have any luck with your fire scrying, wait for seven days and try again.

James Kambos

NOTES:

November 10
Sunday

2nd ♓

Color of the day: Gold
Incense of the day: Eucalyptus

Invisible Pentacle Spell

This is such a simple spell. You need just three things: water, salt, and a container. Use this spell to mark any space as your own, like your home, office, desk, kitchen table, front door, or coven space. The pentacle will appear when the water dries and is easily wiped away when you're done with your magickal working.

Here is what you'll need:

- 2 ounces salt

- 4 ounces room-temperature water

- A cup, bowl, or glass big enough to hold the water

Pour the salt into the container, then add the water. Stir until the salt dissolves. This might take a few minutes. When the salt is dissolved, dip your finger in the water and draw a pentacle on a surface. As soon as the water evaporates, you'll see the pentacle.

Phoenix LeFae & Gwion Raven

November 11
Monday

2nd ♓

Color of the day: Lavender
Incense of the day: Hyssop

Veterans Day –
Remembrance Day (Canada)

The Power of Eleven

Today is a day to honor our veterans for their service. The peace treaty to signify the end of World War I was signed in 1918 on the 11th hour of the 11th day of the 11th month. The number 11 is associated with duality and relates to spiritual messages. Open yourself up to the possibilities that the universe is trying to share with you on this day.

You will need a notecard or sticky note that you can carry with you to write on throughout the day. When you see or hear something today that stands out to you, write it down. Take note especially when you see the clock hit 11:00 or 11:11 in the morning or evening. Write down what you notice in the moment. At the end of the day, look back to see what messages the universe had for you.

Charlynn Walls

November 12
Tuesday

2nd ♓

☽ v/c 1:13 am

☽ → ♈ 1:26 am

Color of the day: Black
Incense of the day: Basil

Kitchen Witchin' Scrying

To perform a simple but effective scrying ritual, get any bowl or good-size mug from your kitchen cupboard. Fill the bowl or vessel approximately halfway with water. Next, use your intuition to grab a cooking oil of your choice, and pour a small amount in the vessel, making sure it covers about half of the water's surface.

Fetch a fancy spoon and one powdered cooking herb of your choice. Sprinkle a dash of the herb on the surface of the water.

With notebook and pen in hand, go to a pitch-black room with a single candle safely lit somewhere behind you. Take deep breaths, blur your vision, and ask your spiritual guides and guardians to gift you vision.

Take note of what you see, and decipher the symbolism tomorrow. Extinguish the candle.

Raven Digitalis

November 13
Wednesday

2nd ♈

Color of the day: Yellow
Incense of the day: Honeysuckle

A Spell for Prosperity

Like so many spells, this one is simple, but it packs a wallop. You'll need a glass dish, a silver spoon, and half a cup each of white sugar, brown rice, and pink Himalayan salt. Silver draws down the nurturing energy of the moon. White sugar entices and summons. Brown rice grounds the energy of fertility and abundance so it can be made manifest. Pink salt protects, but with a loving and kind energy.

Put the sugar, rice, and salt in the glass dish, and place the spoon on top, with the bowl of the spoon facing up. As you place the spoon, say:

I summon the powers of nourishment and protection so that my spoon may never be empty.

Leave the bowl somewhere out in the open, but also in a place where it will not be disturbed. Wash the spoon once a month and repeat the chant. After a year and a day, empty the bowl and repeat the spell with fresh ingredients.

Charlie Rainbow Wolf

November 14
Thursday

2nd ♈

☽ v/c 1:50 am

☽ → ♉ 1:59 am

Color of the day: White
Incense of the day: Jasmine

Family Love

L ove comes in many different
flavors. One of these is what the
ancient Greeks called *storge*, or familial
love. This is a subtype of platonic
love, which is based on affection
rather than sex or romance.

Storge takes as much care and
maintenance as romantic love, just
in different ways. Turn off your
electronics and pay attention to each
other. Shared meals, game nights,
and cuddle piles are all good. Pagan
families may work spells or rituals
together.

This work is sacred to Hestia, the
Greek goddess of home and hearth,
who also oversees family ties and a
happy home life. If you have a fireplace, that's the best place to set up
an altar to her; otherwise the kitchen
or living room is good. Include a
statue of Hestia, a symbol of fire, and
family photos. Dedicate the altar to
her with these words:

Hestia, goddess of happy homes,

*Bless this household and all
who dwell within it.*

*May we always love and
cherish one another.*

Elizabeth Barrette

NOTES:

 November 15
Friday

2nd ♉

☾ull Moon 4:28 pm

Color of the day: Purple
Incense of the day: Yarrow

Rhythm Ritual

This year's Drumming Day falls on a full moon—a great opportunity to recognize the power of percussive rhythm in ritual. Drums are among the most ancient of instruments and are still a driving force in rituals today the world over. They help us keep time, energize us, and unify our movements. Many people play drums at circles and events, but few recognize that it's important not only to make a noise but also to listen to what's happening around them. When we listen as we play, we connect to the heartbeat of the group and become one.

One of the best things about drums is that almost anything can be a percussive instrument. You don't need a fancy drum to make a beat. Buckets, pots, mugs, and even cauldrons can be drums, and by hitting them with chopsticks, wooden spoons, or other tools, we can make a variety of sounds.

Gather a small group together, each with an improvised drum. Choose one person to start and let them go for about one minute with a slow, steady beat. Add another drum "voice" when the next person feels comfortable and so on, until everyone is drumming. Experiment with where the energy takes you—it will build up and release naturally!

Laura Tempest Zakroff

NOTES:

November 16
Saturday

3rd ♉

☽ v/c 2:03 am

☽ → ♊ 2:09 am

Color of the day: Blue
Incense of the day: Rue

Pendulum Power Attunement

This is a great ritual to do when you know you want to engage in new self-care practices but you're not sure which ones would be most powerful for you.

To begin, relax and call on the Divine. Write the word *Home* on a piece of paper. Then ask yourself, "What area of my home can I bring into greater harmony?" Contemplate various areas of your home while checking in with your pendulum. When you get a "yes" answer, write the name of that area down. Ask for clarification as needed. (For example, ask whether you should clean, clear clutter, or redecorate.)

Next, write the word *Body*. Bring various health practices and body parts to mind while checking with your pendulum. Continue to check for specifics until you get an obvious and definite hit, like "yoga" or "more sleep." Record what you receive.

Write *Mind* next. Once again, check in with your pendulum about various topics and skills to research, and write down what you get.

Finally, write *Spirit* and look for various practices and modalities you could incorporate into your spiritual path.

Tess Whitehurst

Notes:

November 17
Sunday

3rd ♊

☽ v/c 11:09 pm

Color of the day: Orange
Incense of the day: Juniper

Crafting Peace

Potions have been a witch's tool since the beginning of time. Water is a great transmitter. It opens itself readily to infusing with herbs, and the spirits love to glide across it.

As harvest celebrations approach, and with them stress and anxiety, a good witch's potion is in order. This one is called Peace Water. It is simple to make on the surface, but for it to be effective, drawing on witchy skills is in order. The skills required are control of your thinking and the ability to transfer your special healing energies into the potion—no small task. With patience and willpower, the perfect Peace Water will be created today.

Gather your materials: an 8-ounce spray-top bottle, a tiny funnel, and 2.5 ounces each of orange flower water, lavender water, and rose water. If you do not have a bottle or funnel, you can use a stainless steel or Pyrex bowl. Use a stainless steel dipper or large spoon for stirring.

Clear your head before beginning to work. Deep breathing and silencing your devices is a must. Once you are calm and clearheaded, add the waters to the bowl, saying:

With this orange flower water, I ask spirit for energy. Ashe!

With this lavender water, I ask spirit for relaxing energy. Ashe!

With this rose water, I ask spirit for strength. Ashe!

Stir gently. Use the water when you feel anxious, depressed, or tapped out. You can spritz it over and around your head or add small portions to your bathwater.

Stephanie Rose Bird

NOTES:

 November 18
Monday

3rd ♊

☽ → ♋ 3:50 am

Color of the day: Silver
Incense of the day: Clary sage

Books and Us

The first book printed in English, Chaucer's *Canterbury Tales*, appeared on this date in 1476. It was printed and sold by William Caxton, a merchant who brought the first printing press to England.

Books printed on real paper seem to be disappearing today. Devices seem handier. Nevertheless, if our civilization is to survive, we need real books and libraries. Cast your circle and state your intention to protect books and libraries. Appeal to the goddesses and gods of wisdom:

*O Great and Wise Ones—
Seshat and Thoth,*

*Athena and Tir, Sarasvati
and Ogma—*

Step forward today.

*Bring your powers both
magical and practical,*

*And share those powers with
us who love and read books.*

*Help us tell the world about
library cards and*

*Great novels and the works
of philosophers,*

Works of history and social progress.

*Help us preserve our books about
magic and our holy days and rituals.*

So mote it be. So must it be!

Barbara Ardinger

NOTES:

November 19
Tuesday

3rd ♋

Color of the day: Gray
Incense of the day: Cinnamon

Gratitude Simmer Pot

With Thanksgiving right around the corner, now is the perfect time to bring the energies of gratitude and abundance into your home. A perfect way to do that is by filling your home with the sweet aroma of autumn. Enrich your senses and make your dwelling cozy by creating a simmer pot of your favorite aromatic autumn herbs and spices. We like to use citrus peels, star anise, cinnamon sticks, whole cloves, cardamom, rosemary, and sage. These can all be either dried or fresh. Add your combination to a pot of water and put on simmer. (Remember to keep an eye on the water level to avoid scorching the pot.) You can even write things you are grateful for on bay leaves and toss those in the pot. As the words blend into the water, imagine your home filling up with those sentiments.

Amanda Lynn & Jason Mankey

November 20
Wednesday

3rd ♋

☽ v/c 6:20 am
☽ → ♌ 8:51 am

Color of the day: White
Incense of the day: Lilac

Aye, Captain!

On this day in 1820, an eighty-ton sperm whale sank the Essex, a whaling ship from Nantucket, Massachusetts. This event was the inspiration for Herman Melville's famous fictional story *Moby Dick*. Nantucket is a beautiful, mystical, magical seaport. I once rode the ferry to Nantucket, and I'll never forget the experience. I clearly felt the energies of past lives upon me.

Are you the captain of your ship, or are you the crew? Do you command your voyage, or are you fighting fictional monsters that may thwart your success? Bring a spring upon 'er! Right your vessel so you may sail in the direction of your dreams.

For this spell you will need a bowl of water. Use your breath to blow upon the water, creating waves. When the water stills, say:

I am the wind, I am the captain of my ship. I hold steady, I hold the course. Though far away my sights may be, I have the power to manifest my destiny!

Najah Lightfoot

 **November 21**
Thursday

3rd ♌

☉ → ♐ 2:56 pm

Color of the day: Turquoise
Incense of the day: Nutmeg

Blow It Off Spell

Use this spell to shake off unpleasant feelings following stressful situations or interactions with hostile people. Go outside with a pinch of black pepper in your hand. Hold the pepper in your closed hand as you let any unpleasant thoughts and feelings flow freely into the spice. Try to step back and be an observer of these energies as you pour them into the pepper.

Once you're finished transferring the unwanted energies into the pepper, open your hand, close your eyes, and blow the pepper off your palm while visualizing that you are blowing away these unpleasant thoughts and emotions. Turn around and open your eyes. Don't look back in the direction that you scattered the pepper.

Melanie Marquis

November 22
Friday

3rd ♌

☽ v/c 8:15 am

☽ → ♍ 6:01 pm

4th Quarter 8:28 pm

Color of the day: Pink
Incense of the day: Mint

Seeing Clearly

The windows in your home allow literal *and* metaphorical light to enter. Both help us see more clearly, and in a metaphorical sense, light increases self-awareness and the ability to clearly perceive dynamics in the world around us. Giving your windows a magical cleaning boosts your inner and outer sight, helping you identify limiting patterns so you can embody your fullest potential.

In a spray bottle, prepare a window cleaner with 2 cups distilled water, ½ cup white vinegar, and 10 drops lemon essential oil. Holding the bottle in both hands, feel the energy of the sun cascading into your crown chakra and flowing down your arms and out through your hands into the bottle. Shake to combine. Spray your windows, wiping with a cloth as you say:

Welcome, Sun, into this home,
Shedding light on things unknown.

My sight is clear, my wisdom true.
The Light empowers all I do.

Melissa Tipton

November 23
Saturday

4th ♏

Color of the day: Indigo
Incense of the day: Sandalwood

A Spell Against Gossip and Slander

If you are the victim of gossip or slander, try this spell. You'll need a sheet from a newspaper and a pen. You'll also need a hoe or shovel. On the newspaper, write what has been said about you. You may write directly over the print. Now crumple the paper up with anger. Go to a secluded area away from your home. With the hoe or shovel, dig a small hole. Throw the crumpled newspaper into the hole. Grind it into the hole with anger. Cover the paper with soil. With your tool, tamp down the soil firmly as you say:

Gossip and slander, go rot.

Gossip and slander, you hurt me not!

Gossip and slander I smother.

*Gossip and slander, you'll
never hurt me or another!*

Walk away, hold your head up, and don't look back.

James Kambos

 # November 24
Sunday

4th ♏

Color of the day: Gold
Incense of the day: Hyacinth

Peaceful Home Spell

Before a big family gathering, perform this spell to keep things smooth and drama-free. Take a small bowl and fill it halfway with water. Add a pinch of sugar, a pinch of dried lavender, a pinch of dried rosemary, and a pinch of dried chamomile.

As you put all the ingredients together, allow yourself to feel peaceful and calm. Allow this to infuse your mixture. As you visualize the bowl glowing with a soft blue light, use the first two fingers of your dominant hand to mix these ingredients together. As you do this, say:

Peace, calm, love, and sweetness,

Getting along is the goal for today.

Peace, calm, love, and sweetness,

All is well, all is well, all is well.

Use this mixture to anoint the bottoms of all the chairs and the doorknobs. Toss the rest of the mixture out your front door, so all your guests will have to walk through it as they enter your home.

Phoenix LeFae & Gwion Raven

November 25
Monday

4th ♏

☽ v/c 12:35 am

☽ → ♎ 6:20 am

Color of the day: Ivory
Incense of the day: Narcissus

Sacred Self-Care Spell

Monday is associated with the moon, the home and family, nurturance, deep personal needs, and our habits and reactions. The moon represents the way we take care of ourselves daily—our sacred self-care.

Put on the kettle and boil some water. Find your favorite cup. Favorite items carry a high-vibrating energy. Place one fragrant tea bag in your cup. I love rooibos or apple spice tea with a bit of cinnamon. Scent is important.

When the water is boiling, pour it over the tea bag. Wrap your hands around the cup and "feel" the warmth. Say: *I am loved.*

Smell the aroma of the fragrant tea. *I am worthy.*

Look at the steam rising from your mug. *I am sacred.*

Take a small sip and taste the tea. *I am blessed.*

Throughout the week, take regular small breaks to make tea, attending to your deepest needs.

Dallas Jennifer Cobb

November 26
Tuesday

4th ♎

Color of the day: Scarlet
Incense of the day: Ylang-ylang

Embracing the Hermit

Today is the feast day of Basolus, a French Benedictine monk. He was known for being a hermit, so today we will work with the Hermit tarot card to capture wisdom. For this meditation you will need a piece of paper, a pen, and an image of the Hermit. You can use a card from your favorite tarot deck or an image from the internet.

Place the card or image in front of you where you can focus on its imagery and what it is trying to convey to you. Take a deep breath and relax your body. Study the card or image and write down anything important that you notice or that pops into your head. Close your eyes and hold the image of the Hermit in your mind. Walk along with him on his path and see if he gestures toward anything or shares with you an image that can help you on your own path. Add anything you discover to your notes.

Charlynn Walls

November 27
Wednesday

4th ♎

☽ v/c 4:14 am

☽ → ♏ 7:21 pm

Color of the day: Brown
Incense of the day: Marjoram

Steps for Success

R ed brick dust is powerful protection magic. It's easy to make
with a red brick, a hammer, and a
mortar and pestle—breaking up and
grinding down the brick—or it can be
purchased from magic shops online
or in person. This spell uses four
cups of hot water and a pinch each of
red brick dust, cinnamon, and brown
sugar. You'll also need a small bucket
or similar container, a scrubbing
brush, and a washcloth.

Put the hot water in the bucket and
add the dry ingredients. Mix well. Use
the scrubbing brush to wash a doorstep or threshold with this solution.
(If using this on a threshold, reduce
the quantity of water.) Scrub with
the brush in a spiral, going clockwise,
until all the mixture has been used.
Dry the doorstep or threshold with
the washcloth, starting on the outside
and moving inward. Envision favor-
able energy moving toward you as
you do so. This spell can be done at
any time but is particularly effective
on Wednesdays.

Charlie Rainbow Wolf

NOTES:

November 28
Thursday

4th ♏

Color of the day: Crimson
Incense of the day: Balsam

Thanksgiving Day

Thanksgiving Day

Thanksgiving Day is a time for celebrating abundance. The harvests have all come in. Livestock has been secured in the barns, and the surplus butchered for the fall and winter feasts. Families gather together in joy.

Consider focusing on traditional and local foods. The Three Sisters of corn, squash, and beans are the major agricultural crops commonly grown together by many farming tribes of Turtle Island/North America and thus traditionally featured in many feasts or harvest festivals. The Americas also gave rise to peppers, tomatoes, potatoes, sweet potatoes, wild rice, quinoa, sunflowers (including sunchokes), black walnuts, pecans, peanuts, American persimmon, cacao, vanilla, and maple syrup. Many classic dishes originated here, such as mashed potatoes, wild rice casserole, chili, cornbread, pumpkin pie, pecan pie, and chocolate cake. Three Sisters soup is delicious and filling. Put out birdseed or corn for All Our Relations so the animals can feast too.

Cooking your feast as a family gives you time to bond. When you sit down to eat, give thanks for the food and the ancestral farmers who developed these crops for us to enjoy. Name other things you appreciate, whether magical or practical. Acknowledge deities of field and forest.

Elizabeth Barrette

NOTES:

November 29
Friday

4th ♏

Color of the day: Rose
Incense of the day: Vanilla

A Protection Sphere of Vanquishing

A fellow mystical friend recently told me about (and gave permission to share) a unique protection spell that can be performed whenever one desires.

It's best to perform energetic shielding on a daily basis. As with all protection shields, regular upkeep and maintenance can go a long way. By reinforcing shields through visualization and spoken affirmation, the shields continue to be active both externally and unconsciously.

Simply close your eyes, breathe deeply, and visualize a glass-thin shield around you at arm's length. Every time you exhale, the shield becomes stronger. When ready, declare:

All good things are welcomed here,
and all that harms must disappear!

When negativity enters your sphere, know that it will bounce off the shield and dissolve. If you are aware that aggression, judgment, or anything you deem negative is being projected toward you—or if you believe it is—see it hitting the shield and instantly disintegrating into nothingness.

Raven Digitalis

November 30
Saturday

4th ♏

☽ v/c 1:19 am

☽ → ♐ 6:53 am

Color of the day: Blue
Incense of the day: Pine

Conjuring the Spirit of Citrine

Citrine, one of the birthstones of November, is named for lemon, which is reflected in its color. This stone is reminiscent of the sun and symbolically represents its cleansing power, energizing effect, and ability to elevate the mood. Citrine is also deeply associated with the solar plexus chakra. For this meditation you need to put one small piece of citrine in an ice cube cell. Cover it with spring water. Allow enough time for it to completely freeze. Take the citrine out of the freezer and pop it into your hand. Put in a glass.

Remove your clothing and lie down on a light blue towel or cloth. Place the ice-covered citrine on your solar plexus. This will be very cold, but be as still as possible and let it melt. As it melts, let it dissolve any evil thoughts that have been directed toward you and free up your imagination. Allow negativity to melt away and success to enter your soul through your solar plexus. Stay focused and your wishes will come to pass.

Stephanie Rose Bird

December

December features a palette of cool colors: white snow, silver icicles, evergreen, and, of course, blue—the bright cerulean sky on a clear, cold winter's day, or the deep navy velvet of the darkening nights, culminating on the longest night of the year, the winter solstice. This hue is reflected in December's birthstones: turquoise, zircon, tanzanite, and lapis. The notion of a stone representing each month has been linked to ayurvedic beliefs that suggest correspondences between the planets and crystals. It wasn't until the eighteenth century that associating stones with a birth month became a popular practice in the Western world.

Even if you weren't born in December, you can still tap into the power of this month's special stones. Zircon increases bone stability, which is good for moving over icy terrain. Use turquoise, a rain-making stone, to summon snow. Turquoise also heals and brings peace. Engage tanzanite's powers for psychic visions for the impending new year. Lapis—the mirror of the winter night sky, and a stone that can be found in the breastplate of the high priest—brings wisdom and awareness.

Natalie Zaman

December 1
Sunday

4ṭ ♐

New Moon 1:21 am

Color of the day: Amber
Incense of the day: Almond

Manifesting with holly

One of the most cherished abilities of the witch is to manifest wishes by setting a strong intent. One celestial aid to this type of work is the new moon, which just so happens to be gracing us today.

Dr. Bach's flower remedies encapsulate tiny portions of selected plants. The flower remedy we turn to today is fitting for the coming winter season—it is holly. This is one of the more beautiful and spiritually medicinal plants that exists. It is enveloped in rich traditions of folklore, mythology, and storytelling.

Today's work couldn't be a simpler way to harvest holly energy. You will obtain the Holly flower remedy. This Bach flower remedy is a small vial containing a tincture. Take the number of drops directed under your tongue three times a day. Like melting snow, anger, jealousy, suspicions, and judgments will magickally diminish, and you'll find that your heart feels kinder and lighter.

Stephanie Rose Bird

December 2
Monday

1st ♐

☽ v/c 10:47 am

☽ → ♑ 4:09 pm

Color of the day: Gray
Incense of the day: Lily

Letting Go Spell

Occasionally in life, it becomes necessary to let go of some aspect of ourselves. Maybe you are holding on to habits that no longer serve you. Perhaps your way of thinking has become outdated and your beliefs don't align with how you see your future. This spell uses a lock of your own hair. Hair has long been seen as a place where people carry their energy and life force. All you need is a cast-iron cauldron or fire-safe bowl and some matches or a lighter. Place a lock of your hair in the cauldron. Safely light the hair with the matches. As the hair burns, chant:

Goodbye, old self. Thank you.
Hello, new self. I am ready.

Alternatively, if you are letting go of a habit, say:

Goodbye, old habit. Thank you.
Welcome, new habit. I am ready.

Do not leave the burning hair unattended. Once the hair is fully burned up, clean out the cauldron with blessed water or salt water.

Phoenix LeFae & Gwion Raven

December 3
Tuesday

1st ♑

Color of the day: Maroon
Incense of the day: Ginger

Giving Connections

Today is Giving Tuesday. Held on the Tuesday after Thanksgiving, this holiday reminds us to think of those less fortunate. Turn your attention to deities of compassion, like Quan Yin, Eleos, and Clementia, or of generosity, such as the Charites (or Gratiae), the Vanir, and Lakshmi. Service to the gods is about more than just saying a prayer or casting a spell. It's about doing their work in this world, where human hands and hearts are well scaled for the tasks, while a divine touch is often a bit too much.

Today, manifest a compassionate or generous patron deity by serving food at a soup kitchen, taking a care package to a neighbor, inviting unemployed friends to dinner, donating to a food or clothing bank, and other charitable acts. Don't just think of these people as needy—think of them as people to form relationships with. The community you build may be there to support you when you need it someday. What you do returns to you three times over.

Elizabeth Barrette

December 4
Wednesday

1st ♑
☽ v/c 6:34 pm
☽ → ♒ 11:21 pm

Color of the day: Yellow
Incense of the day: Lilac

A Gratitude Jar

During the holiday festivities, we often get busy with what we need to do rather than taking time to be thankful for what's already been accomplished. I believe the road to abundance is not paved with gold; it's paved with gratitude. This is a gentle spell the whole family can do together. You'll need some colored paper, some pens, and a lidded jar.

At the end of the day, have everyone write down something they're thankful for and put it in the jar. In the past, our family has done this without discussion, just adding the papers, while other times we've done it over tea, talking about our choices.

Keep this up for the rest of the month. At the end of the year, gather together and open the jar, reading aloud what the papers say. This enables you not only to recall the good things that have surrounded you in the past, but also to create a thankful mindset as you enter a new month—or in this case, a new year. Outlook changes everything!

Charlie Rainbow Wolf

Page 239

December 5
Thursday

1st ♒︎

Color of the day: White
Incense of the day: Myrrh

Cleansing Divination Tools

This spell makes use of *all* your divination tools. As many Witches know, the herb mugwort is utilized frequently in spells both to cleanse tools and to open the third eye. Gather all your divination tools in one place, whether Tarot decks, scrying mirrors, crystal balls, dowsing rods, runes, or anything else.

Call upon your guides and guardians. Sit in a calm space with only candlelight or moonlight to illuminate it. Brew a very strong cup of mugwort tea and let it cool. Anoint all your divinatory tools with this tea. Place some on your brow. Take a sip of the tea to further align with the plant's essence. If possible, burn some mugwort to further cleanse the tools.

While doing all of this, say the following nine times whenever it feels right:

I open my eyes and cleanse all
these tools. I serve self and
others each time I use.

Raven Digitalis

December 6
Friday

1st ♒︎

☽ v/c 7:01 pm

Color of the day: Coral
Incense of the day: Orchid

A Cold Winter's Rest

In 1872, Victorian poet Christina Rossetti felt inspired to write "A Christmas Carol," a long poem that describes the world's terrible winter before the birth of Jesus. Read the first verse aloud to get the feeling:

In the bleak midwinter,
frosty wind made moan,

Earth stood hard as iron,
water like a stone;

Snow had fallen, snow on
snow, snow on snow,

In the bleak midwinter, long ago.

But while our winter may be cold, it is not bleak! We know the planet is naturally spinning into its season of rest. Many animals need to hibernate. Many trees need to store up their sap. Many plants need to refresh their roots. The land itself needs to rest before everything wakes up again. Instead of suffering in the cold, let's acknowledge it and celebrate it as our ancestors did. Cast a circle to bless the land and the plants and animals in their resting time. Now feed the birds and start planning your Saturnalia.

Barbara Ardinger

December 7
Saturday

$1st \, \approx$

$\mathbb{D} \rightarrow \mathcal{H}$ **4:49** am

Color of the day: Brown
Incense of the day: Sandalwood

Candle Love

Candle Day is celebrated every year on the first Saturday in December. There are many candle spells available in this book and elsewhere, so I'm not going to give you another one. Instead, here are some ways to share the candle love, especially if you're looking for some fun gift ideas for friends and family.

You can, of course, make your own batch of candles from soy, beeswax, or paraffin if you're up to the task. But if you don't have the time, space, or materials for making candles, here are some ways to take generic store-purchased candles to a new level:

1. Choose a theme and color for the year to come (such as healing, prosperity, love, etc.).

2. Carve a sigil or symbol that embodies your theme into each candle.

3. Anoint/dress the candles with an oil or tincture that connects with your theme.

4. Write up a small explanation of your candle spell on parchment or pretty paper.

5. Wrap the candles in tissue paper to protect them and place in a fabric bag for gifting.

Laura Tempest Zakroff

NOTES:

December 8
Sunday

1st ♓

2nd Quarter 10:27 am

Color of the day: Yellow
Incense of the day: Marigold

Salamander Spirit

Salamanders are the elemental guardians of fire. While fire has the potential to do great harm, it also has the capacity to provide energy and renewal. The salamander knows the difference and finds a balance between the extremes. Today being a Sunday allows us to tap into the energies surrounding this creature and channel its spirit.

You will need an incense such as dragon's blood or patchouli. Light the incense in a heatproof container or vessel. Let the incense move over you. Take your hands and direct the smoke over yourself while saying:

As flame and smoke arise, let me capture the energy and brave courage of the salamander.

Repeat this verse three times and finish with a deep breath.

Charlynn Walls

December 9
Monday

2nd ♓

☽ v/c 3:45 am

☽ → ♈ 8:38 am

Color of the day: White
Incense of the day: Neroli

Shrug It Off

When you're feeling stressed or you'd like to connect more deeply with your body, find a place where you won't be disturbed for five minutes. Lie on your back on a rug or carpet. You want a firmer surface (so don't do this in bed) but with enough padding that you feel comfortable. Bend your knees and plant your feet on the ground a comfortable distance from your hips. Take a few moments to focus on your breathing, gradually lengthening each inhale and exhale. Close your eyes and allow your attention to move inward.

Keeping your shoulders resting on the ground (don't lift them toward the ceiling), slowly shrug them up toward your ears, exaggerating the movement. Get a sense of which muscles are engaging to generate this movement. Now, very slowly, release your shoulders back to the starting point, bit by bit. Try doing this to the count of ten, feeling the engaged muscles gradually releasing. You can repeat this three times, and with each round, visualize your energy

unspooling, loosening, and returning to its natural flow.

Melissa Tipton

NOTES:

 **December 10**
Tuesday

2nd ♈

☽ v/c 5:13 pm

Color of the day: Red
Incense of the day: Cedar

healthy habit
Empowerment Ritual

It's a great day to magically empower a healthy new habit, like getting more sleep, eating more vegetables, or exercising more regularly. (Why wait for New Year's?) First, safely light a red candle and some cinnamon incense. Relax your body and center your mind. Call on a divinity of your choice. Next, in the present tense, write down a desired habit in a journal or notebook, such as "I get at least seven hours of deep sleep per night."

Now get creative and write down some fun ways you could immediately support this new habit. Staying with the sleep example, you might think of ways to make your bed more comfortable and your bedroom more restful. Also list adjacent habits that will support your primary habit, such as (in the case of sleep) regular exercise and limiting screen time at night. Now conjure up a sense of excitement for all these positive changes. Thank the divinity, extinguish the candle and incense, and get started on your new habit today.

Tess Whitehurst

December 11
Wednesday

2nd ♈

☽ → ♉ 10:55 am

Color of the day: Brown
Incense of the day: Honeysuckle

Yuletide Candle Divination

Bleigiessen (which translates as "lead pouring") is an old German Yuletide tradition where lead in a spoon is heated up over a candle flame and then poured into cool water. The shapes of the lead are then interpreted to see what the new year will bring.

Because heating up lead feels both messy and dangerous, in our house we have adapted this tradition using candles. Instead of heating up lead, pillar candles are lit and the wax is allowed to drip into a large bowl of water. The cooled pieces of wax are then interpreted to catch a glimpse of our futures.

The best type of candle for this work is a long pillar candle, which will comfortably keep your hands far away from the candle flame. Be sure not to use "dripless" candles for this form of divination, since the drips are the most important part! Yuletide candle pouring can be done alone or with friends. It makes for a great holiday activity.

Amanda Lynn & Jason Mankey

December 12
Thursday

2nd ♉

Color of the day: Purple
Incense of the day: Carnation

Manifestation Spell

Use this spell to manifest a physical resource. Find a bare patch of ground and use a stick to scratch the shape of a pentacle into the dirt. Invite the four elements and the spirits of the land to enter into the space of the pentacle. Open your mind and extend your awareness into the surrounding environment. Do you sense any spirits that dwell there, any spirits tied to the land, any guardians or keepers of the location? If so, acknowledge them and express your respect and gratitude, then tell them directly what you need. Think clearly of the physical object you seek to hold in your hands. If you don't sense any spirits around or you're not certain, touch the center of the pentacle you scratched in the dirt as you think of the resource you need. You could say:

*Spirits of the land, rulers of the
night and day. Put this in my sight!
Bring this to me right away!*

Keep your eyes open, take advantage of any good opportunities, and expect to have the resource you seek (or the means to obtain it) manifest quickly.

Melanie Marquis

December 13
Friday

2nd ♉

☽ v/c 7:39 am

☽ → ♊ 12:22 pm

Color of the day: Rose
Incense of the day: Vanilla

holiday Protection Spell

Many of us travel over the holidays, gathering with family to celebrate. Let's use the power of Friday the 13th to cast a holiday protection spell. Friday is Venus's day, a day to attract beauty, comfort, luxury, and goodness to you. Venus governs love and romance, desires and passion. It also rules what you value and how you relate to others, and 13 is Venus's lucky number. Say:

I call on Venus to protect and guide.
May her pleasures always abide.

May thirteen further bless
all my people with happiness.

Venus, gorgeous, bright, and clear,
draw your protective energy near.

Wrap me in your loving arms
and keep me safe, happy, and warm.

Because Venus rules this time and place,
I embody her feminine grace.

May she bless all festivities.
Venus, protect and guide me, please.

So mote it be.

Dallas Jennifer Cobb

December 14
Saturday

2nd ♊

Color of the day: Gray
Incense of the day: Rue

Relief from holiday Stress

This time of year can leave us feeling frazzled, impatient, anxious, ill-tempered, or even depressed. We can feel a lot of pressure at this time of year, which is the exact opposite of what this season is supposedly about. Many people can't wait for the holidays to be over, whether they celebrate them or not. This spell gives you permission to chill out amid the stress. You will need:

- Comfy clothes
- A white candle
- A fireproof candleholder
- Your favorite calming essential oil or relaxing scent
- Soft, gentle music
- A place where you will not be disturbed

Put on your comfy clothes and light your candle in the holder. Anoint yourself with your favorite calming scent, or simply inhale the aroma. Play your choice of soft, calming music. Allow yourself to be in this space until you feel relaxed. Extinguish the candle when done. Repeat as necessary.

Najah Lightfoot

December 15
Sunday

2nd ♊

Full Moon 4:02 am

☽ v/c 9:32 am

☽ → ♋ 2:21 pm

Color of the day: Gold
Incense of the day: Juniper

Pulling the Year Forward

This spell is best performed on the last full moon of the year. Here is what you'll need:

- A small Mason jar with a lid
- Water to fill the jar
- Quartz crystal pebbles or points

On the day of the full moon, gather water from a spring, river, ocean, or other free-running source of water. Rainwater or tap water will also work. Put the quartz pebbles or points in the jar and fill with the water. Seal the jar and place it in a special place, like on an altar. As it becomes dark and the moon begins to rise, take the lid off and place the jar outside. As the water begins to collect the moon's energy, think back over the past year. Remember all the joyous times. Name them, speak them out loud, and say:

*I pull this joy into the new year.
Let these crystals focus my energy,
bringing joy and happiness with
me. Let this moon water be a
reminder of happy times.*

If hard times come your way, open the jar and anoint yourself with your magickal tools with this water. Safety note: It's best not to drink this water.

Phoenix LeFae & Gwion Raven

NOTES:

December 16
Monday

3rd ♋

Color of the day: Silver
Incense of the day: Clary sage

Stress-Free Traveler Spell

No matter when you get on a plane, it often feels like all the bin space has already been claimed by your fellow passengers. To make sure we can always get our bags in the bins, we carry sachets for luck and success in all our carry-on luggage.

To make the sachet, you'll need a small piece of fabric, a piece of string, and a few dried herbs from your kitchen pantry. You can use whatever herbs you want here (be sure they are dried!), but we recommend basil, rosemary, bay leaves, chamomile, and cloves, because you are likely to already have a couple of these at your house. Crush all the herbs up and place them on your piece of fabric. Lift the four corners of the fabric up and tie your sachet shut while saying:

My journeys shall be easy and stress-free.

All the space I need shall come to me!

Place one sachet in every bag for which you need overhead space.

Amanda Lynn & Jason Mankey

December 17
Tuesday

3rd ♋

☽ v/c 1:33 pm

☽ → ♌ 6:39 pm

Color of the day: Gray
Incense of the day: Basil

Stay Calm Spell

This ritual will help you cope with those last-minute holiday nerves. Perform it first thing in the morning. Begin by standing and facing east. Ground and center, then say:

I will watch my words,
I will watch what I say,

I am perfect calm,
I am perfect peace,

Today and every day.

Still facing east, raise your power (dominant) hand and visualize a blue light streaming from it. Begin to turn clockwise, still seeing the blue light. When you return to your original position, lower your power hand. The blue light will remain with you throughout the day. As you go about your day, if you find yourself in a stressful situation, remember your Words of Power and your shield of blue light. You will make the right choices and say the right thing. You may even see the blue light at a time like this. You'll make it through the rest of the holiday season just fine.

James Kambos

December 18
Wednesday

3rd ♌

Color of the day: White
Incense of the day: Lavender

Cookies for the Queen of Heaven

This is Bake Cookies Day. Have you heard the term "Cakes for the Queen of Heaven" before? Many Pagan traditions included one or more days for baking special cakes, cookies, or other treats for their goddess—or god, as in Egypt it was for Osiris.

Now is a perfect time to make Pagan cookies. Find cookie cutters shaped like pentagrams, deer, cats, trees, stars, goddesses, gods, or whatever other themes suit your patron(s). You can also make round cookies and write runes or blessings on them with icing. Nuts or seeds work well for dedicating cookies to a god, and dried fruit for an orchard deity. As you work, charge them with positive energy by saying:

Cookies for the Queen of Heaven,

Cookies for the King of Earth,

Cookies for my friends and family,

In the season of our mirth!

Once done, you can serve the cookies for a celebratory feast or use them during the cakes and ale portion of a ritual.

Elizabeth Barrette

December 19
Thursday

3rd ♌

Color of the day: Turquoise
Incense of the day: Mulberry

A Pre-Yule Invigoration Flame

Can you believe it's almost the Winter Solstice? Also called Yule, Midwinter, and many other names, this is a sacred time for those of us who walk in alignment with the seasons. (For folks in the Southern Hemisphere, it is currently approaching Midsummer.)

Because we are soon to formerly welcome back the Holy Sun/Son at this time, let's put a little fire in our step to amp us up in preparation!

At nightfall, simply light a candle of any color. (Black, white, and fire colors are ideal.) When alone and all feels calm, take deep breaths and admire the flame. Declare:

Approaching Yule, I'm so excited;
the sacred flame is now ignited!

Briefly touch your right hand to the flame and then touch all your chakra points. Jump over the candle if you wish. Let it safely burn out after any additional prayers or rebirth-centered magick has been completed.

Raven Digitalis

December 20
Friday

3rd ♌

☽ v/c 12:19 am

☽ → ♍ 2:37 am

Color of the day: Pink
Incense of the day: Mint

To Freeze Time

At this time of year, time often seems to be running short, because there is so much to do before the festivities of the new year. This spell will help you stretch what little time you have so that you can accomplish more. You'll need a pen, some small pieces of paper, an ice cube tray, and your kitchen freezer.

Write down what you still need to do this year. Be careful how you word this. For example, you don't want to write "present for Mary," because that could freeze the energy in a way where you would never get her present finished! Instead, write things like "more time in the kitchen" or "more time for art."

When you have written down what you wish to freeze, put the pieces of paper in the ice tray compartments, fill the tray with water, and put it in your freezer. This will help you freeze time so that you can get everything accomplished. Once the urgency has passed, thaw the ice and dispose of the papers.

Charlie Rainbow Wolf

December 21
Saturday

3rd ♍

☉ → ♑ 4:21 am

Color of the day: Blue
Incense of the day: Ivy

Yule – Winter Solstice

The Mysterious Lessons of Winter

In many locales there is a definite chill in the air. We crave warmth, color, and brightness, but often we see and feel the opposite. Today is the shortest day of the year. Witches realize the age-old battle between the Oak King and the Holly King is being acted out, ultimately leading to renewal and rebirth.

You can savor the stories of olden times, but participating in the drama of the day is even better. Dress your home for Yule! Gather holly, cedar, and pine clippings and set them out in a large circle on your dining room table. Follow the circular shape, inside and out, with tall green, white, and red pillar candles in holders. In the center, place an edible Yule log. (You can pick one up at a bakery or find a recipe online.) Invite guests to take in the symbols and scents of the Yule season with you. Light all the candles. Sip some wassail, nibble your goodies, and savor the mysterious lessons of winter.

Stephanie Rose Bird

December 22
Sunday

3rd ♏

☽ v/c 8:27 am

☽ → ♎ 2:08 pm

4th Quarter 5:18 pm

Color of the day: Orange
Incense of the day: Frankincense

Be Like Scrooge
(the Next Morning)

S ometimes abundance is more than your checkbook. People who seem poor often have hidden riches that are not merely financial, and people who seem fabulously wealthy are sometimes discovered to be poor at heart. Consider what Ebenezer Scrooge's night of lessons taught him. Next morning:

> He became as good a friend, as good a master, and as good a man, as the good old city knew…. Some people laughed to see the alteration in him, but he let them laugh, and little heeded them; for he was wise enough to know that nothing ever happened on this globe, for good, at which some people did not have their fill of laughter…. His own heart laughed: and that was quite enough for him.

Cast your circle and set your checkbook on your altar. Ask it how it defines and rules your life. Ask it how you can find abundance that is not tied to money. Resolve to be like the new, reformed Scrooge. Be generous and laugh at the skeptical world.

Barbara Ardinger

NOTES:

December 23
Monday

4th ♎

Color of the day: Lavender
Incense of the day: Hyssop

Fertility Spell

Sometimes nature needs a helping hand. There are individuals and couples who want to conceive and may need an extra magical push to help them along the way. Today, with the energies of the moon, we will work to increase fertility. Lunar energies are all about the feminine and potential. We will be working on increasing the potential for a new life to be created.

You will need a small egg-shaped object to symbolize the creation of life and serve as a focal point. The object could be made of wood, stone, or crystal. Once you have selected the object, rub it on the abdomen of the person trying to conceive (whose consent you have asked for and received) in a clockwise motion. As you do so, say aloud:

Symbol of fertility, bring a
child into being. This child
will be wanted and loved.

Charlynn Walls

December 24
Tuesday

4th ♎
☽ v/c 5:44 am

Color of the day: White
Incense of the day: Cinnamon

Christmas Eve

Offering of Thanks

As the year winds to a close, leaving food offerings to the spirits who have helped you on your journey over the past twelve months is a wonderful way to end the season with gratitude, feeding your relationships with unseen allies. For a liquid offering, you might choose milk sweetened with honey; cider, beer, or wine; or a tea made from herbs that have special significance to you. For food, little cookies, cakes, or bread; fresh or dried fruit; or nuts and candies work well. If you have pets, you can leave the offerings in a closed room.

Before bed, arrange the offerings in a spot that feels meaningful to you, imbuing the food with the energy of love as you do so. Feel free to decorate the area with crystals and perhaps an LED candle or two. Write out a list, however short or long you'd like, of what you're grateful for. Read it aloud, envisioning love and gratitude beaming outward to your spirit allies. Then place the list next to the offering.

Melissa Tipton

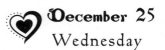

December 25
Wednesday

4th ♍︎

☽ → ♏︎ 3:06 am

Color of the day: Topaz
Incense of the day: Bay laurel

**Christmas Day — hanukkah begins
at sundown (ends Jan. 2)**

holiday Unity Candles

Christmas this year is especially poignant, as it occurs on the first night of Hanukkah, which begins at sundown. For this spell you'll need five chime candles with holders. (The colors are up to you.) Wait for the sun to set and find a place in your home to set your candles that resonates with you, such as an altar or mantelpiece. As you set your candles down, say:

*On this dark and holy night, a
night shared by so many, I share
the five energies of love, peace,
unity, belonging, and hope.*

*I seek these qualities within myself
and in this world. Blessed be.*

With each candle you light, say the names of the five energies outlined above, and stop to think about how you can better manifest those powers in your life and the lives of those around you. As the candles burn, reflect on the qualities that unite us as people. Extinguish the candles when you're done.

Amanda Lynn & Jason Mankey

December 26
Thursday

4th ♏︎

Color of the day: Green
Incense of the day: Balsam

**Kwanzaa begins (ends Jan. 1) —
Boxing Day (Canada & UK)**

Moving Forward

The end of the year is near. On this day, some people may begin the celebration of Kwanzaa, or they may celebrate Boxing Day if they live in Canada or the UK. Others may be resting, feasting on leftovers, or spending the day watching their favorite movies or TV shows. Some may be going for a long winter hike or sitting still in nature. It is truly one of those days to let go and be, and we're blessed that this day falls during the waning moon cycle, which is a period for letting go of things that no longer serve us.

Tonight, if possible, go outside. Gaze at the stars and contemplate the vastness of the universe. Know that you stand in the crossroads of time. Perhaps you'll see a shooting star or feel the mysteries of the divine. Lift your hands to the sky and say:

Thank you. Blessed be.

Najah Lightfoot

December 27
Friday

4th ♏

☽ v/c 9:24 am

☽ → ♐ 2:46 pm

Color of the day: White
Incense of the day: Rose

Worth It Spell

Time off from work and holiday pay? That's something to celebrate! Today, as you get dressed, wear some of your favorite clothes.

With each garment that you put on, quietly affirm: *I am worth it.*

Black cotton bikini underwear with lace: *I am worth it.*

Perfectly fitting, soft T-back bra: *I am worth it.*

Comfy curvy-fit black jeans: *I am worth it.*

A pink long-sleeve cotton T-shirt: *I am worth it.*

A sensuously soft black turtleneck cashmere sweater: *I am worth it.*

Hand-knit, multi-colored socks: *I am worth it.*

Pearl earrings and a single-pearl drop necklace: *I am worth it.*

Your favorites will be different from mine. Favorite clothing can uplift and empower us. As we dress up in our favorite clothes, our self-worth and self-esteem spiral up.

Dallas Jennifer Cobb

December 28
Saturday

4th ♐

Color of the day: Indigo
Incense of the day: Pine

Deep Renewal and Reset

This nighttime self-care ritual will help you recharge your batteries. First, clean and clear clutter from your bedroom. Also cleanse the energy in your bedroom with white sage smoke or aromatherapy spray, or another herbal smoke or spray of your choice. Shower or bathe. Then brush your teeth, comb your hair, and otherwise care for your body according to your preference. Safely light your bedroom with candles. Put on your comfiest pajamas and some relaxing music. Sit comfortably on your bed. Close your eyes, breathe deeply, and relax. Say:

Great Goddess, thank you for helping me sleep deeply and restfully tonight. Thank you for sending me magical dreams of healing so that I awake in the morning refreshed and renewed.

Now imagine that you are held in a pillar of indigo light. See or sense that light completely surrounding you and filling you. Breathe it in and out, and let it relax both your body and your mind. When you feel ready, extinguish the candles and go to sleep.

Tess Whitehurst

December 29
Sunday

4th ♐

☽ v/c 6:34 pm

☽ → ♑ 11:37 pm

Color of the day: Amber
Incense of the day: Heliotrope

A hope Chest

Have you accomplished everything you wanted to this year? If you want to keep your wishes organized in a magical way, create a hope chest. In it you put photos, drawings you create, or even a small toy representing the things you are hoping for.

First, go to a craft shop and purchase a box. You'll probably want a plain one you can decorate. Next, pick out any supplies you may need, such as paints, markers, glitter, etc. Also have on hand some dried lavender or a lavender sachet.

Now begin to decorate your hope chest. Remember to have fun! You want good vibes to surround your chest. When done, scatter the lavender or place the lavender sachet in the bottom of the box. Lavender draws happiness and good fortune, and that's what we want. Lastly, begin filling your chest with tokens of the hopes and dreams you have: a new home, a car, a new career—anything you wish. During the coming year, add or remove things as your hopes change.

James Kambos

December 30
Monday

4th ♑

New Moon 5:27 pm

Color of the day: Gray
Incense of the day: Rosemary

New Moon, New Start Spell

Use this spell to help you let go of baneful people or bad habits. Scoop a few spoonfuls of dirt from near your property and place in a small bowl. Stir the dirt around with your fingertips as you think of the harmful people or habits you wish to cut out of your life. Then transport the dirt to a crossroads and dump it in the middle of the intersection as you say:

I leave this here to get lost forever!
I turn my back and walk away!

Turn around and walk away, and don't look back. As soon as possible after casting the spell, sprinkle your hands and the bowl with salt, then rinse thoroughly with cool water. Do all you can to keep your commitment to leave the person or habit behind. This spell will help you find the strength and confidence to take the actions necessary to free yourself safely. Depending on the situation, such actions might include seeking outside support.

Melanie Marquis

December 31
Tuesday

1st ♑

Color of the day: Scarlet
Incense of the day: Bayberry

New Year's Eve

New Year's Braid

New Year's Eve marks the transition from the old year to the new, which makes it a great time to weave in new possibilities for a prosperous year to come.

Collect three narrow ribbons or some embroidery floss in the following colors (about one foot of each):

- Black (to represent the wisdom you've gained this past year)

- White (to signify new opportunities to come in the new year)

- Green or gold (to call forth growth and prosperity)

Knot the three cords together at one end, leaving a little tail so you can tape the length down for easier braiding. As you braid the cords together, say:

From wisdom true and old

To future bright and gold,

On this eve I weave with three.

Fortune be, new and bold!

Knot the loose ends together so your braid holds, then tie it around your front door knob. When you open the door to the new year, the braid will be there to remind you of good things to come.

Laura Tempest Zakroff

NOTES:

Daily Magical Influences

Each day is ruled by a planet that possesses specific magical influences:

Monday (Moon): peace, healing, caring, psychic awareness, purification

Tuesday (Mars): passion, sex, courage, aggression, protection

Wednesday (Mercury): conscious mind, study, travel, divination, wisdom

Thursday (Jupiter): expansion, money, prosperity, generosity

Friday (Venus): love, friendship, reconciliation, beauty

Saturday (Saturn): longevity, exorcism, endings, homes, houses

Sunday (Sun): healing, spirituality, success, strength, protection

Lunar Phases

The lunar phase is important in determining best times for magic.

The new moon is when the moon and sun are conjunct each other. It corresponds to all new beginnings and is the best time to start a project.

The waxing moon (from the new moon to the full moon) is the ideal time for magic to draw things to you.

The full moon is when the sun and moon are opposite each other. It is the time of greatest power.

The waning moon (from the full moon to the new moon) is a time for study, meditation, and little magical work (except magic designed to banish harmful energies).

Astrological Symbols

The Sun	☉	Aries	♈
The Moon	☽	Taurus	♉
Mercury	☿	Gemini	♊
Venus	♀	Cancer	♋
Mars	♂	Leo	♌
Jupiter	♃	Virgo	♍
Saturn	♄	Libra	♎
Uranus	♅	Scorpio	♏
Neptune	♆	Sagittarius	♐
Pluto	♇	Capricorn	♑
		Aquarius	♒
		Pisces	♓

The Moon's Sign

The moon's sign is a traditional consideration for astrologers. The moon continuously moves through each sign in the zodiac, from Aries to Pisces. The moon influences the sign it inhabits, creating different energies that affect our daily lives.

Aries: Good for starting things but lacks staying power. Things occur rapidly but quickly pass. People tend to be argumentative and assertive.

Taurus: Things begun now do last, tend to increase in value, and become hard to alter. Brings out an appreciation for beauty and sensory experience.

Gemini: Things begun now are easily changed by outside influence. Time for shortcuts, communications, games, and fun.

Cancer: Stimulates emotional rapport between people. Pinpoints need, supports growth and nurturance. Tend to domestic concerns.

Leo: Draws emphasis to the self, to central ideas or institutions, away from connections with others and emotional needs. People tend to be melodramatic.

Virgo: Favors accomplishment of details and commands from higher up. Focus on health, hygiene, and daily schedules.

Libra: Favors cooperation, compromise, social activities, beautification of surroundings, balance, and partnership.

Scorpio: Increases awareness of psychic power. Favors activities requiring intensity and focus. People tend to brood and become secretive under this moon sign.

Sagittarius: Encourages flights of imagination and confidence. This moon sign is adventurous, philosophical, and athletic. Favors expansion and growth.

Capricorn: Develops strong structure. Focus on traditions, responsibilities, and obligations. A good time to set boundaries and rules.

Aquarius: Rebellious energy. Time to break habits and make abrupt change. Personal freedom and individuality are the focus.

Pisces: The focus is on dreaming, nostalgia, intuition, and psychic impressions. A good time for spiritual or philanthropic activities.

Glossary of Magical Terms

altar: A table that holds magical tools as a focus for spell workings.

athame: A ritual knife used to direct personal power during workings or to symbolically draw diagrams in a spell. It is rarely, if ever, used for actual physical cutting.

aura: An invisible energy field surrounding a person. The aura can change color depending on the state of the individual.

balefire: A fire lit for magical purposes, usually outdoors.

casting a circle: The process of drawing a circle around oneself to seal out unfriendly influences and raise magical power. It is the first step in a spell.

censer: An incense burner. Traditionally a censer is a metal container, filled with incense, that is swung on the end of a chain.

censing: The process of burning incense to spiritually cleanse an object.

centering yourself: To prepare for a magical rite by calming and centering all of your personal energy.

chakra: One of the seven centers of spiritual energy in the human body, according to the philosophy of yoga.

charging: To infuse an object with magical power.

circle of protection: A circle cast to protect oneself from unfriendly influences.

crystals: Quartz or other stones that store cleansing or protective energies.

deosil: Clockwise movement, symbolic of life and positive energies.

deva: A divine being according to Hindu beliefs; a devil or evil spirit according to Zoroastrianism.

direct/retrograde: Refers to the motion of a planet when seen from the earth. A planet is "direct" when it appears to be moving forward from the point of view of a person on the earth. It is "retrograde" when it appears to be moving backward.

dowsing: To use a divining rod to search for a thing, usually water or minerals.

dowsing pendulum: A long cord with a coin or gem at one end. The pattern of its swing is used to answer questions.

dryad: A tree spirit or forest guardian.

fey: An archaic term for a magical spirit or a fairylike being.

gris-gris: A small bag containing charms, herbs, stones, and other items to draw energy, luck, love, or prosperity to the wearer.

mantra: A sacred chant used in Hindu tradition to embody the divinity invoked; it is said to possess deep magical power.

needfire: A ceremonial fire kindled at dawn on major Wiccan holidays. It was traditionally used to light all other household fires.

pentagram: A symbolically protective five-pointed star with one point upward.

power hand: The dominant hand; the hand used most often.

scry: To predict the future by gazing at or into an object such as a crystal ball or pool of water.

second sight: The psychic power or ability to foresee the future.

sigil: A personal seal or symbol.

smudge/smudge stick: To spiritually cleanse an object by waving smoke over and around it. A smudge stick is a bundle of several incense sticks.

wand: A stick or rod used for casting circles and as a focus for magical power.

widdershins: Counterclockwise movement, symbolic of negative magical purposes, sometimes used to disperse negative energies.

About the Authors

Barbara Ardinger, PhD (English—mostly Shakespeare), has been writing for the Llewellyn annuals since 2004. Her work has also been published in devotionals to Isis, Athena, and Brigid. She is the author of *Secret Lives*, a novel about crones and other magical folk, and *Pagan Every Day*, a unique daybook of daily meditations. Her other books include *Goddess Meditations* (the first-ever book—published by Llewellyn—of meditations focusing solely on goddesses) and *Finding New Goddesses* (a parody of goddess encyclopedias). Her blogs and/or stories appeared every month for over a decade on Feminism & Religion, https://feminismandreligion.com, where she was a regular Pagan contributor. She lives in Long Beach, California, with Schroedinger, her rescued calico cat.

Elizabeth Barrette has been involved with the Pagan community for more than thirty-three years. She served as the managing editor of *PanGaia* for eight years and the dean of studies at the Grey School of Wizardry for four years. She has written columns on beginning and intermediate Pagan practice, Pagan culture, and Pagan leadership. Her book *Composing Magic: How to Create Magical Spells, Rituals, Blessings, Chants, and Prayers* explains how to combine writing and spirituality. She lives in central Illinois, where she has done much networking with Pagans in her area, such as coffeehouse meetings and open sabbats. Her other public activities include Pagan picnics and science fiction conventions. She enjoys magical crafts, historical religions, and gardening for wildlife. Her other writing fields include speculative fiction, gender studies, and social and environmental issues. Visit her blog, *The Wordsmith's Forge* (https://ysabetwordsmith.dreamwidth. org), or website, *PenUltimate Productions* (http://penultimateproductions. weebly.com). Her coven site, which includes extensive Pagan materials, is *Greenhaven: A Pagan Tradition* (http://greenhaventradition.weebly.com).

Stephanie Rose Bird is a practicing Green Witch and Hoodoo. She is a magick maker and is passionate about African diasporic spirituality, folklore, and mythology. Bird contributes to several of the Llewellyn annuals and writes a column for *Witches & Pagans*. She is the author of seven books, including *Sticks, Stones, Roots & Bones* and her most recent, *The Healing Power of African American Spirituality* (Weiser) and *365 Days of Hoodoo: Daily Rootwork, Mojo & Conjuration* (Llewellyn). She also contributed to *Llewellyn's Complete Book of North American Folk Magic*. Bird is an avid swimmer, artist, herbalist, aromatherapist, mom, and wife. Visit her

website, www.stephanierosebird.com. Follow her on Instagram @s.r.bird, Twitter @stephanierosebi, and Facebook at https://www.facebook.com /stephanierosebirdauthor.

Dallas Jennifer Cobb lives an embodied life. Studying somatics, trauma therapy, astrology, and magic, she spends time in nature, where all of these converge. A Pagan, mother, feminist, writer, and animal lover, she has conjured a sustainable lifestyle with an abundance of time, energy, wisdom, and money. Widely published, she writes about what she knows: trauma and neurological recovery, magic, herbs, astrology, deep ecology, and vibrant sustainability. She is eager to connect with like-minded beings. Contact her at jennifer.cobb@live.com.

Raven Digitalis (Hawaii/Montana) is the author of *The Empath's Oracle* deck, *Esoteric Empathy, The Everyday Empath, A Witch's Shadow Magick Compendium, Planetary Spells & Rituals,* and *Goth Craft.* Originally trained in Georgian Witchcraft, Raven has been an Earth-based practitioner since 1999, a Priest since 2003, a Freemason since 2012, and an empath all his life. He holds a degree in cultural anthropology from the University of Montana, co-operated a nonprofit Pagan temple for sixteen years, and is a professional Tarot reader, DJ, card-carrying magician, and animal rights advocate. Feel free to contact him for signed books, professional Tarot services (sliding-scale), and other occult/spiritual services. Visit www .ravendigitalis.com or www.facebook.com/ravendigitalis.

James Kambos is a writer and an artist from Ohio. He writes articles and essays about folk magic, occult lore, and living a magical life. He raises many wildflowers and herbs. When not writing, he paints in an American primitive style. He holds a degree in social sciences and geography from Ohio University.

Phoenix LeFae (she/her) started on the path of Witchcraft in 1993. She has trained in several Witchcraft traditions, always looking to learn more and expand her knowledge. She is initiated in the Reclaiming Tradition of Witchcraft, the Avalon Druid Order, and Gardnerian Wicca. Phoenix is a professional Witch, author, reader, teacher, and owner of the witchy shop Milk & Honey in Sebastopol, CA (www.Milk-and-Honey.com).

Najah Lightfoot is a multi-award-winning author of *Powerful Juju: Goddesses, Music & Magic for Comfort, Guidance & Protection* and the best-selling *Good Juju: Mojos, Rites & Practices for the Magical Soul.* She is

a regular contributor to the Llewellyn annuals and a contributor to *The Library of Esoterica, Volume III: Witchcraft*. Her magickal staff is part of the permanent collection at the Buckland Museum of Witchcraft & Magick, located in Cleveland, Ohio. Najah is a fellow of the Sojourner Truth Leadership Circle, sponsored by Auburn Seminary. She lives in Denver, Colorado, where the blue skies and the power of the Rocky Mountains uplift and fill her soul. She can be found online at www.instagram.com /NajahLightfoot, www.facebook.com/NajahLightfoot.

Amanda Lynn has been dedicated to Witchcraft since childhood. For thirteen years she was a priestess in her local community, where she developed a penchant for ritual creation and spellcraft. These days, when she's not taking long walks in cemeteries or circling with one of her covens, she studies aromatherapy, esoterica, and intuitive magic. You can often find her checking out new music and wearing lots of glitter.

Jason Mankey is a third-degree Gardnerian High Priest and helps run two Witchcraft covens in the San Francisco Bay Area with his wife, Ari. He is a popular speaker at Pagan and Witchcraft events across North America and Great Britain and has been recognized by his peers as an authority on the Horned God, Wiccan history, and occult influences in rock and roll. He is the author of *The Horned God of the Witches* and coauthor of *Modern Witchcraft with the Greek Gods* (with Astrea Taylor) and *The Witch's Book of Spellcraft* (with Matt Cavalli, Amanda Lynn, and Ari Mankey), all from Llewellyn. You can follow him on Instagram and Twitter @panmankey.

Melanie Marquis is an award-winning author, the founder and producer of the Mystical Minds Convention, and a local coordinator for the Pagan Pride Project. She is the author of *Llewellyn's Little Book of Moon Spells*, *Carl Llewellyn Weschcke: Pioneer and Publisher of Body, Mind & Spirit* (IPPY Award Gold winner for Best Biography), *A Witch's World of Magick*, *The Witch's Bag of Tricks*, *Beltane*, and *Lughnasadh*, as well as the coauthor of *Witchy Mama* (with Emily A. Francis) and the creator of the *Modern Spellcaster's Tarot* (illustrated by Scott Murphy), all from Llewellyn. She is also the creator of the independently published *Stuffed Animal Tarot* (with Aidan Harris). Melanie offers tarot readings, handwriting analysis, witchcraft services, and customized classes in tarot and magick. She is also a folk artist and crafter. Connect with her at injoyart@yahoo.com, https://www.melaniemarquis.com, or facebook.com /MelanieMarquisauthor, or on Instagram @magickalmelaniemarquis.

Gwion Raven is a tattooed Pagan, writer, traveler, musician, cook, kitchen witch, occult shop owner, and teacher. Although initiated in three magickal traditions, Gwion describes his practice as virtually anything that celebrates the wild, sensuous, living, breathing, dancing, ecstatic, divine experiences of this lifetime. He is the author of *The Magick of Food: Rituals, Offerings, & Why We Eat Together* and coauthor of *Life Ritualized: A Witch's Guide to Honoring Life's Important Moments* (with Phoenix LeFae). Born and raised in London, England, he now resides in Northern California and shares space with redwood trees, the Pacific Ocean, and his beloved partner.

Melissa Tipton is a Jungian Witch, Structural Integrator, and founder of the Real Magic Mystery School, where she teaches online courses in Jungian Magic, a potent blend of ancient magical techniques and modern psychological insights. She's the author of *Living Reiki: Heal Yourself and Transform Your Life* and *Llewellyn's Complete Book of Reiki*. Learn more and take a free class at www.realmagic.school.

Charlynn Walls is an active member of her local community and a member of a local area coven. A practitioner of the Craft for over twenty years, she currently resides in Central Missouri with her family. She continues to expand upon her Craft knowledge and practices daily. Charlynn shares her knowledge by teaching online and at local festivals.

Tess Whitehurst is the author of *The Oracle of Portals*, *The Magic of Flowers*, *You Are Magical*, and lots of other books and oracle decks. She's also the founder and facilitator of Wisdom Circle Online School of Magical Arts. Find lots of free spells, rituals, guided meditations, and magical inspiration at TessWhitehurst.com.

Charlie Rainbow Wolf is an old hippie who's been studying the weird ways of the world for over fifty years. She's happiest when she's got her hands in mud, either making pottery in the "Artbox" or tending to things in the yarden (yard + garden = yarden). Astrology, tarot, and herbs are her greatest interests, but she's dabbled in most metaphysical topics over the last five decades, because life always has something new to offer. She enjoys cooking WFPB recipes and knitting traditional cables and patterns, and she makes a wicked batch of fudge. Charlie lives in Central Illinois with her very patient husband and her beloved Great Danes.

Laura Tempest Zakroff is a professional artist, author, creatrix, and Modern Traditional Witch based in New England. She holds a BFA from the Rhode Island School of Design and her artwork has received awards

and honors worldwide. Her work embodies myth and the esoteric through her drawings and paintings, jewelry, talismans, and other designs. Laura is the author of several best-selling titles from Llewellyn, including *Weave the Liminal*, *Sigil Witchery*, and *Anatomy of a Witch*, as well as the artist/author of the *Liminal Spirits Oracle* and *Anatomy of a Witch Oracle*. Laura edited *The New Aradia: A Witch's Handbook to Magical Resistance* and *The Gorgon's Guide to Magical Resistance* (Revelore Press). She is the creative force behind several community events and teaches workshops worldwide. Visit her at www.LauraTempestZakroff.com.

Notes

Notes

Notes

Notes

Notes

Notes

2023

SEPTEMBER
S	M	T	W	T	F	S
					1	2
3	4	5	6	7	8	9
10	11	12	13	14	15	16
17	18	19	20	21	22	23
24	25	26	27	28	29	30

OCTOBER
S	M	T	W	T	F	S
1	2	3	4	5	6	7
8	9	10	11	12	13	14
15	16	17	18	19	20	21
22	23	24	25	26	27	28
29	30	31				

NOVEMBER
S	M	T	W	T	F	S
			1	2	3	4
5	6	7	8	9	10	11
12	13	14	15	16	17	18
19	20	21	22	23	24	25
26	27	28	29	30		

DECEMBER
S	M	T	W	T	F	S
					1	2
3	4	5	6	7	8	9
10	11	12	13	14	15	16
17	18	19	20	21	22	23
24	25	26	27	28	29	30
31						

2024

JANUARY
S	M	T	W	T	F	S
	1	2	3	4	5	6
7	8	9	10	11	12	13
14	15	16	17	18	19	20
21	22	23	24	25	26	27
28	29	30	31			

FEBRUARY
S	M	T	W	T	F	S
				1	2	3
4	5	6	7	8	9	10
11	12	13	14	15	16	17
18	19	20	21	22	23	24
25	26	27	28	29		

MARCH
S	M	T	W	T	F	S
					1	2
3	4	5	6	7	8	9
10	11	12	13	14	15	16
17	18	19	20	21	22	23
24	25	26	27	28	29	30
31						

APRIL
S	M	T	W	T	F	S
	1	2	3	4	5	6
7	8	9	10	11	12	13
14	15	16	17	18	19	20
21	22	23	24	25	26	27
28	29	30				

MAY
S	M	T	W	T	F	S
			1	2	3	4
5	6	7	8	9	10	11
12	13	14	15	16	17	18
19	20	21	22	23	24	25
26	27	28	29	30	31	

JUNE
S	M	T	W	T	F	S
						1
2	3	4	5	6	7	8
9	10	11	12	13	14	15
16	17	18	19	20	21	22
23	24	25	26	27	28	29
30						

JULY
S	M	T	W	T	F	S
	1	2	3	4	5	6
7	8	9	10	11	12	13
14	15	16	17	18	19	20
21	22	23	24	25	26	27
28	29	30	31			

AUGUST
S	M	T	W	T	F	S
				1	2	3
4	5	6	7	8	9	10
11	12	13	14	15	16	17
18	19	20	21	22	23	24
25	26	27	28	29	30	31

SEPTEMBER
S	M	T	W	T	F	S
1	2	3	4	5	6	7
8	9	10	11	12	13	14
15	16	17	18	19	20	21
22	23	24	25	26	27	28
29	30					

OCTOBER
S	M	T	W	T	F	S
		1	2	3	4	5
6	7	8	9	10	11	12
13	14	15	16	17	18	19
20	21	22	23	24	25	26
27	28	29	30	31		

NOVEMBER
S	M	T	W	T	F	S
					1	2
3	4	5	6	7	8	9
10	11	12	13	14	15	16
17	18	19	20	21	22	23
24	25	26	27	28	29	30

DECEMBER
S	M	T	W	T	F	S
1	2	3	4	5	6	7
8	9	10	11	12	13	14
15	16	17	18	19	20	21
22	23	24	25	26	27	28
29	30	31				

2025

JANUARY
S	M	T	W	T	F	S
			1	2	3	4
5	6	7	8	9	10	11
12	13	14	15	16	17	18
19	20	21	22	23	24	25
26	27	28	29	30	31	

FEBRUARY
S	M	T	W	T	F	S
						1
2	3	4	5	6	7	8
9	10	11	12	13	14	15
16	17	18	19	20	21	22
23	24	25	26	27	28	

MARCH
S	M	T	W	T	F	S
						1
2	3	4	5	6	7	8
9	10	11	12	13	14	15
16	17	18	19	20	21	22
23	24	25	26	27	28	29
30	31					

APRIL
S	M	T	W	T	F	S
		1	2	3	4	5
6	7	8	9	10	11	12
13	14	15	16	17	18	19
20	21	22	23	24	25	26
27	28	29	30			